IELTS  SPEAKING

All of you wish to use English freely during the IELTS Speaking Test, but making this wish a reality
remains a puzzle for most of you out there.

十天突破

雅思口语 剑8版

慎小嶷/编著

Pat's Ten-Day Step-by-Step Guide
to the Speaking Test

机械工业出版社
CHINA MACHINE PRESS

本书针对 IELTS 口语的应试技巧进行了深入分析并极为系统地介绍了在海外真实使用的 IELTS 口语应试所需的语言。全书包括三个部分：正文、附赠的学习手册与光盘。

本书剑 8 版的正文按照天数划分内容，在十天里紧密结合《剑 8》对最新口语测试特点与应试策略进行了详尽剖析，并结合《剑 8》所体现出来的考题特点增加了富有针对性的必备语言点，便于考生使用。

本书作者有多年的海外生活经历，在使用最真实的海外地道英语表达对口试题库进行透析的同时，还对中国考生容易陷入的误区进行了中肯的提醒。附赠学习手册汇集了国外口语常用表达法的精华，考生可以随身携带随时学习。

光盘部分的录音紧随正文和附赠手册的变化，由英籍专业人士朗读，便于考生模仿、练习。

本书作者对于真实海外生活和中国学生的口语瓶颈均具有极为深刻的了解，并著有畅销书《十天突破雅思写作》和《十天突破 IELTS 写作完整真题库与 6-9 分范文全解》。

图书在版编目（CIP）数据

十天突破雅思口语／慎小嶷编著. —3 版. —北京：
机械工业出版社，2010. 6（2011.7重印）
ISBN 978 - 7 - 111 - 31143 - 0

Ⅰ.①十…　Ⅱ.①慎…　Ⅲ.①英语-口语-高等教育-
自学参考资料　Ⅳ.①H319.9

中国版本图书馆 CIP 数据核字（2010）第121946 号

机械工业出版社（北京市百万庄大街22 号　邮政编码100037）
策划编辑：孟玉琴　　责任编辑：孟玉琴　于　雷
版式设计：张文贵
责任印制：杨　曦
保定市中画美凯印刷有限公司印刷

2011 年 7 月第 3 版·第 13 次印刷
184mm×260mm·26. 5 印张·600 千字
65001－70000册
标准书号：ISBN 978 - 7 - 111 - 31143 - 0
　　　　　ISBN 978 - 7 - 89451 - 592 - 6（光盘）
定价：55.60 元（附赠 1 张 CD 光盘＋必备掌中宝）

IELTS 口语的 "脉"

你是谁

对 the IELTS Speaking Test 的持续跟踪让我深感 IELTS 口试的话题极为广泛。事实上，它们几乎已经涉及到了海外生活的所有领域。

以《剑8》的口语部分为例，仅四个 tests 中就涵盖了从 neighbours, friends, television, newspapers and magazines 这样的日常生活话题直到像 questionnaire, evaluation of courses and instructors, food production, meetings between international leaders 这样即使让英语为母语者进行讨论也并不轻松的话题（在本书各章里我们将对《剑8》里的这些话题进行深入分析）。而且这只是 Cambridge ESOL 提供的四个 speaking tests 的样本所涉及到的范围，实战形势则更加复杂。以 2011 年 5 月 14 日周六下午 2:00 ~5:35 的短短三个半小时为例，中国大陆（与澳洲在同一天的笔试题相同但口试题不同）就轮换出现了从 a peaceful place 到 the oldest person you know 等跨度很大的 12 道卡片话题，而同期出现的第一、三部分考题经过排列组合之后的可能性更远多于此。

与 Cambridge ESOL 出题者们明显 "有备而来" 相比，多数国内口语考生（希望您是一个例外）则仍处在采取顽固拖延战术或者根本就没有战术、慌不择路的 "非正规军" 状态。下面的官方统计数据残酷展现了这支 "非正规军" 在 IELTS Speaking Test 中是怎样被剑桥击溃的：

Median Band Score for the Most Frequent Countries or Regions of Origin
（Source: www.ielts.org）

		Place of Origin	Speaking
Germany	7.2	Philippines	6.8
Nigeria	7.1	Malaysia	6.6
Brazil	6.8	Russia	6.6

Place of Origin	Speaking	Place of Origin	Speaking
Greece	6.5	Myanmar	6
Colombia	6.4	Turkey	6
France	6.4	Jordan	5.9
Mexico	6.4	Nepal	5.9
Spain	6.4	Bangladesh	5.8
Sri Lanka	6.4	Libya	5.8
Cyprus	6.3	Taiwan	5.8
Egypt	6.3	Thailand	5.8
Iran	6.3	Japan	5.7
Italy	6.3	Korea, South	5.7
Iraq	6.2	Kuwait	5.7
Sudan	6.2	Saudi Arabia	5.7
Pakistan	6.1	Vietnam	5.7
Hong Kong	6	Oman	5.6
India	6	United Arab Emirates	5.4
Indonesia	6	China（People's Republic）	5.3
Kazakhstan	6	Qatar	5.3

结论 在 IELTS 考生最多的 40 个国家或地区中，大陆考生的口语中位值成绩（median band score）①与 Qatar（卡塔尔）考生的表现并列最后一名，而低于其他全部亚、非、欧国家，其中包括不少文化被普遍认为比中国文化更"内向"的国家。显然，导致这种分数差距的根本原因并不是缺少肢体语言，也不是缺乏目光交流，而只能是实打实的语言能力。咱们也许真的应该反思一下"是不是一直都把错了 IELTS 口语的脉？"

---

① median（中位值）是海外大学学习与生活中的常见概念，它表示各有一半的统计数据在这个数值以上或以下。进行成绩统计时 the median core 比 the average score 更加客观。

考官是谁

"印度大妈"、"光头杀手"、"灭绝师太"、"笑面虎老爷爷"、"5 分中年男"……国内考生中关于口语考官的种种轶闻已经足可以写成一本精彩的武侠小说（a swordplay and chivalry novel）了。但这些故事的盛传，恰恰证明了多数考官其实都是普通人。

事实上，不仅是雅思口试，世界上截至目前为止的任何一种口试（包括求职时要做的 interview）都难以实现绝对的标准化，IELTS 也确实难以排除存在评分不负责任的 examiners，但口语考官们总体来说是敬业的。Pat 自己在国内从事雅思培训期间接触到了十几位现任和前任的 IELTS 口语 examiners，我可以肯定地说他们/她们无一例外都是"正常"人。而且相对于英美社会的整体情况而言，客观地说这些考官的平均文化素质是不错的，如果连这些人您看了都觉着"不顺眼"，那么真要到国外长期居住您恐怕就得"大跌眼镜"了。

而且在评分能力方面，他们/她们全都体现出了下面的 5 个共同点：

❶ They are native English speakers.

这确保了考官们能够使用并且充分理解在英美被大家普遍接受的英文，但同时也意味着他们/她们也许无法理解"罕见"的英文。

❷ They at least have an undergraduate degree.

您肯定知道 degree 和 diploma 的区别，其实口语考官们的整体教育背景在英美社会中是不算低的，但脸长成什么样那是人家的自由……

❸ They all have Teaching English as a Foreign Language (TEFL) qualifications.

这点说明口语考官们把从事语言相关工作当成自己 career path 职业规划的一个重要部分，所以大多数考官其实并不像传说中的"口语杀手"们打分那么"潇傻"。

❹ They need to re-certificate every two years.

考官资质每两年都是需要再次重新认证的，除非彻底不想干了，一般没必要让自己的打分屡遭 remark 推翻。

❺ They have at least three years of English teaching experience.

三年英语教学经验也不算很短了。这一条事实上确保了多数考官对孩子们的"症结"

还是能适当有所体谅的，但这同时也往往意味着考官对常见的技巧其实玩儿得比你都熟。

结论 对口语考官的过度恐惧或者过度谄媚都是没有必要的，只需要像尊重其他所有人一样去尊重他/她就足够了，向考官"献媚"（butter up the examiner）牺牲掉的是本应花在组织自己英语表达上的宝贵时间和精力。尽管无法完全排除特例，但总体上 IELTS 口试打分仍然是公正的而且能够体现出考生水平的，绝大多数考官注意力的焦点是你的语言。

怎样使用本书收效最大

基于以上这些原因，在创作本书的全过程中，Pat 始终希望能够把 21 世纪第 2 个十年里在我身边受过良好教育的英语为母语者们每天正使用着的真实口语和他们/她们的实际生活状态介绍给中国的同学们。坦白地说，写这样一本书并不轻松，因为在评析每个 IELTS 话题时我都是在不自量力地扮演着"文化传播者"的角色。

但让我感到欣慰的，除了考生朋友们越洋寄来的诸多 thank-you notes 之外，还有下面这个令人振奋的事实：

在《剑 8》问世八个月之前开始在中国大陆发行的《十天口语》上一版里 Pat 着力推荐的 *in terms of*, *sort out*❶, as well, flock to❷, *in the spotlight*, *an eye-opener*, *not necessarily*❸, practically❹, normally, regardless of, in particular, check out, It's a shame❺ enormous, venue, approach... 等等实用表达均在《剑 8》文本里密集地现身，这强有力地证明了《十天口语》对剑桥官方所偏爱的口语风格的把握是准确的并带有一定前瞻性的。*That's the best compliment a test-prep book author can possibly get*, *huh*?

---

❶ sort out 是一个在英美生活里极为常用的 phrasal verb，意思很像中文里的"搞定"。这个短语在本书旧版 p. 248 和《剑 8》p. 149 都被使用了。

❷ 它酷似中文的"蜂拥而至"，在本书上一版的 p. 162 和《剑 8》p. 133 它均有出现；

❸ 挺有特色的一个短语，完全等于中文说"不一定"。在本书旧版 p. 81 与《剑 8》的 p. 140 和 p. 144 您能三次看到它。

❹ 真实海外生活里人们经常用它来表示"几乎"，请看本书旧版 p. 52 与《剑 8》p. 148。

❺ 在当代英文口语里这句话其实已和"羞耻"完全无关，而是"很可惜"的意思。连这句话也被本书老版 p. 49 和《剑 8》p. 140"共享"了。

希望备考时间比较充裕的同学能够经常地翻阅您手中的这本书。我可以肯定地说本书里的每句话都是自己很用心地写的，值得您花时间细读，看这样的书不会浪费您宝贵的时间。即使只是每次只浏览三、五分钟，您也能拿走一些此时此刻正在海外被人们**真实使用**着的词句。出国以后您就会明白真实的英文口语其实是简洁有效的，反而比用来"唬人"的英语好学。此次更新的剑8版《十天口语》不仅针对今年的最新考题引入了很多新的地道英文表达，而且新版的每一章都使用《剑8》里的口语题为例来帮您解惑，必备的关键词还配有由剑桥官方唯一指定的 *Cambridge Advanced Learner's Dictionary* 的用法例句。通过认真学习本书中的每一章，您将对 Cambridge ESOL 所偏爱的英文口语风格获得极为清晰的把握。

而对于考试迫在眉睫但根本还没开始准备的考生来说（Pat 深知这样心理素质"过好"的同学虽然人数正在减少，但却永远不会彻底消失），请您立即停止采用拖延战术，登录 blog. sina. com. cn/ieltsguru 打印出本月口语预测，然后按照下面的顺序快速学习本书：Day1（2，3，4，10）→ Day 2（前三节）→ Day 3（有空你就背吧，反正也没剩几天了，小册子随身携带）→ Day 4（第一节的表格必看）→ Day 6（至少结合光盘文件把单词发音的那部分练一练）→ Day 7（本月预测里出现了的话题要掌握）→ Day 8 & Day 10（从本月预测里找出对应考题的分析，<u>不要背答案</u>，但要虚心借鉴会拿分的英文表达而且花点时间体会剑桥例句）→ Day 9（有空时记一些，出国上学时也很有用）→ 附录 D（用 10 分钟通读）。还有，分布在全书各章节结尾处的"超短线"和页边侧的 V 型标识也会为您提供指南针的（要去 UK 的则是指西针）。

结论　充分了解每月出题动向诚然是必要的，但同时必须尽量多积累地道的英文表达并至少对当代英美社会和文化具备适当的了解，才有可能真正帮助国内考生扭转多年来持续稳定在"倒数前三"、甚至连 fluctuation 都从没有过的宿命。也只有踏踏实实地提高自己的语言能力，您才算是把住了 IELTS 口语的"脉"。

Deepest appreciation goes to my parents and my sister Meg, without whom I wouldn't possibly have embarked upon this "cottage industry". Your loving and unwavering support means everything to me.

Special kudos goes to Ms. Meng Yu-qin, the editor of this book, whose intelligence and resourcefulness make a real difference in the creation of this book.

Most of all, I wish to dedicate this book to the students who made up my classes in the Global IELTS Institute (Beijing). Their example has continually spurred me to keep working on this book. I hope it will be a nice reminder of our delightful time together.

小懿

2011 年 7 月于新泽西

英文自序

Preface

All of you wish to use English freely during the IELTS Speaking Test, but making this wish a reality remains a puzzle for most of you out there. In my observation, many Chinese candidates perform poorly on the test because they "over-prepare" for the test. The error-free templates and picture-perfect "model answers" that have been force-fed into test-takers' brains have made the entire preparation process a strategic failure — few of us would try to learn the piano if we only attempted to sound like Mozart, right?

To get a high score on the IELTS Speaking Section, students must understand what the examiners realistically want. Personal preferences may vary as far as words, structures and concepts go, but the reality is all examiners appreciate spontaneity. Throughout the test, the examiner can see and hear the candidate. It is fairly easy for him / her to spot the thoughtless spouting of prepared answers because there are no natural pauses between the sense groups in the answers. There also tends to be a dramatically hesitant response when the examiner asks for further elaboration on those answers. In most cases, this hesitancy substantially erodes the candidate's credibility in proving his/her English proficiency and he/she is penalized for this. Thus, unlike the majority of prep books on IELTS speaking, this volume is not designed to be memorized by rote but rather, to be studied as an approach to a testing method which values a spontaneous performance when students communicate with the examiner. To this end, I have built most chapters around themes that are not only IELTS-oriented, but current and thought-provoking as well. The perspective offered on each theme challenges you to think beyond the common treatment of these themes, and all themes have a One Step Beyond component, which serves as a springboard for addressing related topics at a more sophisticated level.

As this book is a cumulative study, I recommend beginning with Chapter 1 and continuing consecutively. It is true that speaking a second language is partly a talent, but it is mostly a skill, and just like any other skill, it improves faster with continuous practice. Studying and using the English you will learn in this volume over an extended period of time will be an intelligent and effective way to become a competent IELTS Speaking candidate.

Pat,

May, 2011

Contents
目　录

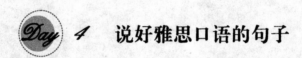

Day 3　雅思口语的词

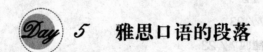

Day 4　说好雅思口语的句子

Day 5　雅思口语的段落

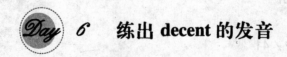

Day 6　练出 decent 的发音

7 **反正 Part 1**

Day 8 **剑 8 时代的 Part 2 真题全集**

Day 9 **激辩 Part 3**

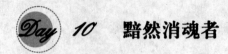 10 黯然消魂者

 附录

Pat 回北京最爱做的事就是下馆子了，因为说实话，美国和加拿大的餐馆里实在没什么好吃的菜，而英国菜嘛……可更是出了名儿的不"给力"，除了 fish 'n' chips。

有次在北京的一家餐馆里，Pat 突然发现英文菜单上很彪悍地写着"stir fly"（炒苍蝇）。我完全被老板的勇气震撼了，心想正常人胆儿再大也不至于连苍蝇都敢吃，而且居然还是炒着吃，仔细研究之后才发现原来应该是 stir-fried（炒的）。

还有一次 Pat 看到一家北京餐馆的菜单上对"干煸四季豆"这道菜的英文描述竟然是："This website is temporarily closed. Please check back later." 这显然是因为餐馆老板在网上搜索这个菜的英文名称，但网站却没有正常运行而得到的不是答案的答案。

Pat 在北京时还曾经见到过"四喜丸子"被叫做 four happy meatballs（四个快乐的肉球），"鸡肉"被翻译成 muscle，而咱们中国的经典古语"知之为知之，不知为不知，是知也"竟被翻译成："Know is know. No know is no know. That's know."

本书就献给这些可爱的 glitches。

No sweat.

Day

> ## 最真实的谎言
> *True Lies*

Pat's Guide
To the Speaking Test

Using lies as alibis
Is the same game
Played in different ways
It's just a waste of time
Made for gullible minds

✦❀✧ 长期困扰中国口语考生的 10 个问题 ❀✧✦

○ 口语考试是不是必须回答"积极"的答案？口试是不是一定要回答"新颖"的答案？

○ 口语考试是每个月的最后一场最简单吗？口语下午2:00 的考题和下午5:00 的考题有什么区别？周六考和周日考或者周一考有没有区别？

○ 口语考官打分到底凭什么？

○ 口语用词是越难越拿分吗？

○ 口语要准备模板吗？

○ 发音在口语评分中到底有多重要？

○ 如何选择口语考点？

○ 看口语机经有用吗？

○ 口语考试要不要"套磁"？

○ 考官问的问题根本没有听懂怎么办？

Bonus Question

○ IELTS 口语考时事么？（高分内容）

○ 怎样正确看待口试的 Predictions？（高分内容）

Pat's Answers

1. 口语考试是不是只能回答 "积极" 的答案? 口试是不是一定要回答 "新颖" 的答案? (***Do I have to sound positive or optimistic? Do I have to present completely original, creative or unconventional answers?***)

国内考生甚至一些培训教师普遍相信下面的错误观点:

A) 不能给考官 "I don't like..." "Actually, I don't know much about..." "Well, I disagree..." 这类否定语气的答案。

B) 必须要给出非常有创意 (original)、与众不同 (unique)、引人入胜 (engaging) 的答案才能拿高分。

我们来看看一位口语考官是怎样理解这个问题的 (Clark: 29): "One important point to emphasize (强调) here is that the marking system does NOT include references to the following points:

* Interesting content
* Amusing or funny answers
* Body language
* The truth
* Appearance or dress

更发人深思 (thought-provoking) 的是,这位考官同时还给出了自己评分的实例 (Ibid, 29): "Many years ago in an IELTS speaking test, I interviewed a young lady who was arrogant (傲慢的), impolite, impatient and quite rude — but I awarded this lady a score of 8 only because her spoken English matched the descriptions in the marking system for band score 8."

像这样一个集所有讨厌于一身 (obnoxious, intolerable) 的女士,因为英语说得并没有明显问题,还是从考官那里拿走了口语 8 分的高分。

而我在环球雅思北京总校的同事,前任口语考官 Martin Renner 就更加直白地评价: "It's not what you say. It's how you say it."

这两位货真价实的考官的肺腑之言完全符合 Pat 自己对学生口语成绩的长期跟踪调查：口语的分数，只看你的英语水平和答案是否具体、充实，和所谓的"新颖"或者是否"积极"完全没有关系。说得更直接一点：考官坐到口试的小房间里的任务不是测智商，也不是搞心理分析，剑桥交给他/她的唯一任务是要确定考生的英语口语水平怎样。我们需要做好的，只是力争去说正确的流利的英文，但是实在没必要给自己设计更多的条条框框了（hard and fast rules）。

2 口语考试是每个月的最后一场最简单吗？口语下午 2:00 的考题和下午 5:00 的考题有什么区别？周六考和周日考或者周一考有没有区别？(***How will the timing influence my performance?***)

A/ 过去已经有过多次新题在月末出现的实例。所以我建议同学们根据自己的申请计划来安排报名就好了。每个月的 3~4 次考试哪一次最难或者最容易的概率（probability）都是一样的，新题出现在哪一次都有可能。

B/ 根据七年来我观察到的规律，同一个半天里面的 Part 1 问答题目通常很接近，但是 Part 2 口语卡片题确实有可能在同一个半天内换题。例如周六下午 4:00 多经常有可能要换一次卡片，而周日上午 10:30 左右也有可能换一次卡片，周日下午还有可能再换一次。所以各位在"蹲点"的时候也要考虑同一个半天里 Part 2 换题的可能性。口试第二部分的卡片题最有价值的信息来自于和你同一个半天内考试的其他考生（包括同一半天中考试的外地考生在网上回忆出的信息）。

3 口语考官打分到底凭什么？(***How should I interpret the marking system?***)

大家都知道口语有四项评分标准，但是那个标准很学术，一般考生难以望其项背。通过下面这个表格，我们可以总结出一个"草根版"的口语评分标准。

Pat 的"草根版"雅思口试评分标准

	5分	6分	7分
Fluency 流利度	句子中经常出现不必要的停顿，还有些同学习惯用"er…""ah…"这些 fillers，甚至中间出现长时间没话说	能说出完整的句子，但是每隔几句一定会有不连贯的地方。有可能出现	语速比较自然，只在很少的地方由于思考答案出现了不必要的停顿

（续表）

	5分	6分	7分
	"干在那儿"（get put on the spot）的尴尬情况。而 5 分得主的另一个极端是超级流畅，说话完全没有轻重缓急，甚至已经听不出来喘气，看不到眨眼，这种考生说中文时都没有的灵异现象（supernatural phenomenon）只能被考官解读为是在背书	较长时间的令人尴尬的停顿，但是次数不多	
Grammar 语法	不能准确区分单词是否要加 ed 或者 s，甚至出现 he/she 不分的情况	每隔几句都有少量的时态或者单复数错误	基础语法错误已经基本消除，但仍存在一些高端的语法错误（比如介词或者连词使用不准确）
Pronunciation 发音 （本书 Day 6 将详解口语考试对发音的要求	考官可以听懂你的内容，但是某些地方他/她需要仔细分辨才能听懂，考官不会享受和你的对话，只希望考试时间快点过去	考官能比较容易地听懂你的内容，但是有些单词发音很明显是错误的，语调上不是很自然	发音自然，但还是偶尔出现发音错误，考官已经开始享受和你的交谈过程
Vocabulary 词汇量	使用小学或初一单词过多，这是一种可能。 但对国内考生而言还有另一种更常见的可能，就是字典英语痕迹明显，使用大量在国外生活里从来不用的超级大词，Pat 管这叫做"词汇恐怖主义"（verbal terrorism）	用词已经比较准确，在适当的时候可以用出来一些有难度的词汇，但是遗憾的是，这些难词大约有 1/3 是被错误使用的	可以分辨在哪些地方应该用小词，哪些地方可以用大一点的词汇，偶尔有用词不当，但是不影响整体意思的表达

我们用《剑 8》test 4 中的一道题为例来说明低分与高分口语答案的区别：

Do you enjoy the advertisements on television?

典型的 5 分答案：

> No, I don't. I think they are very boring.

典型的 6 分答案：

> I don't like them. Advertisements on television just waste my time. They suddenly stop interesting TV shows and the things they try to sell are useless.

典型的 7 分答案：

> *I would say I enjoy some of them because they are creative and witty. But it's true most ads just spoil the fun of watching TV, and the information they bring us tends to be misleading.*

下面我们再通过《剑8》test 1 的考题来体会低档、中档与高档分数之间的差异：

Do you think it would be a good idea for schools to ask students their opinions about lessons?

典型的 5 分答案：

> I think it's a good idea. That can make lessons more interesting. So the students will like their school much more.

典型的 6 分答案：

> It sounds like a good idea. We can give the teachers our opinions and help them improve their lessons. This method will make us feel we are part of our school, too.

典型的 7 分答案：

> *It may be a good idea if it's well-managed. Students can get their voices heard when they evaluate the lessons. Then the school will know how to keep up with the students' demand. But on the other hand, some opinions will be extreme, which may hurt teachers' feelings.*

还可以通过这道《剑7》test 2 的考题看看口语7分到底是怎样炼成的：

Do you like making other people laugh?

典型的 5 分答案:

> Yes I do. I'm a funny person and I always tell my friends jokes.

典型的 7 分答案:

> *Sure. I know lots of jokes* and *really enjoy sharing them with friends of mine. It seems like I just happen to have a unique sense of humor. I tend to believe humor is essential to a good mood at work and at home as well.* ☺

下面再用一个每场考试 Part 1 都会有人被问到的常考问题实例来说明一下 5→6→7 的飞跃 (leap):

What's your favourite subject at school?

典型的 5 分答案:

> It's English because English is very useful and interesting.

典型的 6 分答案:

> It's math because math makes us smart and math is very useful for learning some other subjects such as chemistry.

典型的 7 分答案:

> *Humm, I guess it's PE,* which *stands for physical education. Sometimes we call it the gym class. PE* not just *keeps us physically fit, it gets us more focused on academic subjects* as well.

再看一个 5→6→7 的三级跳 (hop, skip, jump):

What's your favourite season?

典型的 5 分答案:

> I like winter best. I enjoy the snow in winter. It's so beautiful.

典型的 6 分答案:

> It's spring because everything is fresh in spring. Sometimes we have light rain. Spring is gentle and comfortable.

典型的 7 分答案：

> *Well*, I would say … summer. *Actually*, the summer in Beijing is really hot … scorching, you know. *But* in summer, my friends and I can just hang out together in places *like* malls. The summer vacation is long, *much longer than* the spring break. *And the coolest thing* about summer is we *can just* wear casual clothes like tees and shorts …

我们的结论

☆ 5 分是挣扎着说出来的（或者另一个极端是无敌流利地喷出来的），和考官的交流要不然就是基本无效，要不然就是特生硬

☆ 6 分是思考着说出来的，和考官的交流开始有效，但是并不充分而且不很流利

☆ 7 分是快速思考之后较为连贯地说出来的，但中间会有呼吸和短暂思考需要的自然停顿。和考官的交流比较充分而且已经有一定的层次关系，但允许出现不导致严重误解的语法、用词或发音错误

口语用词是越难越拿分吗？（***Should I equate big words with higher scores?***）

这绝对是中国孩子考 IELTS 口语的最大误区之一。

很多上过外教口语班的同学问我为什么外教讲雅思话题的用词总是比他们/她们自己的用词更好懂，其实这种现象并不仅限于英语教学课堂。出国之后刚下飞机您立马就会发现：在国外生活中真的没有人整天把大词挂在嘴上，那样的英语太怪异了（weird）。有些朋友在 21 世纪的第二个十年里所说的英文仍然带有明显的"文革英语"的痕迹，那些被频频用错地方的大词和畸形长句（convoluted sentences）实在难逃其咎。

请看下面这个由剑桥考官给出的口语 7 分实战案例：

What's your favourite colour?

> *Well*, to be honest, *I don't really* have an actual favourite colour but *I guess if I* were buying clothes, *then* I'd usually go for something like blue or grey — *kind of* dull colours, *nothing too* bright.

也许您觉得这样的用词"不配"拿7，但其实这个考生的答案除了开始处的 Well，to be honest...还显得比较"假"之外，风格已经很接近于多数 native speakers 的真实交流风格了，而且内容也还算充实，所以拿7并不过分。

这种英语风格同样也是 Pat 自己在上大学的时候天天都能听到的真实海外大学英语：

Sample
Rachel & Kyle

Rachel: *Say, Kyle, are you ready for the big exam coming up this Friday?*

Kyle: *No. I guess I'm nowhere near ready. Maybe it's all because I really have no interest in biology.*

Rachel: *So you'd better start studying.*

Kyle: *I have an idea. The test is on Friday, so maybe on Thursday night you could* （其实像虚拟语气这样国内孩子们压根儿不敢用的特殊语法现象在真实的口语里反倒是用得不少，上面的那个 7 分实例同样也用了，详情请看 *Day* 4）*come over to my apartment and help me cram* （突击学习）.

Rachel: *It wouldn't be very smart to try and rush through half a semester's information in just three hours. We could compare notes, anyway.*

Kyle: *I'm busy every night this week. I've got a date tonight and tomorrow I'm playing basketball. I'll just pull an all-nighter* （熬夜学习）.

Rachel: *I don't think studying all night is going to do you any good if you fall asleep during the test.*

Kyle: *Humm, I guess you're right. I'll change my date to after the test and then I'll be free to study this week.*

同时，Pat 还希望各位不要轻视由一些简单词汇组成的短语（phrases）。经常跟"老外"聊天的同学们一定已经发现了，很多短小的词组在英文口语里面异常活跃，比如下面几个例子在雅思口试中都有机会用到：

To keep fit, I work out （=exercise) in the gym for an hour every day.

I'm studying hard coz I don't want to let my parents down （=disappoint sb.).

DIY stands for Do-It-Yourself.

The work piles up （=becomes more) but I will keep at it.

We played games to liven up the party. (=to make the party more lively)

I need to polish up (=improve) my English before I go to Australia.

Steven Chow's（周星驰）comedies never fail to crack me up. (=make me laugh)

It was handed down from my grandmother.

Reading helps me wind down (=relax).

These old photos bring back memories of my childhood.

> ⚠ WARNING 但 Pat 反对您在雅思口试里使用 wanna, ain't, dude, gal, yucky 这些在国外日常生活里其实并不太常用的过于口语化的表达。通读完本书后，您的口语用词风格将非常接近受过良好教育的英语为母语人士的用词风格：浅易、自然、平实，但也不是"痞话连篇"。

5 口语要准备模板吗？(*Will templates work?*)

近期刚听过一个口语模板，实在太经典了，记录在这儿：

……如果考官问你的问题答不出来，就可以深情地跟考官说，"Humm, that is a very good question. Let me think about it…" 然后眼珠转两圈（而且还规定好必须是"两圈"），假装沉思，猛然惊醒，对考官大声说，"Ah！Sir, I finally found a good answer to your question. But…I'm not sure if I understood your question correctly… So, could you please say that question again?"

I was totally dumbstruck by it. 自己说吧，其实你没那么差。如果你执意要背模板的话，本书 Day 5 和 Day 9 提供了一些英文正确的模板，但还是少用为宜。书面沟通与口头交流是不同的。正常人用母语写作时也常常会使用"套句"（例如《剑8》p. 167 的那篇考官范文就是集议论文套句之大成的范例），但在说话时还频频使用套话只会让英语为母语者觉得呆板甚至怪诞。

6 发音在口语评分中到底有多重要？(*How important will my pronunciation be during the actual test?*)

2008 年 8 月开始，剑桥对口语考试的发音部分评分推出了新的细则。这个标准听起来很美，实施起来却很难（The examiners will have a hard time putting it to good use.）。想把发音这样不可能量化的内容去量化，最后只能变成画蛇添足（like gilding the lily）。我强烈建议各位：不要过多考虑发音的评分细则。另一方面，努力提高自己的发音水平是绝对必要的，因为对今后出国生活也有好处。本书的 Day 6 为大家提供了非常实用的发音训练，可以帮你在很短时间内练出至少不让考官讨厌的发音（但是要达到让人主动喜欢您的水平确实还需要一个比较长的过程）。

7 如何选择口语考点？（*Where am I supposed to take the IELTS speaking test?*）

关于考点，我们可以明确三件事：

A 考题难度在不同的考点没有任何差异。这听起来很绝对，但这么说的依据是我自己七年来一直跟踪不同考点考题的实践。Pat 想特别提醒大家，全国所有考点在同一天的考题都一样。很多同学不理解这一点。其实大家好好看看 www.51ielts.com 上的当天考生回忆，你会发现全国当天考题确实是同步的（这个网站上的当天考生口语考试回忆可以作为"蹲点"的重要补充，而且零风险，业内行话称为"网蹲"）。

B 考官给你的打分会受其他考生水平的影响。口语考试是主观性考试，这就决定了它的评分必然带有主观性，完全标准化的口试评分不仅雅思没有，世界上也并不存在。我也确实听到不少水平一般的北京孩子去外地考试考到 6.5 或者 7 分的实例，所以如果总体来看，我们应该承认北京、上海、广州等大城市竞争更激烈一些。

C 但具体到某一个考生，还是存在不确定性（uncertainty）的。我们不能说他/她去外地就一定能比北京口语考分高。比如有可能给你考试的那个外地考官天性（by nature）就是"刺儿头"（cranky），或者说英语带有较重的"外地"口音，再比如你为了去外地而长途旅行，考前没能休息好等。这些具体的个案因素不能完全排除（can't be ruled out）。

结论：总体上二三线城市口语打分的大环境确实要好一些，但是还要看自己的行程安排是否方便，而且单个考官的个性（individuality）其实比区域大环境更重要。

8 看口语机经有用吗？（*How can I use online collections of past test questions wisely*?）

口语机经是对过去考题的总结，挺好，但美中不足的（a fly in the ointment）是题目数量惊人，所以对于非专业人士而言最好还是结合近期动态来准备效率更高。各位可以随时登录我的博客 blog. sina. com. cn/ieltsguru，Pat 会及时公布最新口语考题，供您随时参考。

9. 口语考试要不要"套磁"？（*Am I supposed to butter up the examiner*?)

To tao or not to tao, that is the question.

像这类"第二十二条军规"（*Catch 22*）的问题其实永远都会吵个没完。但这样来看这个问题你就能看得更清楚：套磁并不会明显加分，但是如果套不好却可能导致扣分，因为考官被套一点也不影响他/她用英语提出问题，可集中精力用英语套磁却会让你没有精力去好好回答问题。再说，即使考官真的对你的套磁感兴趣了，他/她撇开考试真跟你聊起来了你吃得消吗？（Are you really up to it?)

10. 考官问的问题根本没有听懂怎么办？（*What should I do when I can't fully understand a question*?)

国内考生的通常做法是说，"I beg your pardon?" / "Sorry I didn't quite catch the question. Could you ask it again?" 或者 "I'm sorry I missed that one. Could you repeat it?"

但是 Pat 认真观察后却发现，如果考生没听懂，一半以上的情况其实是因为问题里面有生词，那么即使考官真的 nice 到愿意给你再重复一遍，重复之后多半也还是听不懂，而这次却要被扣掉 fluency 那部分的分数了。

所以，请敢于面对这个事实（face up to reality）：如果第一次没听懂，90% 以上的可能是这道题你不会再拿分了，但你仍然有可能逃过因为没听懂而被扣分的命运。

> 下面两个方法可以让您即使听不懂问题也至少不被扣分：
>
> ◈ 如果你的考官态度还算客气，那么请跟他/她说，"Could you please rephrase（转述）your question?" 如果他/她愿意换个说法替你转述一遍，那么就应该可以躲开原题里的生词了。
>
> ◈ 如果对方的态度不温不火甚至根本看不清他/她的态度，你没有自信他/她会愿意替你转述，那么请直接告诉他/她，"Well, my best guess would be..." 这么说的好处是诚实，坦白承认你就是在猜，那么即使后面你所猜测的内容有一点跑题，至少这一道题他/她应该可以原谅你，认真听他/她的下一个问题就好了。

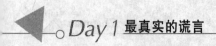

Bonus Question

IELTS 口语考时事么？（高分内容）（***Am I supposed to constantly update my knowledge about current events for the speaking test?***）

最近有不少考生发来邮件问 Pat 如果近期考试的话是否要准备一些关于福岛核危机（Fukushima nuclear crisis）或空袭利比亚（air strikes on Libya）的知识，而且每次到逢年过节的时候大家在来信问候之余也少不了要问问关于该节日的英语会不会在口试里被"盘查"。

这种担心是完全正常的，毕竟 IELTS 口试是面对面的交流，很容易让人联想到考官是否会"实时"出题。但令人遗憾（或者令人庆幸）的是，每一次 IELTS 口试的考题均是由剑桥统一提供的，考官个人并没有"出题权"，他/她只被允许从剑桥提供的该次考试出题范围里选题来考，而且 IELTS 口语不考查最新的时事知识。

《剑8》里的官方真题最真实地展现了 Pat 连续观察七年来所体会到的雅思口试"只考趋势，但不考时事"的准确定位：

✳ Do you think there will be a greater choice of food in shops in the future, or will there be less choice?

✳ Do you think it is possible to be friends with someone if you never meet them in person?

✳ Do you think it will be a good idea for schools to ask students their opinions?

✳ Do you think that meetings between international leaders will become more frequent in the future?（您可以在后面的 Day 9 看到对这些题的深入分析）

虽然这种"只管趋势，但不管时事"的严格定位在一定程度上导致了口试话题的空洞与乏味，但只要想想其实考官一天下来要把有限的那几十个问题轮番问这么多不同的人，你心里也就平衡了，甚至会开始同情考官（但也应该想到考题范围有限将进一步增加口语只机械背诵答案的风险）。更重要的是：考查范围明确也就保证了 IELTS 口语的难度对参加考试的全体考生来说是公平的，而不会因为考官突然"发挥创意"而导致不同考生间出现明显的考题难度不公。

因此，我们可以非常明确地说：考口语不需要担心"核辐射"（nuclear radiation）。

怎样正确看待口试的 **Predictions**？（高分内容）

对于备考时间很紧的考生们来说，不论英语水平高低，提前看看口语预测里的题目都是高效率的备战方法。而且，由于雅思口试是分阶段更换题库而并不是每次考试都更换题库，因此口语预测的命中率还是挺高的。客观说准备口语预测不算浪费生命。但有3点Pat要请大家特别注意：（a）对于那些过于简单、你肯定能答得出来的预测题，可以跳过去不必准备，有侧重点地备考是明智而非偷懒；（b）性质接近的话题完全允许合并。虽然你不是考官，但考官也不是你，多数考官也就是一般人而不是 mind reader。当然，合并话题还是要自然，太牵强也不行；（c）Pat 坚决鼓励您把自己原创的想法加到预测题的回答里去，即使有点幼稚也还是比完全放弃自己的思维就地卧倒可贵得多。至于如何扩展思路，读完 Day 8 即知。

Let's get the show on the road.

The Ultra-Short Track

对于备考时间过短而且又天生胆小不敢去蹲点的孩子来说，"网蹲"是个合理的选择。请注意以下几点：

❶ 考生回忆最集中的是 www. 51ielts. com，大家可以在首页上方中部看到红色的"x 日笔试、口语"的醒目标题；

❷ 如果打算"网蹲"请务必安排好时间（plan ahead）。距离你的口语考试时间越近的回忆信息就越新，但不要因为沉迷于网站上的信息而忘记了自己的考试时间，一定要留出足够的时间在路上。只要是同一天的口语题就都有一定的参考价值；

❸ 不要只找和自己同城的考生回忆（很多新手会犯这个错误）。事实上在同一个半天里，全国各考点的题库全都是同步的（但请注意澳洲和新西兰的笔试题虽然与大陆同步，但口试题却不同步，大陆考生不要参考同一天里这两个地区的口语回忆），只要是大陆当天考题就应该汇总起来，越全越好，并迅速思考自己将会如何回答。

网蹲虽然不是在考场进行，但却是一场"没有硝烟的战争"。对它做好计划同样是IELTS 口试总体行动部署的重要一环。

Conduct your search safely.

Day 2

 雅思口语的本质是
什么？

The Untold Story

Pat's Guide
To the Speaking Test

When I look into your big blue eyes,
I start to quiver and shake
Talk to me, talk to me,
All I want is just a nice little conversation

对于从来没有近距离接触过外国人的那部分中国孩子，第一次进考场和考官面对面可能会有"坐电椅"的感觉。经常点击上面这个网站上的 interviews（在右上角的 search 栏里填入 interview 即可），能让你更了解地道英语的风格和"LW"们说话时独特的面部表情，让你从战略上藐视敌人。

▶ *We just have adopted a laid-back approach, even though we take the test seriously.*

Part 1 的实质是什么？

关键词：chat

雅思口语第一部分用剑桥的官方定义来说，是"关于你的背景、爱好、兴趣和习惯的基础问题"。但这听起来也太虚伪了吧？用普通人的话来讲，Part 1 的本质就是一个 chat，跟考官聊聊你自己的基本情况。从答案长度上来讲，每道题平均能回答 3 句话左右就相当不错了。当然，如果确实遇到了准备充分的题目，那你也不必"嘴下留情"，尽管发挥就好了，只要能确保流利就成。

一般来说在国外聊天儿的时候人们是比较随意的（laid-back）。既然咱们铁了心要去考官们的国家，那就得按照他们的习惯来了。如果 Part 1 说得就跟背书（regurgitation）似的，人家就会怀疑你跟他/她聊的诚意。所以，在 Part 1 里，请放松您的心态，跟 examiner 好好地聊一次吧！

Part 1 的考题也是口试三个部分中最接近考生自己的生活的，比如下面都是《剑8》给出的 Part 1 考题：

◆ How often do you see the people who live next door to you?

◆ What kinds of problem do people sometimes have with their neighbours?

◆ How do you think neighbours can help each other? (您可以在 Day 7 的 Topic 9 看到聊 neighbour 所需的全部常用英文)

◆ Which magazines and newspapers do you read? [Why?]

◆ What kinds of article are you most interested in? [Why?]

◆ Have you ever read a newspaper or magazine in a foreign language? [Why?]

◆ Do you think reading a newspaper or magazine in a foreign language is a good way to learn the language? [Why? / Why not?] (您可以在 Day 7 的 Topic 5 看到对报纸杂志类考题的详细分析)

◆ Do you like to have flowers in your home? [Why? / Why not?]

◆ Where would you go to buy flowers? [Why?]

◆ Are flowers important in your culture? [Why? / Why not?] (在 Day 7 的 Topic 19 您将看到与 flowers 有关的地道英文)

◆ How often do you watch television? [Why? / Why not?]

◆ Do you enjoy the advertisements on television? [Why? / Why not?]

◆ Do you think most programmes on television are good? [Why? / Why not?] (您可以从 Day 7 的 Topic 4 了解到大量涉及到电视的常用英文表达)

Part 2 的实质是什么?

关键词:description

对于 Part 2,剑桥的官方定义是"In Part 2, the examiner gives you a topic card. You have one minute to prepare and make notes. Then you'll be required to talk about the topic for one to two minutes. "

不过现在在很多考点考官其实都已经不再是发一个 card 了,而是发一张大纸,上面在一个很小的角落上印着一个 topic 和几点提示。

Part 2 的本质是要你做一个 description(描述)。为了更充分地理解什么是" description",您可以回想一下自己小时候上语文课的时候,老师向你描述一个事物时和老师平时说话有什么不同。

"描述"与"闲聊"至少有下面三个不同:

·☆ 描述时一定会有适当的思考和停顿(pause)。

我们说过,Part 1 基本可以看成是 chat,但是有些考生在 Part 2 因为正好遇到可以调动自己准备过的答案(a prepared speech),就直接把答案无比流畅地背出来。这明显不符合正常人描述的习惯。

☆ 描述需要有一定的规划,需要有秩序。

"描述"需要更加精确的语言。而且和 Part 1 与 Part 3 不同,Part 2 需要在同一个话题的不同方面之间做数次转换,所以对答案的秩序性要求要高一些。不过既然是口语,毕竟与写作的严谨度要求不同,所以也不用太呆板(rigid)。

☆ 句式会有一些变化(variations),但是并不会像 Part 1 的 chat 那么多样(diversified)。

这一点听起来可能不好理解,但其实您自己试着用母语描述一个话题,1~2 分钟你马上就会发现其中的奥秘:这 1~2 分钟的过程并不是互动(interaction),而只是你自己一个人的独白,不像 Part 1 那样有考官不断给你信息的反馈(feedback)和新的提问(follow-up questions),所以你就不必再为了回应新信息去不停地修改你的句式了。

比如下面这道题是《剑8》test 1 的 Part 2:

> Describe a time when you were asked to give your opinion in a questionnaire or survey.
>
> You should say：
>   what the questionnaire/survey was about
>   why you were asked to give your opinions
>   what opinions you gave
> and explain how you felt about giving your opinions in this questionnaire/survey.

下面这个则是《剑8》test 2 的 Part 2:

> Describe a restaurant that you enjoyed going to.
>
> You should say：
>   where the restaurant was
>   why you chose this restaurant
>   what type of food you ate in this restaurant
> and explain what you enjoyed about this party.

再比如下面几个卡片话题也都是近期常考的:

◆ Describe a place where there is a lot of water.

◆ Describe a naughty thing you did in your childhood.

◆ Describe a place with a lot of noise.

◆ Describe things that you can do to help improve the environment.

◆ Describe a vehicle you wish to buy.

◆ Describe a successful company.

◆ Describe an old person you know.

◆ Describe a walk with a friend.

◆ Describe a quiz show.

◆ Describe a building in your school or university.

如果这些"邪门儿"的 topics 让您感到无所适从，没关系，我们将在后面的 Day 8 和 Day 10 对它们以及整个完整卡片真题库进行深入探寻。

Part 3 的实质是什么？

关键词:discussion

它的本质是一个 discussion（讨论），多数时候 Part 3 的问题与 Part 2 所考卡片的话题有关，但有的题目也可能会离开（deviate from）卡片的话题。其实这部分和 Part 1 的深层区别就是更加"博爱"：Part 1 的多数题是关于"you / your life"，而 Part 3 的多数题目则是关于"people"，"society"或者"your country"，甚至"the world / global issues"。

> 既然是 **discussion**，那么在语言上就必然有下面三个特点：
>
> ☆ 会用到很多表示逻辑关系的连接词。不过大家尽可以放心的是：本书已经为您总结出了雅思口语乃至海外日常口语里所需的全部常用连接词，详见 Day 4。
>
> ☆ 要求考生的答案比 Part 1 要正式一点，无论从用词还是从内容都会比口试前两部分更 formal。
>
> ☆ The good news is: There's no need for you to make it as formal as a job interview. 毕竟 Part 3 还是考口语水平，所以答案也不必过难，Part 3 考题与雅思作文题的难度相比还是有很大差距的。更具体的 Part 3 详情请见本书 Day 9。

所以，如果说 Part 1 是和考官聊天（chat），那么在 Part 3，你的任务就是论述好你的观点（state your case）。

比如《剑 8 》test 2 的 Part 2 卡片话题是 restaurant，相应的 Part 3 就出现了下列问题:

◆ Which are more popular in your country: fast food restaurants or traditional restaurants?

◆ Some people say that food in an expensive restaurant is always better than food in a cheap restaurant — would you agree?

◆ Do you think there will be a greater choice of food available in shops in the future, or will there be less choice?

再比如，2011 年近期的一个常考话题是 a piece of electronic equipment，相应的 Part 3

就出现了：

◆ What kinds of machine are used for housework in modern homes in your country?

◆ How have these machines benefited people? Are there any negative effects of using them?

◆ Do you think all new homes will be equipped with household machines in the future? Why?

Part 1 的话题有范围吗？

Pat 认真总结了近七年里的全部口语 Part 1 话题。分析结果表明不管是新题、旧题、半新半旧或者是半新不旧的题,都一定超不出下面的 20 个方面。其中颜色越亮的话题越放松(laid-back),颜色越暗的越呆板(stuffy)。希望大家对这个图示最好能在头脑里有个大致印象,这样你就将发现 Part 1 的具体问题虽然千变万化,但剑桥的总体出题规律却变得容易把握了。您还将在后面的 Day 7 看到更深入的 Part 2 话题分析。

The Part 1 Topic Pool				
Studies	**Language**	Food	Nature	Sports & Outdoor Activities
Work	**Weather&Season**	Media	Collection	Pets
Building	**Hometown**	Arts	Clothing	Festivals，Holidays & Parties
People	**Reading & Writing**	Colours	Traveling	Shopping

Part 1 的提问方式有规律吗？

整整七年的考题跟踪下来,Pat 很想说其实雅思口语 Part 1 的提问形式是极度缺乏创意的,因为它永远只有两种形式：

① Yes / No 类题

下面一节的真题中使用斜体字的题目都是这种类型,这类问题全都可以用 Yes 或 No 来回答,然后展开。

② Wh-（What/Why/Which…）/ How 类题

如此有限的提问形式,在一定程度上破坏了我们征服 Part 1 应该获得的成就感。It spoils our sense of fulfillment. ☺

Part 1 考什么?

每个月在亚太考区（包括东亚、澳洲和新西兰）最新出现的新题,Pat 都会及时在自己的博客 blog. sina. com. cn/ieltsguru 的口语预测中为大家及时公布。

下面的这些真题是近期亚太区的最新 Part 1 真题（对这些考题的详尽分析请看 Day 7）。

The Most Recent Part 1 Question Pool
最新亚太区 Part 1 真题库

（您还可以在 Pat 博客 blog. sina. com. cn/ieltsguru 中看到实时更新）

The Start of the Test

Please switch off/ turn off your mobile phone.

> What's your full name? / Can you tell me your full name please? ☆
>
> Can I see your ID card please? ☆

☞ ☆ What's your full name? / Can you tell me your full name please?

这是固定的题目,简单地回答 My（full）name is… 就很好。如果你还不放心,一定想要解释名和姓,大家都知道中文的姓名顺序和英文正好相反,所以最好别太具体地说你的 first name /last name 是什么,除非故意想在一开始就弄晕考官,而 surname 那个词又是比较正式的。所以,如果你非要说姓字名谁,那就还是脚踏实地地说 My family name is… and my given name is… 吧。

☞ ☆ Can I see your ID card please?

这个也是固定问题,回答 Here you are. 或者 Here you go. 都成。

Hometown/ Your House/ Your flat/Housework

What do you like about your hometown?

What do you dislike about your hometown?

Do you think your hometown is good for young people?

What's the nightlife like in your hometown? ☆

What would you change about your city? ☆

What types of public transport can be found in your hometown? ☆

Do you often do housework?

Do you have a driver's license? ☆

Do you live in a house or a flat? ☆

Is your landlord charging a high rent for the flat?

Is there anything hanging on the wall?

☞ ☆ What's the nightlife like in your hometown?

What's... like? 就是指……是什么样儿的？

☞ ☆ What would you change about your city?

这里的 would 表示只是你的希望，未必是能实现的，所以可以说得大胆一点。

☞ ☆ What types of public transport can be found in your hometown?

注意，很多同学爱说的 transportation 那个词其实是美国的说法，英国考官会用 transport。

☞ ☆ Do you live in a house or a flat?

flat 是英国人说的公寓，国内同学更熟悉的 apartment 其实是美式说法，如果你拥有公寓的产权则可以叫它 condo。

☞ ☆ Do you often do housework?

常见家务的地道英文表达：wash the dishes/do the dishes（洗碗），do the laundry

（洗衣服，比较少有人说 wash the clothes），take out the rubbish（倒垃圾，这是英式英语，而在美国则叫 take out the trash），vacuum the floor（用吸尘器吸地板，在国内吸尘器都已经快过时了，而英美的绝大多数家庭却都还在坚持使用），mop the floor（擦地板），change the bed linen（换床单、被套），cook（meals），而且在英文里 spring cleaning（春季大扫除）是经常听到的说法。

☞ ☆ Do you have a driver's license?

对于这种考题最好不要只用 Yes/No 一个词就把考官粗暴地顶回去，看在 1550 大洋的份上也要跟他/她多练几句口语，比如可以用在英美人所尽知的一句名言用来解释自己为什么要"考本子"：Driving is not a right. It's a privilege（特许的权利）. 或者很"巨蟹"地说 Driving makes life much easier for me and my family members.

如果没有 driver's license 那也不要说自己一直都在无证驾驶，可以说 The traffic is always tied up so there's no point in getting a driver's license anyway. 喜欢玩深沉的还可以说家乡的司机普遍缺乏责任感（There're an awful lot of reckless drivers out there.）或者就简单地说开车有风险（risky），怕受伤（I'm afraid of getting hurt …）。

☞ ☆ Is your landlord or landlady charging a high rent for the flat?

这里的 landlord/landlady 分别指男女房东，charge 在这里是"征收"，而 rent 当然就是房租了。这道题有些考官也会简单地问成，"Is the rent high?"

Your Studies/ Your Work

Are you working or studying?

（对学生）What do you like about your studies?

What's your major? Do you like it?

Is there anything you don't like about it?

What did you do on your first day in this school university? ☆

（对已经工作的考生）What do you like / dislike about your job?

Do you think people should be paid more if they work at weekends?

☞ ☆ What did you do on your first day in this school/university?

国外学校的第一天经常被称为 Orientation Day，常见活动有 an orientation tour of the campus（其实也就是带着大家看看校园），a Welcome Meeting，a free lunch（但现在经济不好，有些学校已经赖掉了），在有些学校里还能 meet the principal（校长）and other faculty and staff。

Hobbies

Do you have any hobbies?

What do you usually do at weekends? ☆

What do people usually do to relax in your country?

☞ ☆ What do you usually do at weekends?

注意英国考官说"在周末"会说 at weekends 而不说 on weekends。

Sports / Outdoor Activities

What sports are most popular in your country?

Do you think it's important to play a sport? ☆

Do you like doing outdoor activities?

Do you like swimming?

What are the benefits of swimming?

Do you like biking / cycling?

Are bikes popular in China?

How old were you when you first learned to ride a bike?

Do you often play games? ☆

What games are popular in China? ☆

☞ ☆ Do you think it's important to play a sport?

注意：play a sport 是很地道的英文，不是中式英语。

☞ ☆ Do you often play games?

英语国家的常见游戏：

card games，tag（基本就是国内小朋友玩的"捉人"游戏），I-spy-with-my-little-eye（这个游戏可是 Pat 小时候的最爱，但国内孩子似乎不太爱玩，请看 Day 8 的详细解释），spelling bee（拼字游戏），math games and hide-and-seek（捉迷藏）。

☞ ☆ What games are popular in China?

such as chess, mahjong, jumping rubber band（跳橡皮筋），kite-flying, Killers of Three Kingdoms（三国杀），Grows Vegetables and Steals Vegetables（种菜、偷菜），West Illusion Swims（梦幻西游），Dungeon and Warrior（地下城与勇士），Plants vs.（发音/'vəːsəs/）Zombies（植物大战僵尸）。

The Media

What types of TV program do you like watching? ☆

What types of TV program are popular in your country?

Why do we need ads? ☆

What kinds of radio program do you like best?

What types of film do you like watching?

What are the differences between local newspapers and international newspapers?

☞ ☆ Why do we need ads?

最重要的原因肯定是 They keep us informed about the latest products and give us more options. 而且很多广告的娱乐性也很强（entertaining），更不用说还可以在广告中看到 superstars；而对于商家（businesses）来说，ads 则是 marketing tools。

☞ ☆ What types of TV program do you like watching?

⚠ WARNING　IELTS 的惯例：在这类问题中剑桥考官通常都会将 What types of / What kinds of 后面的名词使用单数形式，但注意听到时不要误以为考官只允许你说一种选择，详情请看 Day 7。

The Internet

How often do you use computers?

What are the differences between emails and letters? ☆

What are the disadvantages of writing something by hand?

How can children improve their handwriting?

☞ ☆ What are the differences between emails and letters?

letters 也经常叫做 snail mail（蜗牛信），因为实在太慢了。

Reading & Writing

Do you like reading?

What're your favourite kind of books?

Do you prefer to type things or to write things on paper? ☆

☞ ☆ Do you prefer to type things or to write things on paper?

打字的好处除了更快（more speedy，speedy 是 IELTS 口试里代替 fast 的有用选择）之外，还可以编辑（edit）和剪贴（just cut and paste it）。

Language and Numbers

What do you find difficult about learning English?

Would you like to learn another foreign language in the future?

What're your lucky numbers? Why do you think they can bring good luck?

☞ ☆ Why do you think they can bring good luck?

Lucky numbers sound similar to words that have positive meanings. 详情请看 Day 7。

Clothing

What kinds of clothing do you like wearing?

Do you like fashionable clothing?

Food

How often do you eat out in restaurants?

What are the advantages and disadvantages of eating out?

Is fast food popular in your country?

Which meal is the most important to you, breakfast, lunch or dinner?

Do you like cooking? Why?

Do you think children should learn how to cook?

Do you like vegetables? ☆

☞ ☆ Do you think children should learn how to cook?

"小盆友"们学做饭的好处包括 It makes them more independent（更独立），gives them a basic life skill，而且还可以 keeps them away from junk food。

☞ ☆ Do you like vegetables?

这道题有时候也会被问成是否喜欢水果（fruit），理由除了说好吃不妨加一条 They're rich in Vitamin C and fiber（富含维生素 C 和纤维），形容水果"多汁的"在地道英文里就坚定地用 juicy 这个词来表达。

People

Do you prefer to have old people or young people as your neighbours? ☆

Who does the housework in your family?

What do you usually do with your friends?

In your country, where can you meet new people? ☆

Did you have a happy childhood?

☞ ☆ Do you prefer to have old people or young people as your neighbours?

这是《剑 8》里的题目，年轻邻居的好处是 more sociable（更喜欢社交的），more open-minded，easier to communicate with 等；而老人做邻居的优点则可以强调 They tend to be quiet and more helpful.

☞ ☆ In your country, where can you meet new people?

这里的 new people 指的就是你"新结识的人"，请看 Day 7 的详解。

Arts

What kinds of music do you like listening to?

Do you think it's important for children to learn to play a musical instrument? ☆

What kinds of photographs do you like looking at?

Do you like painting or drawing?

☞ ☆ Do you think it's important for children to learn to play a musical instrument?

　　这里的 a musical instrument 表示"乐器"，各种乐器的地道英文表达请看 Day 7 的 Topic 8。

Buildings

Are historical buildings important?

Do you often go to museums?

How can a museum attract more people?

What are the advantages of staying in a hotel? ☆

☞ ☆ What are the advantages of staying in a hotel?

　　有个拼写类似的词叫 motel，国内翻译成汽车旅馆，但在国外并不只是开着汽车才能去住，其实就是"如家"式的经济型酒店了。

Weather & Seasons

What types of weather do you like best?

What is your favourite season?

How do people feel about rain?

Shopping

Do you like shopping?

How often do you go shopping?

Collection

Why do some people like collecting things? ☆

What do you like to collect?

☞ ☆ Why do some people like collecting things?

详解请看 Day 7 的 Topic 10。

Colours

Do any colours have special meanings in China?

Nature

Do birds have any special meaning in your culture?

Do any flowers have special meanings in your culture?

Are gardens and parks important to a city?

What's your favourite wild animal?

☞ ☆ What's your favourite wild animal?

　　除了 panda, koala, kangaroo 这些考官已经听得比人类都熟悉的动物外，moose（驼鹿），beaver（水獭）和 turtle（海龟）都是英语文化中大家相当喜爱的动物，而且这几个词最大的好处是发音异常简单，考试时绝不会因为紧张而说错。

Pets

What are the advantages of raising pets?

Travel

Do you like traveling?

Why do people like spending time near the sea?

What do you think of traveling by air?

Pollution

How can people control the pollution in your city?

What harm can noise do to our lives?

Festivals，Holidays & Parties

Do you like partying? ☆

What are the differences between formal and informal parties?

Do you think it's important for people to celebrate their birthdays?

What do people usually do at weddings in China?

How do you spend holidays?

What are the most important holidays in China? ☆

Do you think festivals are important?

Do you like dancing?

What are the most popular gifts parents give their children in your country?

☞ ☆ Do you like partying?

您大概还不知道吧，在地道英文中 party 其实经常会当动词用，类似的英文还有 clubbing。

☞ ☆ What are the most important holidays in China?

请看 Day 7 的 Topic 20。

Part 2 考什么?

最近 7 年中所有的雅思口语 Part 2 topics 都是紧密围绕一个神秘的 Map 展开的。

Pat "秘制" 的 Part 2 卡片话题藏宝图
My Personalized Map for the IELTS Card Topics

Cities

Location
History
People
Food
Cityscape
Culture
My own feeling

Natural Beauty

Location
History
People
Activities
Equipment
Atmosphere
My own feeling

Buildings

Location
History
People
Exterior
Interior
Atmosphere
Service
My own feeling

Organizations

History
Members
Location
Work
Influence
My own feeling

Leisure Activities

Who
What
When
Why
How
My own feeling

People		Animals
Appearance		Appearance
Personality		Habits
Hobbies		Habitat
Past experience		Food
Relationship with others		Relationship with humans
My own feeling		My own feeling

Events	Objects	
When	How I got it	
Where	Exterior	
Who	Functions	
What	Price	
Why	Role in my life	
How	Role in society	
My own feeling	My own feeling	

Part 2 的答案还可以合理合法地合并

截至本书剑 8 版完成时雅思口语 Part 2 的话题总数已经达到了 270 多个。2011 年 2 月至 6 月（中间还跳过了春节假期没有考试）在中国大陆累计出现的卡片就超过了 50 个，如果再算上一些比较"火星"的题目总数就更多了。现实地说把 IELTS 口试卡片题库全都准备得很熟练是不可能的（That would be out of the question.）。为此而且我专门询问了环球雅思的几位前任和现任考官，大家一致认为：合并答案这种"偷懒"的做法是可行的。请看：

Describe a teacher who has influenced you.	Describe a neighbor who helped you before.	Describe a person who can speak another language.
Describe someone who helped you before.	Describe an important person in your life.	Describe an old person who you admire.
Describe someone who you have studied or worked with.	Describe a family member.	Describe someone who gave you advice.

很明显,通过描述 an old English teacher,我们不仅可以准备好表格左上角的题目,还可以很自然地描述这个表格里面其他所有的 topics,甚至还可以把一部分内容用到 Describe a subject you liked at school. / Describe the first day of a course you attended at school. / Describe an ideal job. 等 "不搭界" 的考题里。

又比如下面这个表格:

Describe a special meal you had recently.	Describe a difficult thing you can do well.	Describe a skill.	Describe an interesting thing you did in your spare time recently.
Describe a happy event in your childhood.	Describe a birthday party.	Describe a good cook you know.	Describe an exciting experience.

通过准备一个关于 cooking 的详细过程,会让我们对这些题目都有足够的信心。

下面请大家自己感受一下合并 topics 的乐趣,练习下面的话题怎样快速搞定.

?	Describe a person you admire.	Describe a successful person.	Describe a leader.
Describe a famous person / a celebrity.	Describe your favourite book.	Describe your favourite movie.	Describe your favourite character in a TV program.

又比如:

Describe an electronic device (except a computer).	Describe a gift you have received.	Describe an expensive thing you want to buy.	Describe something you lost.
Describe your favourite mode of communication such as mobile phone or email.	Describe something you want to buy if you have a lot of money.	Describe an object you use every day.	**?**

此外,大家还可以在本书的 Day 8 中看到完整的雅思 Part 2 真题库详解。

Part 3 的话题范围

根据过去七年对所有 Part 3 试题的统计，我们可以用下面的表格覆盖口语第三部分的所有话题：

Weather & Season	Food & Health	Nature	Sports & Games	Reading& Writing	Volunteers & Charities（慈善机构）
Buildings（such as Museums & Libraries）	Media & Celebrities	Collection	Animals	Traveling	Employment
Cities & Countryside	Arts（photos, paintings, music, etc.）	Clothing	Festivals & Parties	Shopping	Language

由此可以清晰看出，其实 Part 3 的话题和 Part 1 还是有很多相似之处的，只是 Part 3 的话题更加正式（但当然还是没有雅思写作那么正式）。

Part 3 考什么？

下面的题目都是近期在中国大陆出现的 Part 3 真题，可以让大家充分领略 Part 3 的出题风格，对 Part 3 的详解您可以在后面的 Day 9 看到。缩写 "cf." 是 "参阅" 的意思，出国之后大家在大学论文里经常会看到这个拉丁词。

◎ In your opinion, what's a healthy lifestyle?

（思路提示：eat low-fat and low-calorie food / get more fruits and vegetables 注意 fruit 在表示不同种类的水果时可加-s / watch less TV/ early to bed and early to rise 这不是中式英语而是很地道的英文：早睡早起 / exercise regularly）

◎ What materials can be recycled?

（思路提示：paper / wood / aluminum cans "易拉罐儿" / glass containers 玻璃

容器／tyres 轮胎，blah，blah，blah…）

○ Why are gardens and parks important to a city?

（思路提示：places where people can exercise / breathe the fresh air / improve our mood / make us calm and peaceful / gorgeous views）

○ Do you think TV programs can teach us about history?

（思路提示：plenty of history programs on TV / but some of them are not based on facts / fabricate history 杜撰历史/ just to attract more viewers）

○ What are the differences between modern buildings and traditional buildings?

（思路提示：traditional buildings are more eco-friendly 有益于环保的/ modern buildings are less efficient in terms of the use of energy / modern buildings are stronger and taller / traditional buildings represent the history of a town，a city or a country）

○ Which are better，big classes or small classes?

（思路提示：Small classes: more opportunities to express themselves / more discussions / students are more attentive in class / students can receive more individual help from the teacher；Big classes: a larger number of classmates / lower costs / more experience with peers of different backgrounds）

○ Who can give good advice to us?

（思路提示：our parents/our teachers/our friends who're more experienced with certain things / or other people who really care about us）

○ How do TV programs affect education?

（思路提示：some TV programming（请注意这个词跟可数的 programme 不同，不可数名词 programming 是电视节目的总称，它在地道英文中谈媒体时与 programme 一样常用，可惜 Pat 在北京期间却从来没听到过国内考生用这个词）can be pretty educational，like National Geographic and Discovery. They're real eye-openers. / some TV programs may be addictive/some TV shows may make kids violent…）

○ How can veterinarians help people?

（思路提示：cf. Day 7: Pets become sick sometimes / They give the pets shots / make them safe to us /prevent the spread of viruses…）

○ Why do some people like traveling to other countries? (cf. Day 7: travel)

○ Who like shopping more, men or women?

(思路提示：men tend to be more attracted to items like electronic and digital stuff, such as iPod touch（Pat 发现国内媒体喜欢把这个简称成 iTouch，但事实上在国外并没人这么说，大家都还是讲 iPod touch），iPhone 4, Blackberry and PSP... and of course fancy cars / women tend to be more interested in things like snacks, cosmetics（化妆品）and clothing...)

○ What are the advantages of 24-hour stores?

(思路提示：more business / more customers / more convenient / more flexibility)

○ What are the differences between Chinese movies and Western movies?

(思路提示：Apparently, Chinese movies tend to be more focused on the Chinese way of life while the Western movies tend to deal with the Western issues / As I see it, Western movies can be more entertaining and more creative / Chinese movies are sometimes a bit too predictable / even in China, most box-office hits are Western movies.)

○ What do Chinese think of nutritious food?

(思路提示：it's something that's essential to your good health / it should be something that helps you keep fit, like vegetables, fish, eggs and grains / it contains more vitamin more protein / low-fat stuff)

○ Do you think the government should move factories to the countryside?

(思路提示：it depends / the factories that get the environment seriously polluted should definitely be moved to the country or closed / but factories that are "green" can stay where they are now)

○ What do you think of giving children gifts when they behave well?

(思路提示：it may be an incentive（给人动力的东东）to them / on the other hand, some kids may be spoiled by doing that / basically, it would be better to reward them with words than with gifts)

○ Why do some people like eating out at restaurants?

(思路提示：better taste / more choices / socialize with others / family reunions /

But that has made some of us seriously overweight)

○ **What skills can be learned at home but cannot be learned at school?**

（思路提示：cooking skills / gardening skills / sewing and knitting skills 这个基本上就是中文的"缝纫"了，国外的 grandma 们也都爱没事儿时打个毛衣什么的，其实西方并不像国内朋友们想象的那么"前卫"）

○ Is it important for us to have a global language?

（思路提示：Currently, English is used as a global language / It seems this trend is positive coz it really helps people from different countries communicate with one another more efficiently / especially at business meetings / and of course it's good news for scientists /we can understand the English-speaking cultures much better than before / On the other hand, English being used as a global language is unfair to those who can't speak this language / Many other languages are dying out from this world each year…）

○ If they could choose, would most people become lawyers or police officers in your country?

（思路提示：lawyers make tons of money / lawyers enjoy high social status / lawyers are intelligent / being a police officer may be dangerous coz theses days, lots of criminals carry guns with them / but some lawyers are dishonest）

○ What's your idea of success?

（思路提示：success gives you a sense of fulfillment / even if it's just something as ordinary as cooking a nice meal, to some people, it may be a great success / some other people are real go-getters, they always strive for success）

○ Is money important to us?

（思路提示：Money talks / money can help you fulfill your dreams, like getting a big Mercedes or a posh house / but money is not everything / love makes the world go around /money may make people cold and cruel…）

○ How can we solve the global warming issues?

（思路提示：reduce the number of cars / encourage people to take the public transport / cut down on car emissions / control the number of heavy-industry factories /

raise the environmental awareness)

   ○ Do you think laws should protect celebrities?

（思路提示：celebrities are also citizens, and more importantly, they are also taxpayers / paparazzi should be punished if they break the law)

   ○ What are the differences between individual sports and team sports?

（思路提示：team sports like soccer and basketball cultivate team spirit / Team sports tend to be more stressful 'cause people play multiple roles / Team sports can be more fun coz you cooperate with your teammates / People are more focused when they do individual sports, like jogging and swimming / Individuals sports may give you a stronger sense of achievement / Some individual sports can be very competitive, like golfing and running)

Pat 指南

Part 3 的题目不管听起来多么怪异（weird），也一定一定不要想得太高深了。时刻牢记：雅思口语无论再高分的答案也还是说话（spoken），而不是写作（written）。

Part 3 出题有规律么？

☆ 除了那些与 Part 1 类似的问题之外，Part 3 的一个重要特色（feature）是经常会有 1~2 个涉及比较不同讨论对象间的差异（comparison / contrast）的问题。

例如下面的《剑 8》考题实例：

★ Do you think there will be a greater choice of food in shops in the future, or will there be less choice?

★ Do you think we meet different kinds of friend at different stages of our lives?

下面这个表格展示了最近七年出现过的所有比较类型，其中的符号 vs（versus）表示"与……相比较"：

Government (Incl. Law) vs Citizens	Males vs Females	Traditions vs High Technology	Individuals vs Teams	Elderly People vs Children	The Present vs The Future

★ 考生在 Part 3 还经常会被问到 1~2 个涉及利弊（advantages / disadvantages）的问题。比如，《剑 8》中出现了如下考题：

What would the advantages for schools be if they asked students their opinions about lessons?

Would there be any disadvantages in asking students' opinions?

★ 另外，Part 3 中考生还经常会被问到 1~2 个要求分析原因或者解决方法（Why/causes / solutions）的题目。比如《剑 8》中出现了如下 Part 3 考题：

Why do you think people go to restaurants when they want to celebrate something?

Why do you think world leaders often have meetings together?

我们将在本书的 Day 9 中对更为详尽的 Part 3 答题技巧进行讨论。

超短线
The Ultra-Short Track

对于雅思口语 Part 1 和 Part 3 中的问答题，有六个用来快速思考理由的关键词，可以供备考时间过短或者口语基础太"潮"的同学在考试时实在想不出思路被"干"在那儿时解围使用：

Time

Cost

Mood

Health

Safety

Knowledge

* 其中 health 除了身体健康 physical health 也包括心理健康 psychological health

比如我们来看一道 Part 1 中较难的考题：

Do you think children should be allowed to drive?

这个题的视角很蹊跷，但是没关系，不妨试试六字诀：

Time →Kids can get to school earlier if they are allowed to drive.

Cost →It would cost more for teenagers to learn to drive.

Mood →Driving is exciting for youngsters, no doubt about it.

Health →If children got hurt in an accident, they would suffer more physically and psychologically.

Safety →Some teens may will NOT be able to drive safely.

Knowledge →It would be nice if children could learn more about traffic rules through driving.

这只是给您的一点提示，当然，您也可以完全用这六个提示词想出属于自己的 ideas。

需要提醒的是：六字诀对口试的 Part 1 和 Part 3 问答题最有效，而对于 Part 2 卡片题的思路来说，则还是沿着本书 Day 8 中每类话题里的展开思路表格思考更有效。

但也有特例，比如最近在大陆考区有道十分著名的 Part 2 卡片熊经常出没：

Describe a TV show that you dislike（不喜欢）.

喜欢的电视节目比较好说，但描述自己不喜欢的节目却不太容易深入下去。

也用六字诀试试：

Time →Too late (around midnight) and terribly long

Cost →It cost（cost 的过去时还是 cost）a huge amount of money to produce.

Mood →It's totally heavy（沉重的）and depressing（非常压抑的）.

Health →Filled with violent scenes and is psychologically damaging to youngsters.

Safety →I'm even afraid it would lead to some youth crimes.

Knowledge →It doesn't bring any fresh ideas and is often interrupted （节目中间被

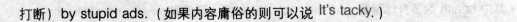

打断）by stupid ads.（如果内容庸俗的则可以说 It's tacky.）

这样一个 TV show 足以给人 nightmare 了吧。

在头脑中使用六字诀需要对它们大量练习，熟练掌握才能在考场中运用自如。如果觉得自己已经很有把握了，那么可以再加上 View（美观还是丑陋）这条补充理由作为备用，如果连前面六条还没记熟就不考虑这条视觉理由了。

最后还是要强调：六字诀只是在实在没招儿了时作为救命稻草，对于能自己快速想出 ideas 的题就完全不必依赖它们，毕竟在雅思口语里流利度是相当重要的一个指标。

Think hard. Think well.

Day 3

 雅思口语的词
IELTS Speaking Building Blocks

Pat's Guide
To the Speaking Test

Talk in everlasting words,
And dedicate them all to you.
I'm here if you call me.
You think that I don't even mean a single word I said.
They're only words.
And words are all I can possibly have.

这个网站上的网友来自世界各地,大家可以经常上去看看。

它的英语风格其实就很接近雅思口语高分答案的风格:不是很难,但也并不是很"痞";有一定的描述性,但绝不是背书。

We just have adopted a laid-back approach,
even though we take the test seriously.

试的时候词汇用得好会加分,这是不争的事实。可到底什么叫好词,在国内培训界却很有争议。

英文有句名谚,"A man travels across the world in search of what he needs and returns home to find it."中文可以叫"舍近求远"。

其实大家准备雅思口语备考的过程,也多半如此。我经常告诉自己的学生们:"老师教的'亮点'词句,只是用来点缀(spice up)你的答案的。很多内容其实完全可以用简单一点的英文自己说。口语的本质是交流,而不是用来吓人的。"

请您仔细体会《剑8》Test 2 的高分答案:

Do you think it's possible to be friends with someone if you never meet them in person?

It's not only possible, even lifelong friendship can be formed *this way. I heard about pen friends or "pen pals" who didn't really meet up in person but could still* communicate *well. And these days it's popular for people to make new friends on social networking sites like Facebook and Twitter. Just choose such friends* wisely.

这样用词简易的答案之所以会是高分答案,是因为它没有"语不惊人死不休"的难词怪词,但却意思清晰、内容充实。

下面的《剑8》Test 1 高分答案同样用词平实,但也能有效地传达意义并且层次清晰,牢记"交流"才是口语的唯一目的:

How do you think neighbours can help each other?

There can be plenty of ways, such as helping elderly *neighbours with their housework or* walking their pets *for them. And when new neighbours move in, we can show them around the community, give them information about the* community *services and tell them some useful phone numbers.*

再请看下面的答案:

What's your favourite subject at school?

I guess... it's history, especially the world history. I like it so much coz it explains

---

> *lots of things to us, like why Americans wanted to get independence from Britain two centuries ago. And why Hitler wanted to attack other countries during the Second World War. Probably the most important reason I adore this subject is the history tests are always so easy...*

这样的答案,如果能比较流利地说出来,至少会有 8 分,但它却只用了两个词"点缀"(independence, adore),而且这两个词今天我们都会学到。

当然,并不是每个人都需要 8 分,再看这个回答:

> **What kinds of radio program do you like best?**
>
> *Actually I don't really listen to the radio very often. But basically, it seems I tend to pick sports shows and news shows over other kinds of radio programs, simply because they are fun and informative.*

说这样的答案,考生的目的显然是要和考官进行真正的交流,而不是把一堆大词和连考生自己都不明白的句子推给考官后就闪。

即使相对抽象的考题也并不是必须要用大词才能拿到高分的:

再看这个常考题的 8 分答案:

> **Is laughing the same as feeling happy?**
>
> *It seems like there's always some confidence behind our laughter coz after all, we've made the laughing sound, which sometimes could be annoying to the people around us. But feeling happy can really be a private thing. We can just happiness to ourselves.*

像这样的答案,已经绝对是 IELTS 口试中的高分答案了,就因为它们合理(make sense),而且比较像"人话"(human utterances)。

今天就跟各位分享在 IELTS 口语考场上真正能打动考官的词。这些词汇多数貌不惊人,但踏出国门之后您将会真正明白它们在国外生活里是何等地常用。

雅思口语中最常用的"小词"
Colloquial Words and Phrases

◇ 前面标"★"的词句表示极为常用,一定要熟练掌握。

◇ 对于没有标出"★"的词句,如果时间很紧的话那就不要记了。准备 IELTS 听说读写四项都有一个真理:不要为了那些考场里你很有可能想不起来的东西去牺牲(compromise)掉那些考场里你一定会用到的东西。

◇ 此表格充分考虑了英、美两国的英语习惯。对于那些只在美国和加拿大使用,但是英国人并不常用的口语词汇在本书中一律不予推荐。对于没有十分把握的词句,Pat 还专门向我的英国朋友们做了确认。

序号	英文表达	讲解	用法举例
1	★ stuff	东西,口语里面等于 things,但请国内同学们牢记 stuff 永远不能加复数	The stuff in that store is very pricey(贵的).
2	★ folks	= people	Average folks can't possibly afford cars like that.
3	★ pretty	= 副词 very	My iPad is pretty fun.
4	★ fun	= interesting(请朋友们注意 fun 做形容词时其实并不是 funny"搞笑的"意思,但它在日常生活里的出现频率一点也不比 funny 低)	There're lots of fun things to do in the classroom.
5	★ adore	非常喜欢	I adore that singer.
6	shortly	= soon	I'll get these things done shortly.
7	spot	(1)看见 = see ★(2)地方 = place	(1)I spotted some squirrels(松鼠) and woodpeckers(啄木鸟) in Stanley Park. It's a nice spot. 注:Stanley Park 是温哥华的一个大公园,离我家很近,非常美 (2)This park looks like a nice spot for a picnic(野餐).

（续表）

序号	英文表达	讲解	用法举例
8	★ eye-opening	是很地道的英文，"让人大开眼界的"，它的名词 eye-opener 在《剑 8》P. 140 也出现了	Trips to other countries can be reaa-aaaaaaaally eye-opening.（本词原为 really，此处系口语用法。本书中的"sooooo"也是同一种用法）
9	★ decent	上大学英语课时老师可能会告诉你这个词是"体面的"，但在国外真实生活里这个词更多的时候是表示"不错的，挺好的"意思 = quite good	This job offers a decent salary and an impressive set of benefits（"工作的福利"在地道英文里就直接用 benefits）.
10	★ hang out	玩儿。很多时候可以代替 play，注意这个词组后面不能跟宾语	I often hang out in bars at weekends.
11	★ kind of = sort of	有点……, = somewhat	My boss is kind of hard to get along with.
12	★ like…	like 作为连词在口语中极度常用，可以表示"比如说"、"像是……"、"差不多是"	I bought lots of stuff, like carrots, beef and salmon. That program is like, … boring.
13	★ coz = cuz = 'cause	= because	You should watch that movie coz it's very moving（感人的）.
14	★ … as well.	也…… = … too.	Beijing is exciting for its nightlife. And it's culturally attractive as well.
15	… you know…	在你思考的时候可以表示自然的停顿，两个词不要发音太清楚，含含糊糊地哼出来就行了	Kitties and doggies are like, you know, … really adorable（可爱的）.
16	★ … is a piece of cake. =… is a snap. =… is a breeze.	小菜一碟	The IELTS speaking test is just a breeze if you know all the tricks about it.

（续表）

序号	英文表达	讲解	用法举例
17	★ during	表示"在……时候",极度常用,但可惜国内考生普遍都不用	We go hiking and camping **during** holidays.
18	★ know … inside out = know … backwards and forwards	精通……	He **knows** computers **backwards and forwards**.
19	way off base	= totally wrong	Edward **was way off** base when he said money would solve all the problems in this world.
20	is no picnic = is a pain in the neck	很折磨人	Getting the homework done everyday **is no picnic**.
21	get on my nerves	让我很烦	The noise has been **getting on my nerves** lately（近来）.
22	★ kick back and relax =let one's hair down	放松	At parties, we just **kick back and relax**.
23	★ a couple of	几个	I stayed in France for **a couple of** weeks.
24	★ a bunch of	= some 一些	I went there with **a bunch of** new friends.
25	dozens of	几十	I just bought **dozens of** gifts online.
26	★ loads of = tons of = a host of = a multitude of	= lots of	I've got **loads of** work to get through before tomorrow.
27	★ make sense	= be reasonable 合理	The plot（剧情）of that movie didn't **make** any **sense**.

（续表）

序号	英文表达	讲解	用法举例
28	★ …, you name it. = and the list goes on and on	……应有尽有	Beijing has traditions, modern lifestyles, tasty food, exciting night-life, beautiful people … you name it.
29	By doing that, I kill two birds with one stone.	一举两得	When I travel around, I take photos and then sell them online. So you see, I just kill two birds with one stone.
30	★ … is the best +名词, hands down.	……绝对是最……的	The *King's Speech* is the best movie I've ever seen, hands down.
31	… would be the last thing I want to do.	……是我在人生里最不想做的事	Doing the dishes would be the last thing I want to do.
32	That's the way the ball bounces.	命中注定就是这样了（无奈啊……）。一般说这句话的时候，人们还要耸耸肩膀（shrug their shoulders）	Lots of people got fired. Too bad. But that's the way the ball bounces in a recession（经济衰退）.
33	get the hang of	基本了解了怎样做某事	"I've never used a word processor before." "Don't worry — you'll get the hang of it shortly."
34	get… down pat	"完全掌握了……"（请注意这里的 pat 不是我，是小写的！）	If you just memorize all the answers, even if you get all the answers down pat, there may still be questions you haven't thought of during the test. So, …
35	What a shame!	"太可惜了"（在这里 shame 跟"羞耻"无关）	They lost that match. What a shame!

25 个更"痞"的雅思口试常用词(高分内容)
Slang Words and Phrases

这里我们不说 Eminem, Black Eyed Peas 或者 50 Cents 的歌词, 只说雅思口语的常用加分痞语。其实中文里面也有很多痞语, 比如"火"、"大腕儿"、"忽悠"、"牛人"这些词, 真的都"巨"常用对吧? 但对于连在国外都不常用的那种英文, 下表中坚决不予收录。而且如果您觉得自己本身就是比较"板"的人 (a stuffed shirt), 那么这个表格不适合您, Just skip it!

普通版	痞语限量珍藏版	中文解释	例句
fan	★ buff / nut / freak / mania	"迷", 语气一个比一个强, 最后的 mania 基本上是"痴"了	I am a movie buff. I go to the movies whenever I can find some free time.
bookworm	nerd / geek	书呆子	Nerds are often laughed at.
be so surprised	freak out	很吃惊	I totally freaked out when I heard the news.
release pressure	let off steam	释放压力	I often go to the gym to let off steam.
feel uncomfortable / sick	feel under the weather	身体不舒服	When I feel under the weather, I just take a shower, which makes me feel less uncomfortable.
expensive	★ pricey	很贵的	That car was pricey. But he bought it without batting an eyelash (想都没想).
is better than…	★ beats…	比……强	Having the newspaper delivered to your place beats having to go out and buy one, right?
bad	★ lousy	差劲的	That director makes lousy movies.
is boring	★ is a drag	单调的, 烦人的	A nine-to-five job can really be a drag.

（续表）

普通版	俚语限量珍藏版	中文解释	例句
the boring things you have to do everyday	★ the daily grind	每天都一样的无聊事情	I'm sick and tired of the daily grind and want to get away from it all.
is totally unappealing	is totally gross	让人恶心的	The food in that cafeteria (自助餐厅) is totally gross.
is hard to understand	is over my head	我听不懂	The professor's lecture was way over my head.
drive me crazy	drive me up the wall	让人抓狂	The noise really drives me up the wall.
have fun / have a good time	★ have a ball = have a blast	玩得超级开心	The kids are having a ball building their sandcastles.
fancy	funky	新奇的	He's into funky outfits (服装).
clothes	★ outfit	(一件)服装	This outfit looks gorgeous.
attention-getting	flashy	很"炫"的	Some young girls are into flashy accessories (饰品).
beautiful and expensive	snazzy	华丽的,经常用来形容服装	Superstars tend to wear snazzy clothes.
strange	★ weird	怪异的	The noise sounds so weird.
old and uninteresting	corny	很俗的,没创意的	The lyrics (歌词) are meaningful but corny as well.
a person who likes playing video games	a gamer / a vid-kid	超级爱打游戏的人	I'm a vid-kid. I spend all my free time playing games.

Pat指南 🔊

☆ way 这个词在口语里面很多时候作副词,表示"远远……",口语考试时用效果很好。

This movie is <u>way</u> better than the director's last movie.

The professor's lecture is way over my head.

The life in this city is way too stressful for folks who grew up in tiny villages.

That house is way out of my price range.

☆ practically 这个词很多时候表示 almost，是典型的口语说法，在国外生活里相当常用。

Practically everyone likes that song.

Practically everything in that store is good.

☆ 中文的"不错"到底怎么表达？quite good? fairly good?

请你和考官用这个词来表示"不错"，看看他/她的反应：decent。这个词在口语里面和"体面的"没有关系，倒是很像中文的"不错的"。

I can't find a decent house in my price range.

A decent meal in that restaurant costs anywhere near 200-500 yuan.

I just need a decent salary without getting myself overworked.

《那些花儿》
Cool Alternatives to Some Excessively-used Words

有首歌叫《那些花儿》，唱的是年轻时特花心的一男人成熟之后突然反省的故事。当然媳妇儿不能总换，不过对于口语用词来说，能经常替换却绝对是好事儿。需要注意的是，这里说的替换，仅是为了考虑考试的效果，但其实很多意思在生活中使用得最多的就是每组左边那个最普通的词。比如一般在国外生活中说"好吃的"，绝对还是 delicious 这个词听到得最多。但在 IELTS 考场里，这个词存在被国内考生使用过度的可能，那么为了应试就可以试一试 tasty / scrumptious / mouth-watering 这类在国外生活中同样很常用，但是大部分考生却不了解的词汇了。总之，一切为了拿分！

	一般考生的表达	含义	更加分的说法
关于 **number**（数量）	lots of money	一大笔钱	a fortune
	there are so many	大量出现	... are sprouting up all over the city (or the country / or the world)

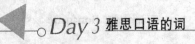
（续表）

	一般考生的表达	含义	更加分的说法
	lots of	大量的	loads of / tons of / a host of / a multitude of
关于 **activities**（活动）	play	娱乐,休闲	hang out
	meet	遇见	run across / encounter
	finish	结束	wrap it up
	help someone	帮助	do someone a favor
	protect	保护(某种资源, resources / old buildings / wild animals 等)	preserve（但如果保护一个人还是要用 protect）
	destroy	破坏	ruin
	do sth.	从事	go about sth.
	relax	休息	kick back and relax
	relaxation	休闲	leisure / recreation
	try my best	尽最大努力	give it my best shot
	easy	简单的	It's a piece of cake. = It's a snap. = It's a breeze.
	difficult	困难的	tough
	interesting	有趣的	stimulating
	boring	没劲的	humdrum / mundane / monotonous
	enjoy ourselves	开心	have a blast
	painful	痛苦的	grueling
	shout	喊	yell / scream
	cheat	骗人	con
	go to bed	去睡觉	hit the sack / turn in
	make trouble	制造麻烦	make waves
	waste time	浪费时间	idle one's time away
	sit in the sun	晒太阳	catch some rays
	save money	省钱	economize

（续表）

	一般考生的表达	含义	更加分的说法
关于 **things** （物品）	valuable	贵重的	precious
	strange	奇怪的	weird
	expensive	贵重的	pricey
	cheap	便宜的	dirt-cheap
	fashionable	时尚的	trendy = stylish = "in"
	popular	流行的	"in"/ big / prevalent / ubiquitous / well-liked（这里的 big 其实也是口语中常用的一个,"流行"）
	good taste	有品味的	chic / classy
	a nice thing	好东西	a knockout
	bad products	劣质产品	trash
	old	老的	worn-out / beat-up
	new	新的	brand-new
	huge	巨大的	enormous / gigantic
关于 **people** （人）	my parents	我的家长	my folks（folks 的"人们"和"家长"这两个意思在生活口语中都极度常用）
	beautiful / pretty	漂亮的	gorgeous
	fat	胖的	overweight
	thin	瘦的	slim
	honest	直率的	straightforward / candid / frank
	strong	强壮的	well-built / well-proportioned
	kind	善良的	caring / considerate / thoughtful
	cute	可爱的	adorable
	polite	有礼貌的	well-mannered
	funny	搞笑的	hilarious
	humorous	幽默的	amusing
	busy	忙的	tied-up
	relaxed	放松的	refreshed

(续表)

	一般考生的表达	含义	更加分的说法
关于 **people** （人）	tired	疲劳的	wiped-out / worn-out / bushed
	hungry	饥饿的	starving / famished
	rich	有钱的	wealthy / affluent
	expert	高手	pro
	high-quality	高素质的（说人一般不能说high-quality）	high-caliber
	become successful	成功	make it big
	people	人们	individuals（正式）/ folks（不正式）
关于 **hobby** （爱好）	like	喜欢	be into / be fascinated by...
	hate	讨厌	dislike / It's not my cup of tea.
	like and dislike	又爱又恨	have mixed feelings about
	don't know any-thing about it	不了解	don't even have a clue about it
	depend on	依赖	count on
	happy	高兴的	delighted
	not happy	不高兴的	in a bad mood / upset
	decide	决定	determine
	can't decide	无法决定	be torn between A and B
	sad	悲伤	in low spirits / blue / down
	boring	枯燥的	It's a drag.
	moving	感人的	touching
	understand	理解	figure out
	make me angry	生气	It makes my blood boil.
	be surprised	吃惊	freak out
	feel afraid	害怕	get cold feet

（续表）

	一般考生的表达	含义	更加分的说法
关于 **weather** （天气）	cold	冷的	chilly（有点冷）/ freezing（很冷的）/ frigid（严寒的）
	cloudy	阴天的	overcast
	hot	热的	scorching
关于 **buildings** （建筑）	tall buildings	高楼	high-rise buildings
	big	宽敞的	spacious
	narrow	狭小的	cramped
	messy	混乱的	cluttered
	quiet	安静的	peaceful / tranquil / serene
	clean	干净的	tidy / spotless
	ugly	丑陋的	It's an eyesore / hideous.
	dirty	脏的	filthy
	old	历史悠久的	time-honored
	important	不可缺少的	essential
关于 **food** （食品）	delicious	好吃的	tasty / out of this world / scrumptious
	smells good	香喷喷的	aromatic（说food）;fragrant（说 flowers / plants）
关于 **time** （时间）	for a long time	很长时间	for ages
	always	总是	constantly

从非常喜欢到极度讨厌的地道英文表达

下面这个表格覆盖了从**非常喜欢**一直到**极度讨厌**的全部常见地道英文表达，在 IELTS 口试的 Part 1 中一定能用到其中的几种：

… is my biggest passion in life.（最喜欢）	I'm not keen on…
I'm enchanted by…	I'm not very fond of…
I'm fascinated by…	I don't care for…
I'm crazy about…	… is not my cup of tea.

I adore…

I love…

I'm a… buff/nut(……迷, 在 buff 前填入喜欢的事物, 比如 car 或 movie)

I'm into…

I'm fond of…

…appeals to me.

I kind of like…

I dislike…

It's a drag.

I thoroughly dislike…

I hate…

I can't stand…

I detest…

I loathe…(最不喜欢)

其实口语里还有语气更强的, 不过基本就是骂人了, 考试用就算了

从**最频繁**到**最偶然**的地道英文表达

下面的表达分别对应从**最频繁**到**最少**发生的各种频率, 只要听到考官强嘴说 How often…的题就要条件反射地想到这样表格:

I… all the time. (总是……)

I constantly …(不断地……)

I… daily. (其实 daily 不止是《日报》, 在地道英文中它也经常作副词, 表示"每天都……")

I… almost every day. (几乎每天都……)

I… every other day. (每隔一天都……)

I… on a weekly basis. (每周都……)

I often …(经常……)

I…every now and then. (时常…)

I…sometimes. (有些时候……)

I…occasionally. (有时……)

I…once in a while… (偶尔……)

I don't… very often. (不常……)

I rarely… (中国考生极其爱用的 seldom 在国外生活中用的却不如 rarely 多)

I hardly ever… (几乎不……)

Maybe once in a blue moon. (表示"极少", 这是个成语, 在国外生活里有时也能听到)

冰天雪地裸求都不给的 30 个"冻人"名词
Top 30 Magical Nouns

名词	注释	举例
leisure	休闲(= recreation)	leisure time / leisure magazines / leisure activities
mood	心情	Colours can really affect our mood.
ambience	氛围, 气氛(= atmosphere)	The ambience there is pretty inviting.
efficiency	效率	Listening to music can actually boost our efficiency at work.
smog	烟雾(最常见的污染之一)	Shanghai is becoming smoggy these days.
necessity	必需品	A car is an absolute necessity in Canada since it's so sprawling (开阔的).
a luxury	奢望	Having a garden is a luxury in Shanghai.
the pace of life	生活节奏	The pace of life in Beijing is very stressful.
competition	竞争	The competition is so fierce today.
encouragement	鼓励	My folks (= my parents) gave me a lot of encouragement.
enjoyment	享受, 乐趣(= pleasure)	Some people play musical instruments just for the enjoyment and pleasure.
gallery	美术馆, 画廊	Art galleries are sprouting up over the CBD of Beijing.
artworks	艺术品(= works of art)	This museum is rich with creative artworks.
pastime	业余爱好	Shopping is my favourite pastime.
preference	偏好	His girlfriend really changed his clothing preferences.
companionship	伴侣关系	People keep pets for companionship or for security.

（续表）

名词	注释	举例
delicacy	美味的食品	In some parts of the world, a jellyfish salad is considered a **delicacy**.
cuisine	一个地区或者国家菜的统称,有点像中文的"菜系"	I'm really into Greek **cuisine**.
status symbol	身份的象征	Fancy cars are not just vehicles. They are **status symbols** in Hong Kong.
fragrance	芳香	The **fragrance** of the garden is fascinating.
family bonds	亲情	Sharing meals together can really make **family bonds** stronger.
potential	潜力	Individual sports help us discover our own worth and **potential**（潜力）.
employment	就业	**Employment** opportunities are rare（稀少的）these days, due to the financial crisis.
blockbuster	大片儿	That movie was a **blockbuster**. Its box office take was incredible（难以置信的）.
satisfaction / fulfillment	满意,满足	Watching their kids grow gives parents a sense of **satisfaction / fulfillment**.
traffic congestion	交通堵塞(= traffic jam)	**Traffic congestion** can be very disturbing（烦人的）.
regulations	规章制度(经常连在一起说 rules and regulations)	It's essential to know the rules and **regulations** of safe driving.
the hustle and bustle	喧闹拥挤(这个词可好可坏,有人喜欢也有人不喜欢,是说 big cities 的必备词)	I'm tired of **the hustle and bustle** of big cities.
the daily grind	每天重复的日常事情	I'm sick and tired of **the daily grind** and it's time for a change.
tourist attractions	旅游景点	Many Vancouver **tourist attractions** are free with the Vancouver Pass.

曾让一个考官面部肌肉不停抽搐的动词短语
Phrasal Verbs

有个学生告诉我,她考口语的时候,用了一些我上课讲的动词短语,那个 SG 考官的眼神里明显有惊奇感,而且面部肌肉开始不停地抽搐。不知道大家有没有发现,当学英语的同学倾向于使用单个动词的时候,地道英文里却经常会用一些动词短语来表达。其实,你也行!

动词短语	讲解	例句
check out	体验,感受	Be sure to **check out** those fun places there.
★ figure out	理解 ＝understand	I just can't **figure out** the difference between them.
bring about	带来	These problems have **brought about** the American financial crisis（金融危机）.
carry out	从事	I always make sure our plans are successfully **carried out**.
★ go about	从事	How you **go about** your work or studies may be asked during the test.
come up with	给出（答案,想法……）＝ present	I'm afraid I can't **come up with** a good solution to this problem.
face up to	承担	They should **face up to** their responsibilities.
★ pay off	有回报	All my hard work **paid off**.
★ take up	开始(一种爱好)	I've recently **taken up** jogging（慢跑）.
think of	想到,想起	The only reason I can **think of** now is there are too many people and so few cabs（＝taxi）.
★ work out	锻炼身体	I go to the gym and **work out** regularly（定期地）.
★ rip sb. off	口语里面说"买东西被骗了"时,大家总是用 cheat,真该学学这个短语了	These stalls（摊儿）owners just **rip you off** they only have fake stuff.

（续表）

动词短语	讲解	例句
★ take... into account	考虑到……	We should take the cost into account as well.
★ get rid of	去掉,消除	We should get rid of the sources of pollution（污染源）.
★ sleep in	睡懒觉	I often sleep in on Sundays.
★ get so worked up	很紧张	There's no sense in getting so worked up about the IELTS speaking test.
adapt to	适应	It's essential for kids to adapt to their school life.
★ participate in	参与	Our professors often encourage us to participate in group discussions（讨论）.
cope with	处理,应付 = deal with	I have to cope with customers' complaints（投诉）every day.
★ get stuck	被……困住了, 陷入……	In Beijing, I often get stuck in traffic.
★ stick to	坚持	Stick to your plan. Don't give up so easily.
brush up on	突击复习……	You'd better brush up on your Spanish before you go to Spain.
★ burn out	累垮了	I will burn out if I keep working like this.
★ wind down	放松 = relax	I really need to wind down after such a hectic day（忙碌的一天）.
let... down	让……失望	I study hard coz I don't want to let my folks down.
★ liven up	丰富,活跃 = brighten up	We played games to liven up the party.
下面这几个词虽然不是 phrasal verbs,但也是相当常用的动词短语		
★ expand our knowledge/ expand our	"开阔眼界"broaden our horizons 已经被国内同学们	Expanding your knowledge won't hurt.

（续表）

动词短语	讲解	例句
outlook/ex- pand our vision	用得过多了	
can never hurt ★ =won't hurt	不会有坏处的	Learning to speak another language can never hurt.
ease your mind ★ release pressure	这两个很像，都是 "释放压力"	Music eases your mind and helps you release pressure.

你早就认识却从不会想到去用的加分形容词和副词
Super-cool Adjectives and Adverbs

Adjectives 形容词

单词	注释	例句
independent	独立的（independence *n.* 独立）	Cats tend to be more independent than other pets.
stimulating	有趣的（ = interesting）	Reading a good book can be very stimulating.
marvelous / am- azing/awesome/ superb	非凡的 = great / wonderful	That garden is marvelous.
pathetic /pə'θətik/	查字典也许会得到 "可悲的" 或近似翻译，但在真实生活里它却常表示 of poor quality	He made a pathetic attempt to explain the failure.

（续表）

单词	注释	例句
punctual	守时的（涉及时间的话题很有用）	Being punctual makes us more productive.
refreshed	精神振奋的（"让人精神振奋的"就说 refreshing）	After a good night's sleep, I feel refreshed.
dynamic	有活力的（替换 active 很棒）	Hong Kong is one of the most dynamic port cities in the world.
speedy	快速的（考试时代替 fast 的好选择）	Charlie is a very speedy worker.
precious	珍贵的（= valuable）	Some people collect precious stones.
inexpensive	便宜的（考试时代替 cheap 非常棒的选择）	I prefer inexpensive clothes.
efficient	效率高的	Working in groups may be more efficient than working separately.
effective	效果好的	This software is effective when it comes to touching up photos.
enjoyable	好玩的,有意思的（它的名词 enjoyment 也挺常用）	That trip was one of the most enjoyable experiences I ever had.
exquisite	精美的,精致的（在 Part 2 我们将会更多地用到这个词）	Some people who collect antique furniture（古董家具）have exquisite tastes（高雅的品味）.
desirable	好的,值得拥有的（很多时候可以代替 good）	That car is really desirable. But... now I'm broke（没钱）.
encouraging/ inspiring	给人动力的	My boss never said any encouraging words to his employees.
appealing	吸引人的（= attractive）	The offer sounds very appealing.
intelligent	聪明的（= bright = smart）	The students are pretty intelligent but it seems the teachers are not so good.
considerate	关心人的（= caring）	She's considerate and thoughtful.

（续表）

单词	注释	例句
delighted	高兴的（＝happy,反义词 upset）	I felt delighted when he complimented（夸奖）me on my English.
state-of-the-art	先进的,最尖端的(这个词和 art 其实并没有什么关系)	This PSP is definitely state-of-the-art.
user-friendly	方便好用的	This laptop is pretty user-friendly.
rewarding	有回报的	This job is pretty rewarding financially as well as emotionally.
gorgeous	非常漂亮的	Vancouver is home to some of the most gorgeous scenic spots（景点）on earth.
flawless	完美的（考试时完全可以用这个词代替 perfect）	His English is flawless.
wholesome	有益于健康的（说 food 和 habits 的时候可以代替 healthy）	I like well-balanced wholesome meals.
nutritious	食物有营养的	Raw vegetable salads are very nutritious.
original	原创性的,有创意的	The plot of this movie（电影情节）is pretty original.
economical	（事物）省钱的（＝coste-ffective）	Biking is economical.
fascinating	迷人的	The fragrance（芳香）in this garden is fascinating.
informative	信息量大的	News shows are informative.
entertaining	娱乐性强的	Game shows are pretty entertaining.
authentic	地道的,正宗的	I hope I'll be able to speak authentic English. （注意:这里不要说 I wish,否则就说明你知道自己这辈子说好英语没戏了）

（续表）

单词	注释	例句
posh	高档的,奢侈的	Some of the posh restaurants offer great service but lousy food.
significant/ essential /vital	这三个词的重要程度从前到后越来越强	Significant changes have taken place in this city.
commonplace	非常常见的(＝very common)	Expensive foreign cars are commonplace in Shanghai.
humdrum / mundane/run-of-the-mill	没劲的(＝boring)	That detective story was totally humdrum.
atrocious / obnoxious	极差的(＝terrible)	Sometimes the traffic congestion (＝traffic jam) in this city can be obnoxious.
worthless	没用的	These impractical suggestions are worthless.
hideous	极丑的(＝extremely ugly)	Those hideous buildings seriously spoil (除了"溺爱",这个词也经常表示破坏本来很完美的东西) the cityscape(城市景观).
messy	乱七八糟的	The layout（布局）of this newspaper is totally messy.
bogus	假的,"山寨的"(＝fake;"山寨版"名词叫knockoff)	Many people sell bogus stuff on the Internet.
mediocre	平庸的,很一般的	That book was so mediocre I threw it away after reading the first 10 pages.
poisonous/toxic	有毒的	Car exhaust fumes（汽车尾气）can be poisonous.
hazardous	危险的(代替dangerous的好词)	In Beijing, biking is hazardous.
exhausting	让人精疲力尽的	Rock-climbing can be exhausting.

（续表）

单词	注释	例句
frustrating	令人沮丧的	The career prospects（工作前景）are frustrating.
disturbing	烦人的	Noise can be reaaaaaally disturbing.（这里可以把 really 的发音拖得很长来强调）
time-consuming	耗时间的	Watching TV can be very time-consuming.
complicated/complex	复杂的	This is a complex issue. The plot of that movie was complicated.

Adverbs 副词

单词	注释	例句
Actually, … Basically, …	这两个词大家应该都认识,但Pat在国内期间却极少听到中国孩子使用它们,与真实英语环境里它们的超高频使用形成鲜明对比,应该力荐一下	Actually, these two words are old hat（老掉牙的）and I'm sure you guys know them already. But … they're still … basically, … worth recommending.
Essentially, …	经常用在句首,表示"本质上看,……"	Essentially, this problem is a problem about the conflicts（冲突）between development and holding on to our traditions.
Specifically, …	经常用在句首,表示"具体来说,……"	The traffic in Beijing is awful. Specifically, there are more reckless（不考虑后果的）drivers in Beijing than in most American cities.
typically	多半（代替 mostly 是很棒的选择）	Seniors（老年人）are typically more laid-back and more understanding.

（续表）

单词	注释	例句
practically	几乎（代替 almost 的极好选择）	I have to work overtime（加班）practically every day.
immediately	立刻（ = right away）	Measures should be taken immediately to cope with this problem.
constantly	比 always 语气更强的	As a salesperson, I'm constantly on the go（总出差）.
currently	现在（ =now =at the moment）	I'm currently working at a design company.
unfortunately/ sadly	不幸的是	Unfortunately, not so many people have meals with their family members today, due to the fast pace of life.
Honestly, …	老实说……	Honestly, I don't know much about this topic.
Normally, …	通常,考试时拿它替换国内孩子们使用过量的 usually 会很酷	Normally, I plan things one or two days ahead.
Hopefully, …	希望能够……（意思很接近于 I hope…）	Hopefully, we'll get the noise controlled shortly.

对分数有野心的人应该熟记的关键反义词
Antonyms for Pros

单词		反义词	
spacious	宽敞的	cramped	狭小的
gorgeous	漂亮的	ugly / hideous	丑陋的
tasty	好吃的	gross	难吃的

（续表）

单词		反义词	
organized	整齐的,有秩序的	messy	混乱的
stimulating	有趣的	monotonous / mundane / humdrum / run-of-the-mill	单调的,乏味的
extravagant	奢侈的	economical	省钱的（说事物）
		frugal	节俭的（说人）
adorable = cute	可爱的（经常用来说小动物或者小朋友）	disgusting	令人厌恶的（可以用来描述任何让你觉得不爽的东东）
promote / boost	促进	restrict / impede	阻碍
preserve	保护	ruin	破坏
encourage	鼓励	frustrate	让人沮丧
inspire	激励		
is accelerating = is speeding up	加速	is slowing down	减慢
is improving	改善	is deteriorating	恶化
fresh air	新鲜空气	stuffy air	不新鲜的空气

下面几组词的反义词只需要加否定前缀：

healthy	un*healthy*
comfortable	un*comfortable*
convenient	in*convenient*
friendly	un*friendly*
expensive	in*expensive*

Part 2 的 100 个核心词汇(7 分内容)
100 Building Blocks in Part 2

对于有很多同义词的词汇,这里都只剩下最拿分的一两个选择。为了准备考试咱们就赤裸裸的了(cheeky)。

☆ 100 个核心词汇按照感官 (senses) 分类

视觉词汇　Sight			
形容词	特漂亮的　gorgeous / breathtaking	壮观的　spectacular / magnificent	
	精美的　exquisite	耐用的　durable	
	新奇有趣的　funky / fancy	小巧的　handy	
	光亮的　glossy / sleek	国际化的　cosmopolitan	
	巨大的　enormous / vast	毛绒绒的　fluffy / furry	
	可爱的　adorable	胖乎乎的　chubby	
	干净整洁的　tidy / spotless	瘦的　slim	
	笨重的 (人) clumsy,(物品) cumbersome	敏捷的　agile	
	破旧的　beat-up / worn-out	凶猛的　fierce / ferocious	
	整齐有秩序的　organized	茂盛的　lush	
名词或者词组	建筑的外观　exterior	建筑的室内装饰　interior décor(发音请注意听录音)	
	建筑的入口　entrance	入口大厅　lobby / hall	
	玻璃幕墙　glass curtain walls	柱子　pillars / columns	
	台阶　steps	喷泉　fountain	
	瀑布　waterfall	灌木　bushes / brush	
	皱纹　wrinkles	有神的眼睛　sparkling eyes	
	浓眉　thick eyebrows	闪亮的湖水　shimmering water	
	中等身材　a medium build	红红的脸庞　rosy cheeks	
	花白的头发　salt-and-pepper hair	强烈的好奇心　an inquiring mind	
	大都市　metropolis	布局　layout	
	花纹　pattern	售货员　shop assistant	
	图书管理员　librarian	购物狂　shopaholic	

（续表）

听觉词汇　Hearing

鸟叫　birds chirping in the trees	烦人的噪声　disturbing noise
悦耳的　pleasing to the ear	轻松的音乐　soothing music

嗅觉词汇　Smell

花香　the fragrance of flowers	香喷喷的饭菜　aromatic dishes

味觉词汇　Taste

非常好吃的　tasty / scrumptious / is out of this world（不推荐大家在考场里用yummy）

感觉词汇　Emotional Perception

神圣的　holy / sacred	重要的　significant / essential / vital
特别棒的　awesome / superb / marvelous	让人很放松的　soothing
有活力的　dynamic	热情好客的　hospitable
慷慨的　generous	直率的　candid / frank
高兴的　delighted	无忧无虑的　carefree
有礼貌的　well-mannered	乐观的　optimistic
有吸引力的　attractive / appealing	开明的　open-minded
幽默的　amusing	勤奋敬业的　industrious / conscientious
有热情的　passionate	有爱心的　compassionate
优雅的　graceful	举世闻名的　world-renowned
志向远大的　ambitious / aspiring	自信的　confident / assertive
遇事冷静的　level-headed	顽强的　tough / tenacious
谦虚的　modest	低调的　low-key
体贴的　considerate	节俭的　frugal
喜欢社交的　sociable	反应快的　quick-witted
多才多艺的　versatile	有远见的　forward-looking
多产的(指作家或者歌手)　prolific	有才华的　talented / gifted
势利的　snobbish	过于现实的　materialistic
多样的　diverse	有回报的　rewarding
时尚的　trendy / stylish	高贵的　classy / chic

休闲词汇　Leisure Activities

唱卡拉OK　sing karaoke	练跆拳道　do taekwondo

（续表）

休闲词汇　Leisure Activities	
滑旱冰 roller-skating	潜水 scuba-diving（在国外是一种需要带专业设备的运动）
滑滑板 go skateboarding	打太极 do taichi
做日光浴 do sunbathing	遛狗 walk one's dog
慢跑 jog	远足 go hiking
宿营 camping	烧烤 have a barbecue

☆ 100 个核心词汇按照 topics 分类

城市　Cities	
绿地 lawns	摩天楼 skyscrapers
有活力的 dynamic / vibrant	雕塑 sculptures
壮观的 magnificent / spectacular	基础设施 infrastructure
某个地方的菜 cuisine	交通堵塞 traffic congestion
勤劳的 industrious	四合院建筑 courtyard houses
乐观的 optimistic	殖民地 colony
势利的 snobbish	多样化的 diverse
小吃 snacks	乐坛 the music scene
一个圣地 a holy place	顽强的 tenacious
国际化的 cosmopolitan	热情好客的 hospitable
城市布局 the layout of a city	物质化的 materialistic
一座名人故居 a celebrity's former residence	举世闻名的 world-renowned
迷人的 enchanting	
中国的政治、经济、文化的中心 the political, economic and cultural center of China	

自然风光　Gardens and Parks	
设施 facilities	喷泉 fountains
水池 pools	池塘 ponds
弯弯曲曲的小路 winding paths	栅栏 picket fence
花坛 flowerbeds	亭子 pavilions
花架 trellises	灌木丛 bushes / hedge

(续表)

自然风光　Gardens and Parks

茂盛的 lush	瀑布 waterfall
宁静的 tranquil and serene	闪亮的水 shimmering water
清澈的水 limpid water	花香 the fragrance of flowers
树上鸟叫 birds chirp in the trees	氛围 ambience
休闲活动 recreational activities	打太极 practice taichi
下象棋 play chess	滑旱冰 roller-skating
遛狗 walk one's dog	露营 camping
约会 go on a date	玩 hang out
感觉焕然一新的 feel refreshed and invigorated	让人放松的 soothing

建筑物　Architecture

外观 exterior	壮观的 magnificent
台阶 steps	主要入口 main entrance
柱子 pillars / columns	玻璃幕墙 glass curtain walls
基座 platform	室内装饰 interior décor
精致的 exquisite	大厅 lobby
电梯 elevators (AmE) / lifts (BrE)	自动扶梯 escalators
光亮的 glossy / sleek	连接 link
美食街 food court	化妆品店 cosmetics stores
电子产品店 electronics stores	服装店 boutiques
时尚的 trendy / stylish	高贵的 classy / chic
售货员 shop assistant	售后服务 after-sale service
书库 stack	多媒体室 audio-visual room
期刊 periodical	图书管理员 librarian

人物　Men and Women

矮胖的 pudgy	胖乎乎的 chubby
瘦的 slim	好看的 good-looking
外表平常的 average-looking	男性身材健美的 well-built
女性身材好的 has a nice figure	优雅的 graceful
有礼貌的 well-mannered	斯文的 urbane

（续表）

人物　Men and Women

敏捷的　agile	体育好的　athletic
浓眉　thick eyebrows	有神的眼睛　sparkling eyes
中等身材　a medium build	红红的脸颊　rosy cheeks
花白的头发　salt-and-pepper hair	口才好的　articulate
知识丰富的　knowledgeable	好奇心强　has an inquiring mind
喜欢社交的　sociable	有活力的　dynamic
热情好客的　hospitable	慷慨的　generous
直率的　frank / candid / straightforward	乐观的　optimistic
无忧无虑的　carefree	开明的　open-minded
幽默的　amusing	勤奋敬业的　industrious / conscientious
有热情的　passionate	有爱心的　compassionate
志向远大的　ambitious	自信的　confident / assertive
谦虚的　modest	低调的　low-key
好接近的　approachable	体贴的　considerate
节俭的　frugal	反应快的　quick-witted
多才多艺的　versatile	有远见的　forward-looking
多产的（指作家、歌手等）　prolific	有才华的　talented / gifted
可爱的　adorable / likeable	举世闻名的　world-renowned
做事有条理的　organized / methodical	收藏古董　collect antiques
电影迷　a movie buff / nut	下象棋　play chess
打麻将　play mahjong	唱卡拉OK　sing karaoke
练跆拳道　do taekwondo	滑板　skateboard
打太极　do taichi	做日光浴　do sunbathing
遛狗　walk a dog	慢跑　jog
远足　hike / do hiking	

动物　Predators and Prey

凶猛的　fierce / ferocious	毛绒绒的　fluffy / furry
温顺的　gentle	庞大的　enormous / vast
神秘的　mysterious / enigmatic	珍稀的　rare
濒危动物　endangered animals	主食　staple food

（续表）

动物　Predators and Prey	
国宝　national treasures	友好的　affable
可爱的　adorable	让人特想抱的　cuddly
物品　objects	
新奇有趣的　funky / fancy	光亮的　glossy / sleek
破旧的　beat-up / worn-out	小巧便携的　handy / portable
娱乐性强的　entertaining	信息量大的　informative
特棒的　awesome / superb / marvelous	不贵的　inexpensive / affordable
性价比　performance-price ratio	耐用的　durable

此外,在本书的 Day 9 中我们还将分析 Part 3 所需的地道加分词汇。

★　　★　　★

今天的必备词汇学习结束之前,Pat 想再次认真地提醒各位:英语从来都不是"贵族语言",它其实是一种极为看重实效(pragmatism)的语言。在欧洲,它没有法语高贵(classy),也没有德语严谨(rigid),但最后英语还是靠着自己的实用性(utility)征服了世界。实用永远是说英文的最高标准。

潜水去也。

Sleep tight.
Don't let the bed bugs bite.

超短线
The Ultra-Short Track

口语考试考的是一种综合素质,想仅靠背单词就通过雅思口语考试并不现实。但是对于备考时间过于紧张的"小盆友们"来说,熟练掌握下面的二十个地道词汇并在口试时积极使用,虽然不能化腐朽为神奇,但至少能减少不做充分准备就去裸考的罪恶感:

名词:

approach 这个词是指用来做某事的方法,比如 a new approach to learning English。

动词：

participate in 参加……,经常代替 join。

involve 涉及到……,在国外有些人只要说到将来的事儿就喜欢把这个词挂在嘴边。

形容词：

comforting 故意躲开那个 comfortable。

entertaining 说一个东西娱乐性强就是它了。

affluent 这是 rich 那个词的替身("替身"目前在英美时髦叫 avatar 了,就因为 James Cameron 的那部电影)。

informative 这个词的意思是:"信息量很大的",用它来描述电视节目或者报纸杂志都不含糊。

appealing / attractive 可比 beautiful 含蓄多了。

mind-numbing 就是比 boring 还枯燥 10 倍的。

efficient 高效率的,说得更直白那就是 It saves time,它的反义词 time-consuming 耗时间的,也是个挺拿分的词。

laid-back 考试时砸锅卖铁也不用 easygoing。

disturbing 只要一个东东让你很烦就可以用这个词描述它,从一个不喜欢的电视节目到一次没有安排好的 trip。

词组：

concerned about 关注……,比如 I'm very concerned about the latest changes in the real estate policy(最近对房地产政策的调控).

类似的地道好词还有很多,但备考时间不够的同学还是先把这些搞定吧,如果再有时间就看看 Day 9 的 284 词汇表。

Day 4

 说好雅思口语的句子
Why Convoluted Sentences Don't Work

Pat's Guide
To the Speaking Test

Why'd you go and break what's already broken?
I try to take a breath but I'm already choking
'Cause everywhere I look, I can see
how you hold back.
How long till this goes away?

不知您是否熟悉 podcast 这种在国外已经相当流行的学习手段，比如在 google 上搜索一下 English as a second language（ESL）podcast，就会有上千个学习资源供你选择，而且都是标准的发音和地道的英文，真的该试一下了。

词汇是砖，句子是墙。

如果墙太长，就变成了长城，会把你封闭起来，让人感觉你很 closed-off。

很多培训老师推荐学生说长难句。其实长难句有两层意思，一是要长，二是要难。环球的大班很多是我教的，我承认讲课的时候老师说长难句对大班授课的效果有好处，可以迅速让学生产生"仰视老师"的崇拜心理。但问题是，是否有必要在考口语的时候让考官"仰视"考生呢？

> 考雅思口语的时候，如果你想让自己的语言听起来不那么机械和怪异，就请尽量少用长、难、怪的句子。正常人在说话的时候是不可能像写作那样"处心积虑"的。

怎样说出不"难"的长句？

长期在国外学习和工作，Pat 可以很坦诚地告诉您：真实生活中的英语句子有一个明显的特点，就是虽然使用的动词、名词和形容词千变万化，但是最常用的连词却只有十几个。即使已经在国外住了很多年，积累了大量实词，但每天用到的连词也还是这十几个。而对于雅思口试而言，考生的分数很大程度上就取决于是否能够把这十几个连词准确、自然、流畅地运用好。

在您的口试过程中请不要过于频繁地使用 Firstly, … Secondly, …Furthermore, …这三个词⊠。严格来说口语里使用它们其实并不是"错误"，而且在国外的学术讨论中这三个词也仍然有它们的位置，但对于 IELTS 口试这样并不是特别正式的交谈中，过于频繁地使用这三个词将导致考官感觉你是一个拘谨、较难接近的人。事实上，在国外日常生活中的对话里引出自己看法的第一点时通常并不使用提示词，或者如果要提示的话也是用 First off, / To start with, / To begin with, 这些更生活化的方式引出第一点。而"其次"在国外日常生活里通常会用 also / as well / as well as 这些更自然的形式或者就更简单地用 and 来表达，生活里说"其次"时使用这些表达的概率比用 Secondly 的可能性要高很多。所以，如果您有用英语交谈时过度使用 Firstly, … Secondly, … 与 Furthermore, …的倾向，请力争在考试之前改掉它。

Pat 总结出的地道口语里最常用的连接词

类别	内容	用法说明与例句
因果	... so... ... so that... ... because = cuz = 'cause = coz... therefore ★	☆ therefore 在地道口语中用得并不算多，如果 IELTS 口试里要用的话，最多也就是用 1~2 次，过多会让对方有压迫感
让步	Although..., ... Even though..., ... ★ Even if..., ... ★ ... as long as...	☆ 注意 Even if..., ...是"即使"，是对还没有发生的情况让步；而 even though..., ...是"尽管"，对已经存在的情况让步 ☆ 例：Even if you take a taxi, you'll still miss the train... ☆ 例：Even though he knew the experiement was dangerous, Ethan went ahead with it. ☆ 例：My parents don't really care what job I get, as long as I'm happy.
转折	But... However, ..., though. ★	☆ 前两个词不必赘述，但..., though. 这个词在地道口语里经常会被放在句子结尾处，听起来很轻巧，意义上则是等于放在句中的 but... ☆ 例：It's hard work, I enjoy it, though.
递进	Apart from..., ... ★ Besides..., ... ★	☆ 例：Apart from being used as a cafeteria, that building is often used for weddings and parties. ☆ 例：Besides camping, I often ride horses on Sundays. 这两个词国内考生用得不多，但其实真的不妨多尝试一下。而写作里面各位很爱用的 In addition to 在日常口语里有时也能听到有人用，但不如这两个表达使用得频繁
修饰	... that... ... who... ..., which... ★	☆定语从句在 IELTS 口语里还是挺常用的，不过 that 有时会被省略，而 which, who, when 和 where 则一般不被省略：

（续表）

类别	内容	用法说明与例句
修饰	… when… … where…	☆ 例：I can't find the books（that）I got from the library. ☆ 例：These are principles which we all believe in. ☆ 例：A skilled workforce is crucial，which is why the training programme is so important.
修饰		☆ 例：《剑 8》例句：Managers who want to apply present knowledge tend to start off by going to an expert. ☆ For most of us, there're some days when everything seems to go wrong. ☆ I have reached the point where I just want to get the project finished.
对比	On the other hand, … … while/whereas… ★ … In/By contrast… ★	☆ … while/whereas…这两个连词表示两种人或物之间的对比，口语里用得不算太多，但偶尔用一下是完全可以的： ☆ I do every single bit of housework while Phoebe just does the dishes now and then. ☆ … In/By contrast…在口语里也出现得不算太多，但偶用一下无妨，表示两种人或物之间的对比 ☆ 例：They need a house whereas we would rather live a flat. ☆ 例：The coastal areas have mild winters. By contrast, the central areas are extremely cold in winter. （句中的生词在 Day 7 中都会见到）
举例和泛指	like… ★ such as… ★ Take… for example. In some cases, … In most cases, … … and stuff like that. ★	☆举例和泛指同样可以帮你比较自然地说出更长一些的句子。举例除了 for instance/ for example/ such as 这些常用说法，其实"like… +n."是日常口语里最常听到的一个 ☆ 例：I'm into reading history books and stuff like that.

（续表）

类别	内容	用法说明与例句
举例和泛指	... and things like that. ... or something like that. ... or whatever.	☆ 写作里司空见惯的 such as 在口语里同样是 native speakers 谈话时举例的常用"例器"： ☆ Lewis enjoys team sports such as basketball and cricket （板球，这是英格兰人相当迷的一项运动，和 Pat 的最爱 baseball 有某些相似之处）。 ☆ In some / most cases, ... 属于泛指，不必具体说明例子但可以让考官觉得你有举例的意识
其它	...as well. ★ ...as well as... ★ in terms of... ★ As far as... (is concerned) instead of / rather than ★	☆ 在地道英文中把...as well. 放在句子结尾是一种相当常见的用法，比句尾的...too. 语气缓和一些： 例：I need a ticket for *Thor*, and one for *Transformer* Ⅲ as well. ☆ 当用在句中时，一般会使用 as well as 的形式，同样也是英文口语里超级常用的连接方式： ☆ Zoe likes the bookstore as well as the reading club. ☆in terms of 在……方面，就……而言，在意义上很像 talking about.../ speaking of...，但那两个词组多数时候出现在句首，而 in terms of 在句子里的位置则更加灵活： ☆ 例：Larry was better off in his last job in terms of salary. ☆ 例：The experiment didn't find any differences in terms of what students could learn. ☆国内同学一般比较熟悉 As far as I'm concerned，但其实这个词组里的第二个 as 后面可以填入任何事物，而且在生活中还经常省略后面的 is concerned 或者把 is concerned 换成 go (es)： ☆ 例：As far as spelling, Alex has never been a good student. But he gets excellent grades in math. ☆ 例：As far as unemployment goes, the UK economy is recovering （恢复）。 ☆rather than 和 instead of 都表示"而不是……"的

（续表）

类别	内容	用法说明与例句
其它		意思，这两个地道词组大家都耳熟能详，但却很少听到各位在口语里面用： ☆ 例：Support was offered by the government rather than private companies. ☆ 例：We can deal with this chapter now instead of waiting until tomorrow. ☺
不是连词却胜似连词的表达	…tend to… ★ basically ★ actually ★ get ★	这三个极端常用的表达其实都不是连词，但仔细分析它们在句子里面又实在没起到什么实际的作用，主要功能还是让 native speakers 把自己的句子更自然地"串"起来。这些会让自己的英文立刻听起来又地道了 3% 的用法实在不应该再惨遭您的忽视了： ☆ 例：The gym tends to （一般会怎样，多半会怎样）get very busy after 6 pm. ☆ 例：We tend to get freezing winters and dry summers in this part of the country. ☆ 例：Basically, the car is in good condition, but the paintwork needs a bit of attention. ☆ 例：Harrison is actually very helpful. ☆ 有些同学可能觉得 get 这样的词绝不会是拿分的词，但 Pat 却要很真诚地对您说：您今后对 get 这个词的使用频率将会与您在英语国家生活的时间直接成正比，因为当您实在想不到合适的词去表达自己意思的时候，往往会发现其实就是这个 get 一直在不远处不离不弃地等着您： ☆ 例：Tyler's gone to the corner shop to get（＝obtain）some milk. ☆ 例：I get（＝receive）junk mail from this company daily. ☆ Things are getting（＝becoming）difficult in this country.

（续表）

类别	内容	用法说明与例句
不是连词却胜似连词的表达		☆ 例：Katie got bored with her job immediately. ☆ 例：Ben'll get his suit dirty (cause sth. to become) in the park. ☆ 例：I'll get this paper finished by tonight. (get sth. done 在真实口语里同样极为常用)

也许你不愿意相信，上面表格中的这些连词，不仅仅是对付雅思口语考试的长句子足够了，甚至对付大家今后几年中的国外校园生活里的长句子也够了。英语口语里的动词、名词、形容词极为丰富，但是连词却真的是相当有限的。

仍然牢记：口语里的长句子是对短句子的使用非常熟练之后，再对这些最常用的连接词自然运用而形成的，而不是刻意去堆砌出来的（Don't just cram them into your sentences）。

可以用来攒人品的词组和句型

攒人品（RP）对于雅思考分的重要性已经越来越高。在一些城市的烤鸭当中正悄然兴起一股利用业余时间帮助公园里老奶奶回收农夫山泉塑料瓶的风潮，据说对提高分数很有效。

下面的这些考试时躲不掉的词组和句型，对于考前攒 RP 也有不可忽视的作用。

Absolutely Essential Words and Phrases for Boosting Your RP

可以攒人品的词组	As I see it, …/ I guess…/ I suppose… As for… = When it comes to… = Talking about（英式）= Speaking of（美式） tons of = loads of = a host of / a multitude of ★ a wealth of… ★ and the like = and stuff like that = and what not

☆ As I see it, …/ I guess…/ I suppose… 我想……

多数国内考生考口语的时候都是 I think 不断，连用 20 多个，听起来实在太像"思想者"了。

I guess… 口语里其实往往不是"我猜"，而只是比 I think 更客气的说法。

In my opinion 口试时可以用 1 ~2 次，但使用过多将会让考生听起来很"顽固"。

As I see it, the number of cars in Beijing should be limited immediately.

☆ As for… （英美通用） = When it comes to… （英美通用） = Talking about （英式） = Speaking of （美式）说起……，谈到……

这几个词组大家都很熟悉，但是不要怕，它们在国外比在国内用得更多，坚决放心用，特别是前两个。

When it comes to traffic, I have to say living in this city is just like a nightmare（恶梦）.

☆ loads of = tons of = a host of/ a multitude of =a lot of

The Internet offers us a multitude of options. （选择=choice）

☆ a wealth of… 大量的

这个词组在国外生活里很常用，后面跟的一般都是 knowledge /information/books 这类积极的事物。

Public libraries offer us a wealth of information.

☆ and the like = and stuff like that = and what not

是"等等等等"的意思，代替 and so on 不错。

I like suspense movies, action movies, romance, funny movies and the like.

可以攒人品的句型	tend to… ★
	I think of… as… = I regard…as…
	is / are supposed to… ★
	are more likely to… ★
	not necessarily ★
	There's no sense in… = It doesn't make any sense. = It's pointless to…
	used to…
	get used to doing sth. = get accustomed to doing sth.
	is the norm ★
	is a luxury ★
	won't hurt ★
	enable sb. to do sth.
	have a hard time doing sth.

☆ tend to... = for the most part 多半……

这两个是口语里经常用来代替 most of 的优秀句型，可惜真的极少在国内听到孩子们用。

例 1: Kids tend to be more active than adults.

例 2: The winter in Beijing tends to be freezing. （地道英文里还有个 frigid 更冷）

☆ I think of... as... = I regard...as...

我把……看做是……

I think of photography as a way to express myself.

☆ is / are supposed to... = should

在口语里代替 should 非它莫属。

Children are supposed to read more books coz that can help them learn a great deal of knowledge.

☆ are more likely to... 更有可能去……

这个连《剑8》p. 167 的考官范文里都俯拾皆是，日常口语里则用得更多。

Children are more likely to copy the violence and bad language in movies.

☆ not necessarily 这个完全等于中文的 "不一定"

Something I thought I'd set up （安排） very well did n't necessarily seem that way to everyone. （《剑8》例句）

☆ There's no sense in... = It doesn't make any sense. = It's pointless to... ……没道理

There's no sense in blocking （封杀） that extremely useful website.

☆ used to... 过去常做某事

I used to stay up late often. But these days I go to bed very early.

☆ get used to doing sth. = get accustomed to doing sth. 习惯去做某事

Speaking English takes some getting used to.

通过举例子给大家说明三种相似表达的区别：

过去时：I bought Pat's books.

说明曾经买过 Pat 的书，至于现在还买不买从这句话看不出来。

Used to: I used to buy Pat's books.

说明过去曾经买过 Pat 的书，现在绝不打算再买了。

Get used to: I've gotten used to buying Pat's books.

暗示可能曾经看着 Pat 的书觉得特别扭，但没想到现在还真就适应了，而且越看感觉越好……

☆ is the norm. ……是最普遍的做法

In traditional schools, rote learning（死记硬背）was the norm.

近义的加分句型还有一个 双重否定句型 It's not uncommon for sb. to... 也是某人通常会怎样去做的意思，在考试时使用听起来比较客气但又不容置疑，是个不错的选择。

☆ is a luxury 是一种奢望

Having your own garden is a luxury in cities like Beijing and Shanghai.

☆ won't hurt 不会有坏处

The house looks good. But a fresh paint job just won't hurt.

☆ enable sb. to do sth. 让某人可以去……

English abilities enable us to find more information on the information highway.（这个词组代替 the Internet，很酷）

☆ have a hard time doing sth. 很难去……

Graduates this year are having a hard time finding a decent job because of the financial crisis（金融危机）.（decent 这个词其实在口语中就是"还不错的"意思，国外生活中相当常用，但国内的孩子们宁可绕弯说 quite good 或者 fairly good，也不愿意用这个既省事又拿分的说法）

雅思口语考试中到底有没有很特殊的句子？

Yes and No.

为什么这么说呢？因为口语的本质就是用来进行实时交流的工具，如果"处心积虑"地搞特殊那就一定不是正常人说的语言了。但是另一方面，下面三种句子还是有点特殊，如果学会使用，偶尔用上一两次，在考试里还是明显会有拿分的作用的。

❶ 虚拟语气

听起来很神奇，其实说白了就是用过去的时态表示现在或者将来的事情，听起来语气比较客气，或者用来表示可能性很小。雅思口语中很常用，而且《剑8》Test 1 的 Speaking 部分就有不少：

Do you think it **would be** a good idea for schools to ask students their opinions about lessons? (《剑8》例句)

What **would** the advantages for schools be if they **asked** students their opinions? (《剑8》例句)

Would there be **any dis**advantages in asking students' opinions? (《剑8》例句)

If I **had** more leisure time, I **would** go to the movies more often. (But I don't have much leisure time.)

If my boss **got** me promoted soon, maybe I **would** continue on with this job. (But chances are that he/she won't do that.)

If the traffic in Beijing **could** be more organized, I **would** ride my bike to work. (But probably the traffic will not become so organized.)

❷ 倒装句

Not only 或者 Only 放在句首，就要倒装，这也就是中学语法知识（说实话，雅思口语所有的语法其实都是中学语法，就看你能不能用对了）。

Not only does this restaurant offer great food, it **also** has top-notch service.

Not only are these flowers gorgeous and fragrant, they are full of special meanings **as well**.

❸ 强调句

It is... that... 意思是：就是……产生了某种效果

It is the pay **that** keeps me doing this job. （pay 作名词在真实口语里其实很常见）

It is the culture in Beijing **that** attracts tons of tourists every year.

It is the climate, the fresh air, the natural scenery and the welfare system **that** attract so many immigrants to Australia.

★   ★   ★

 请注意这些特殊句型一次考试里面最多用 2~3 次，因为用得太多它们压根儿就不"特殊"了。

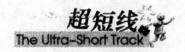

关于雅思备考，我一直坚信而且被大量 7 分或以上的高分考生证明的真谛就是备考必须紧紧围绕剑桥官方所喜爱的英语风格进行，其他的不管听起来多漂亮至少对于 <u>雅思</u> 来说都是浮云。深刻领会剑桥官方提供的《剑4》~《剑8》是体会"剑桥风格"的最好武器。

备考时间已经彻底不够，甚至连书都已经看不下去了的"烤鸭"们其实不妨试试通过练习剑桥听力来提高口语语感的方法：多听剑 4~剑 8 每套题里的听力段子，并且把 <u>剑桥</u> 听力试题的文本（tapescripts）也看上几遍，耳濡目染也能学到不少地道的口语句子。退一万步说，即使这样做之后你的口语还是一点进步都没有，那至少也熟悉了剑桥听力的常考词汇和句型，并没有浪费时间。

比如《剑8》里 的这个听力段子就用到了不少我们已经学到的关于地道英文连词的知识，证实了这些内容的实用性：

I decided people under 18 should be excluded because most of them are students or looking for their first job, and also I decided at this stage just to focus on men who were in employment, and set up something for people who didn't have jobs and for employed women later on. I specifically wanted to do a questionnaire and interviews with a focus group. With the questionnaire rather than limiting it to one specific point, I wanted to include as much variety as possible.

下面这个剑桥段子同样也调用了很多本书里 Pat 推荐的让您的说话风格更接近受过良

好教育的 native speakers 真实口语风格的表达:

At a UK university, as I'm sure you know, you will be in an environment where independent learning is the norm, which takes most students a while to adapt to, and at a time when you'll be separated from your normal surrounding and, in most cases, your family.

不过 Pat 要特别提醒这部分同学的是:一定要先把官方提供的剑 4 ~ 剑 8 听力题都做完 1 ~ 2 遍之后再把它们当成口语资料,而绝不要先把它们当口语书学习,然后再当成听力题来练习,否则你会发现自己每次练都是满分……

Day

雅思口语的段落

Bricks versus Concrete

Pat's Guide
To the Speaking Test

Are you listening?
We write a thousand pages
They're torn and on the floor
Headlights hammer the windows
We're locked behind these doors
And we are never leaving
Coz this place is part of us
And all these scenes repeating are just so cold to the touch

Day

* www. idebate. org *

这个相当酷的辩论网站几乎覆盖了所有的常考口语讨论话题。在页面中部的 A, B 或 C 选择话题并点击 Submit(提交),你就可以立刻找到自己需要的观点和理由。

We just have adopted a laid-back approach, even though we take the test seriously.

怎样才能说出长段落?
(本节只适合"大牛"们阅读,"小白"们请坚定飘过)

如果你上过培训大课,那么口语老师一定给自己的方法起了一个新奇有趣的(fancy)名字,通过它来使这种方法在学生的心目中产生一种神秘感和敬畏感(get you mystified and put you in awe)。这种作法可以增强教师授课的综合效果,但其实如果看穿了,雅思口语 Part 1 和 Part 3 的答案不管多么地有创意,却一定是沿着两条思路展开的:顺延与对比。

中国的传统艺术讲究"起承转合"四个字,咱们用这四个字来形象地分析一下顺延与对比的区别。

1 "起—承—(合)"结构

请先看这道常考题:

Why do some people like collecting things?

下面这个 7 分水平的答案是典型的"起—承—(合)"结构。

I guess there can be a variety of reasons. Some people collect things simply because they have too much spare time and need more personal pleasure. Others may think of collecting stuff as a means to make investments. Actually, I even know some folks who collect things just to show them off to their neighbours...

所谓"起—承—(合)"结构,就是先回答问题,然后沿着这个方向顺着往下再说几句。最后如果有必要还可以再总结一句(合),不过最后的总结很多时候是可以自然省略的。再比如下面这个考题:

What do you think of traveling?

下面的 7 分答案就是典型的"起—承—合"式。

(起)Traveling is... fun... stimulating. I feel energised when I travel...(承)Also, I make friends during trips to other places. (承)And of course, as they say, traveling expands your outlook...(合)I guess that's exactly why so many people travel around these days.

再看这道题:

Do you like shopping?

一个 6 分水平的"起—承—(合)"式答案可能是这样的。

（起）Humm, I'm really into it. （承）At the moment, I have a lot of free time on my hands so whenever I feel bored, I just hang out in malls.

我们再看一个"起—承"，但省略了"合"的结构：

Do you like fresh vegetables?

（起）I just can't get enough of them! （承）They taste good and are *nutritious* as well. （承）Stuff like tomatoes and *celery* don't cost much so I'm certain everyone can afford them…

> "起—承—（合）"式的**优点**：逻辑比较简单明白，向同一个方向展开内容就可以了。
>
> "起—承—（合）"式的**缺点**：口语不太好的同学有时候会发现答案说不长。但客观地说如果您的口语目标只是 6 分，答案本来也不需要很长，基本平均起来 2 ~ 3 句话的答案应付一个 chat 已经足够（当然长度只是一个方面不是机械的，更重要的是看内容和英文表达方式）。

☆"起—承—（合）"结构的常用词汇和句型
（不要都背，否则……肯定记不住！）

（1）起

Yes / No 题		Wh- / How 题	
词汇及句型	说明	词汇及句型	说明
Yes / Yeah / Yup/ Yep ☆	☆ Yup 这个词年轻人很常用，而且通常用升调	Clearly, …	☆ Obviously, … 和 Apparently, … 都表示"很明显"
Sure.		Obviously, … ☆	
You bet.		Apparently, …	
Absolutely.	☆ No way! 语气很强，除非你真的想表示强烈的否定，否则不要用	I'm pretty sure…	☆ 斜体的词汇可以用来引出否定的答案
Certainly.		*To be honest*, …	
Definitely.		*Frankly*, …	
No doubt about it.		*In fact*, …	☆ There are a variety of … 和 There are a wide range of… 也表示"有多种多样的……"
That's for sure.		*As a matter of fact*, …	
No / Nope.		There are a variety of… ☆	
Not really.		There are a wide range of… ☆	
Not necessarily.		There are many types of…	
No way! ☆			

（2）承

词语和句型	备注
First of all, …（但这个应试用已经有点俗了）	☆ For starters = For openers（这两个非常的informal）
The first thing I should mention is…	☆ … primarily because…（首先是因为……）
To begin with, …	☆ … plus… e. g. Beijing is a gorgeous（非常漂亮的）city, plus it has such an amazing history.
For starters = For openers ☆	
For one thing, … For another, …	☆ i. e. 这个拉丁词的正确英文发音就是念出i,e 两个字母,两个圆点不发音。这个词的意思是 that is / that is to say,解释上文用的。受过良好教育的 native speakers 谈话中有时会用起这个词,但也没必要过于痴迷,考试时如果可以准确地用1次可以有加分效果,但过多就贫了
… primarily because… ☆	
Also, …	
Besides, …	
… plus… ☆	
What's more, …	例：This hotel is closed during low season（淡季）, i. e. , from October to March.
Another point I could add is…	
…, too.	☆ As well as this/ As well as that, … 放在句首其实同样可以用来引出进一步的承接,但这在英语中只是一部分人的习惯,用得不算太普及
… as well.	
In addition to that, …	
In other words,…	☆ On top of that, …（这个很赞哟）
That is to say,…	
…i. e. …	☆ 表示强调还可以用 especially…, particularly, in particular 这样的表达
As well as this/ that, … ☆	
Most importantly, …	
On top of that, … ☆	
By the way, …	

注意：如果在"起—承—（合）"式答案最后还想再总结一句结论（合）,可以考虑用下面的表达方式开始：

All in all, ...

In a nutshell, ... (This is an informal phrase. 写作不宜使用,但在日常口语里却经常听到)

In short, ...

So it's no exaggeration to say that ... (可以毫不夸张地说,……)

That's pretty much it.

That's all I can think of now.

 请一定注意结尾句是不可以说"In a word, ..."的,这是很多中国考生,甚至教师频繁出现的错误。In a word 在英文里面永远后面只跟一个单词,而不能跟一个句子,比如 In a word, no.

2 "起—承—转—(合)"结构

请看这个常考问题:

How do people feel about rain?

下面的答案就是典型的"起—承—转—(合)"结构

Humm, it seems to me like some *folks* love rainy days coz rain feels *kind of* romantic.

In contrast, some others may totally hate rain coz they *have a hard time getting* around on rainy days. So you see, the feeling *may vary from person to person.*

"起—承—转—(合)"式就是先回答问题,然后开始说其中一方面,接下来再说另一方面。每方面各说多少其实是比较随意的,没必要太机械,只要确保不说空话(rambling)就可以了。最后的"合"部分,可以选择省略。

比如下面这道题:

Do you like partying?

下面的7分答案就使用了"起—承—转—(合)"式(如果不熟悉斜体的那几个单词,可以在 Day 3 的几个大表格里找到它们,拜托不要照着背诵)。

(起) It really depends. (承) Sometimes when I feel lonely, I go partying with friends of mine. (转) But when I'm busy or when I *feel under the weather*, partying would be *the last thing I want to do*.

> "起—承—转—(合)"式的优缺点和"起—承—(合)"式正好相反：它的内容比较容易说得多一点，因为毕竟两方面都可以说。但是相应的，它的结构也要复杂一些。

☆"起—承—转—(合)"式结构的常用词汇和句型

（不要全背，否则……还是记不住！）

（1）起

Yes / No 题	Wh- / How 题
Yes and no. I can't say for sure. （注意和起—承—合结构中的"起"不同）	It depends. On the one hand, … I'm not sure. It seems like… Let me see… Actually, … It's kind of complicated. （kind of 是"有点"，complicated 是"复杂的"） … may vary from person to person. There are many differences between… and…（仅限于关于 differences 的题目）

（2）承

这个可以参考前面的"起—承—(合)"结构的承接部分表达，因为两种结构的"承"部分是相似的。

（3）转

On the other hand, …

In contrast, …/ By contrast, … ☆

Even so, …

Still, ... ☆

Despite that, ...

Although that's basically true, I would say...

Otherwise, ☆

☆ By contrast, .../ In contrast, ...

表示它后面内容和它前面的内容去对比。这两个在口试里面说并不会过于严肃,放心用好了。

☆ Still, ...

如果放在一句话的开头,那么 still 的意思就不是"仍然",而是"尽管这样"。

☆ Otherwise,

……否则……, e. g. Parents should keep the lines of communication open

with their children. Otherwise, their children may feel ignored.

（4）合

"起一承一 转一（合）"式结构如果要在最后再总结一句（合）,可以用下面的词开头:

Anyway, ...

Anyhow, ...

After all（毕竟）...

On the whole, I guess...

有三个词组 By and large, .../Generally（speaking）, .../In general, ... 很多同学也喜欢把它们放在答案结尾来引出结论。其实这三个词组在国外更多的是直接陈述一个事实,而比较少会放在一组句子的结尾去做总结,e. g. By and large, the people in my hometown are very friendly.

3 "无厘头"结构

在考场实战中,我们其实没有必要使每个问题都有一个明确的结构。所谓的"起一承一

(合)"式和"起—承—转—(合)"式,也只是供参考的思路。很多问题,我们的答案其实是没有明显结构的"无厘头"(off-the-wall)式。答案只要充实,只要英文地道,就没有什么值得我们害怕的。

比如下面的 7 分例子就使用了十分随意的结构,用的都是最简单的连词,但是逻辑已经很复杂了:

How can people control the pollution in your city?(答案中的斜体单词我们都在 Day 3 中学过)

Well, you know, there're plenty of ways to do that. For instance(举例), if we control the number of cars, then there'll *definitely* be less *poisonous* gas. And(并列)if we move the factories to other places, the air just won't be so *stuffy* anymore. But as a matter of fact(转折), it seems it's very unlikely those things could be done immediately *coz*(因果)the city government already has too many things to take care of...

Part 2 结构的 4 种选择

Scenario 1：对于"牛人",我仍然建议你不要太担心卡片答案的结构。把卡片看仔细,然后就开始在考官交给你的纸上展开 brainstorming。基本上只要是相关的内容,不要离题太远都可以。雅思口语其实没有太"神"(wacky)的卡片,否则就不是口语考试而是有奖问答了。理论上来说,任何话题应该都可以扯到 1'30"以上,否则你就不是"大牛"(top guns)。

Scenario 2：对于有一定的英语表述能力的考生,我建议看到卡片之后有一个大致(rough-and-ready)的顺序安排就好了,不用太机械(mechanical)。比如说人物,我们就可以考虑用 Day 2 的 Part 2"藏宝图"里面 people 那一格的几个 items 来安排,这样相对保险,内容也会比较充实。

Scenario 3：对于完全没有口语功底但是又有"野心"想考高分的苦孩子们,也可以考虑背一些结构性的句子。下面是一些不错的结构性句子,每组知道一句就够:

❶ I'd like to talk about...

Well, let me talk about...

I'd like to describe...

省略号处填入你要描述的话题,比如 Beijing, my favourite sport, my cousin...

② I'll get started by looking at...

I guess I'll start off by talking about...

To begin with, I'll talk about (who this famous person is)...

I'll start off by answering the initial question of (what the skill is)...

省略号处填入卡片上第一个提示中的问题。

③ Next then in reply to the second question of...

Now regarding...

Moving on to the matter of...

Concerning the next question of...

省略号处填入卡片上第二个提示中的问题。

④ Continuing with the next point of...

With respect to the matter of...

With reference to the issue of...

Now let's look at...

省略号处填入卡片上第三个提示中的问题。

⑤ Finally, let me take care of the issue of...

Finally, maybe I could wrap up my description with my thoughts about...

Finally, I'd like to explain to you...

省略号处填入卡片上 Explain...后面第四个提示中的问题。

Scenario 4: 下面的几个词组,适合从"大牛"到"菜鸟"(rookies / newbies)的全部考生,因为它们可以帮助你在不同话题之间快速转换,**或者使一个话题引申出一些内容。而且,最重要的是:这个表格里的词组听起来是自然的。对于选择能力不强的考生,建议大家坚定地掌握这些就可以了,最好不要自己编了。**

▶ **in terms of...** （谈到……,关于……）

= regarding = concerning = when it comes to

e. g. In terms of price, this car would be a nice choice.

▶ **And what I need to emphasize here is that...**

= The fact I need to highlight here is that...（我需要特别强调的是……）

= What I need to stress here is that...

e. g. And what I need to emphasize here is that he did that all by himself.

▶ **Specifically, ...** （具体地说,……）这个经常用来进一步深入说明

e. g. He made great contribution to China. Specifically, he donated（捐献）lots of money to the Chinese charity（慈善事业）.

▶ **By the way, ...** 经常用在接近描述结束的部分

e. g. By the way, some parrots can be used as alarm clocks.

▶ **In other words, ...**

= ... that is, ... = By that I mean...

e. g. In other words, people go there not for pleasure, but on business.

把段落说长的更多实用技巧

① 下面的表达都表示"更具体地说",可以用于任何一个英文句子后面的展开部分:

Specifically, ...

In particular, ...

To be more exact, ...

To be more specific, ...

To be more precise, ...

② 口语里最有效的举例方式:

For example...

For instance…

like…

such as…

另外下面这句话也经常用来在雅思口试中引出例子而且并非俗套：

This is best illustrated with the example of…

③ 如果你感觉已经实在没什么可再展开的了可考官却还意犹未尽，那么可以试试：

In other words，…

By that I mean…

… that is to say，…

然后所有你要做的，就是很"流氓（cheeky）"地把前面一句话换个说法再说一遍了……

超短线
The Ultra-Short Track

对于备考时间严重不足的同学们来说，如果本来就没兴趣深入研究口语的段落结构，但又奢望能把自己的回答说得"跌宕起伏"，那么就只能靠下面的四种关系了：

a 因果	b 假设
c 让步	d 对比

如果您现在在图书馆或者自习教室里，请把它们默念五遍，然后再看看本书 Day 4 常用连接词表格里分别对应这四种关系的连接词，并在说英文时积极使用它们，你会发现自己说的内容已经有了一点层次感。当然还有最初级的两种层次关系：转折（But／However）与举例（for example/such as/like），但因为早已溶进咱们的血液里可以脱口而出了，就不用再刻意去记了，毕竟有重点才能有效率。

Day

练出 decent 的发音
Taken at Face Value

李思圆的发音：蒙了，英视的方面发音完全白色到了。50 分 MM

北美英语第二册有声书 BBC 学习网络语、美国大学...、英语有声阅...

Pat's Guide
To the Speaking Test

I take it you already know.
Of tough and bough and cough and dough.
And now you wish, perhaps,
To learn of less familiar traps.

　　要练出不错的发音,除了积极模仿光盘里的英国 SG 和 MM,
还可以登录上面的这个 BBC 官方网站,里面的发音部分相当酷。

▶ *We just have adopted a laid-back approach,*
even though we take the test seriously.

前文已述,地道英文口语里有个相当常用的单词,其意思与中文里的"不错"极为接近: decent。native 的发音需要长期积累,attractive 的发音需要专业训练,但 decent 的发音是有可能在短时间内就练成的。

多短呢?也许,一天……

三大纪律

☆ 少看理论 ☆

关于英语发音的书面理论不管听起来多么神奇,它们其实只会让你的中文 reading 能力越来越强。

☆ 集中精力 ☆

只要开始练习你就应该把 TV set,PC,laptop,PSP,iPhone 全部关掉,完全投入 (Throw yourself into it.),唯一可以留在身边的电子产品是一个录音装置(a recording device)。

☆ 听自己说 ☆

身边放一个录音笔,这样进步更快。实在不好意思就把你身边的人都赶走,并且一个小时之后才能回来。

适合国内同学的英文单词发音测验
A Pop Quiz on Pronunciation

请各位先做三个小测验,都是 Pat 总结的中国考生常见发音错误,看看现在你属于哪种水平。

☆ TEST 1 — EASY

If your English is every bit as good as the average English learner in China, you will have no difficulty pronouncing the following words correctly.

这个测试很简单,是看你能不能达到中国学生发音的平均水平,如果错 5 个以上,那你的英语现在就肯定处在中国人能听懂你的意思,但是外国人完全听不明白你在说什么的状态。测试的时候请随时对照光盘里的录音。

① beach   ② because   ③ yesterday   ④ famous

⑤ invite   ⑥ library   ⑦ night — light   ⑧ slow — snow

⑨ thick — sick   ⑩ said — sad

☆ TEST 2 — HARDER

Your English pronunciation skill is distinctly above average here in China if you can pronounce the following words properly.

这个测试难度大一些,如果这些单词你的发音都正确,你的发音就处在 native English speakers 能轻松听懂的状态。测试的时候请随时对照光盘里的录音。

❶ newspaper   ❷ industry   ❸ quite — quiet   ❹ temperature

❺ sandwich   ❻ thought   ❼ clothes   ❽ kind

❾ comfortable   ❿ loose — lose

☆ TEST 3 — HARDEST

Now you can discover how close you are to native English speakers in pronunciation. The next ten words are no cinch — you will be acquitting yourself creditably if you pronounce eight of them correctly.

这个测试最难,是看你的英语发音可爱指数了。如果这 10 个词你都能正确发音,不用我说,肯定有老外夸过你发音好。测试的时候请随时对照光盘里的录音。

❶ atmosphere   ❷ celebrity   ❸ affluent   ❹ synthesize

❺ photography   ❻ economic   ❼ gorgeous   ❽ unique

❾ resources   ❿ sunbathing

单词发音的七宗罪

听来听去,国内的考生发音其实只有 7 种常见错误(您不是要告诉我刚才的测试里 7 种错误您全都犯了吧?)。如果 7 种错误都能改掉,发音虽然还不完美,但是已经完全可以让老外轻松听懂你的英语了。

1. 应该是长音还是短音?

经常听到学生把 sheet 读成 shit,甚至有人把 beach 说成 bitch。请大家仔细跟光盘朗读下面的单词:

heat   extreme   miss   peak   pick

2. 力度够不够?

北京话讲究轻快,所以很多北京考生说英语力度不够。很多北京孩子读 because 都发

成"笔锛子", sorry 说成"骚瑞",就是因为发音的力度不够。请来自北京的读者仔细跟光盘朗读下面的单词:

net   Patrick   family   kind   easily

3. 有没有儿化音?

北方话,特别是北京话,儿化音超多。像"公主坟儿",如果说成"公主坟",或者"冰棍儿"说成"冰棍",就让人不寒而栗。但是一定要注意,没有 r 这个字母的单词,即使在美国,也不会有儿化音的。

请来自北方的读者仔细跟光盘朗读下面的单词:

famous   panda   grandpa   gorgeous   difficult

4. th 音到底怎么发?

中文里面没有 th 这个音,所以要发好这个音还真要好好练一练。关键是舌尖儿要伸到上牙的外面一点点(不要太多,否则很难看哦),轻轻地碰到上牙,然后轻轻吹口气,效果就出来了。如果是 these 里面的 th,就把舌尖伸出来一点点,轻轻地在上牙上摩擦一下,就可以了。请大家仔细跟光盘朗读下面的单词:

those   thought   synthesize   thread   throw

5. l 和 n 怎么区分?

这两个音在中国南方的一些地区经常有考生分不清,因为一些方言里面没有 n 这个音。另外我还发现一些说粤语的考生,有时候把 fat 里面的 t 省掉了,report 里面的 t 也省掉了,也需要改正。请南方的读者仔细跟光盘模仿下面单词的发音:

night   light   slow   snow   money

6. 重音究竟在哪儿?

重音发正确是比较高端的要求了。重音发错,小错误会听起来别扭,大错误会导致考官无法理解你的意思。请读者仔细跟光盘模仿下面单词的发音:

comfortable   newspaper   atmosphere   celebrity   photography
yesterday   temperature

7. v 和 w 的区别

这两个音区分的关键是牢记发 v 的音牙齿会碰到下嘴唇,但是发 w 的音牙齿不碰下嘴

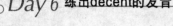

唇。请大家仔细跟光盘模仿下列单词的发音:

invite   wife   swim   win   visit

☆ TEST 4 — TONGUE TWISTER PRACTICE

下面的三个绕口令都是帮助你巩固今天学习的效果的,请跟光盘好好练习朗读一下。

❶ If Peter Piper picked a peck of pickled peppers, where's the peck of pickled peppers Peter Piper picked?

❷ We will wish to visit their wives.

❸ I think this thin thread will go through the eye of this thick needle.

★　★　★

好,单词的发音我们先练习到这里。打开手机看看有没有彩信。

★　★　★

练好句子的发音

现在我们再前进一步,突破句子的发音。还是强调我们练习的三大纪律:

★ 少看理论

★ 集中精力

★ 听自己说

高分考生的发音凭什么拿高分?

经常有学生跟我抱怨,为什么看 Gossip Girl 或者 Prison Break 的时候没有几句话能听懂。其实除了很多国内同学所习惯的词汇与当代真实英语的常用词汇严重脱节外,另一个重要原因就是不熟悉连读、弱化这些发音规则,所以导致很多你认识的单词却听不懂。

不信您试试这个:

http://www.youtube.com/watch? v =ji5_MqicxSo

这个 Randy 教授在英美可是鼎鼎大名的,号召力甚至超过 Obama 和 David Cameron,你能听懂他人生中的最后一次讲座吗?

几年来的教学实践告诉我,发音能真正接近 native English speakers 的考生,一定会注意下面四个方面:

★ 连读	★ 弱化
★ 句子重音	★ 语调

A 弱化与连读 Weak form and Liaison

弱化与连读是区分发音高手和菜鸟的重要依据。这两个技巧效果相似,都是让你的句子更流利更连贯,所以我们把这两项放在一起练习。请仔细听光盘的朗读,认真模仿下面的发音。

part-time

but now

I'll

He'll

what's

Where is she?

Do you want a beer?

Want to go shopping?

give me an answer

three hundred years

but that word is hard

it used to be

You should take care of them.

kick back and relax

the gap between the urban area and the rural area

B 句子的重音 Sentence Stress

一般来说，名词、动词和形容词会倾向于重读，而介词、连词和代词会倾向于轻读。但是要注意别太机械地使用这个规则，其实很多时候最重要的是看你的句子要强调哪一个单词。比如下面的句子，强调的内容不一样，重读的单词就不同。

I don't know where he is now. (Maybe someone else does.)

I don't know where he is now. (So don't keep asking me.)

I don't know where he is now. (But I know where Nancy is.)

I don't know where he is now. (But I saw him last week.)

C 句子的语调 Sentence Intonation

大家都知道，一般来说，疑问句用升调，陈述句用降调。但实际上可没那么简单，native English speakers 说话，每句话里面都会有几次升降调的变化。只是陈述句一般句尾落在降调，而疑问句句尾落在升调。请仔细听光盘录音，体会下面一段话每个句子的升降调，并注意模仿。（放心，这个段落一定不会白模仿的，里面的很多句子在雅思口语 Part 1 和 Part 2 我们都可以用的）

(Please pay close attention to the word stress sentence intonation.)

Three Great Reasons to Learn a Foreign Language

☆ Improve your Chinese

As a person who speaks only one language, you have no basis for comparison; all you know is Chinese. In different languages the same idea is often expressed in different ways. There is a reason most great writers and poets are students of many languages.

☆ Enhance your travel experiences

Traveling is one of the great joys of life and also one of the most expensive. Why not get the most out of your experience? As a person who doesn't know the native tongue you are completely excluded from the culture. Knowing even a few phrases of the language will make a huge difference. You will meet many more people and find it much easier to get around.

☆ Languages are beautiful

Language is what makes us human. It is the medium we use to share our thoughts with the world. Could you imagine thought without language? Great language also has a wonderful musical quality. Learning a new language is like learning a new way to think and a new way to sing.

这一节给大家重点讲的是，如何让你的口语发音进一步接近老外的地道发音。其中最重点推荐的是连读和弱化这两个技巧。今天的最后，给各位介绍几段生活化的口语，这段话体现了地道英语发音的全部特点，请大家认真听，认真模仿。

(Familiarize yourself with the way native English speakers actually speak in daily life, particularly how some consonants and vowels are fused or omitted.)

Larry: Hi, Harry. Great to see you again. I heard you've traveled a lot recently.

Harry: Yup. Actually, in the past three months I traveled to tons of countries in Africa.

Larry: I really envy you, man! Did you pet a zebra?

Harry: Well, I didn't get to pet a zebra, but I was once chased by an elephant, and it was pretty scary!

Larry: Serious?

Harry: Nope, just kidding.

Larry: You really scared the heck out of me, buddy.

Harry: You know, I really missed the comforts of home. And now I just want to take a break. A long break in my super comfy home!

超短线
The Ultra-Short Track

对于备考时间紧但又对自己的单词发音没有信心的同学，如果你对某个词的发音不确定，也许你会选择查字典。试试 http://www. howjsay. com/ 吧。用这个网站学发音可比字典轻松多了，而且朗读者使用的是标准的英音。

Day

反正 Part 1
Opposites Attract

Pat's Guide
To the Speaking Test

Polar opposites don't push away
It's the same on the weekends as the
rest of the days
I know I should go but I'll probably stay
I'm trying to drink away the rest of the day

👉 口语 Part 1 话题库索引

Pat 的 Part 1 完整素材库（时间太紧的读者只要结合我在博客里贴出的本月预测题准备就好了）
Pat's Idea Pool for the Part 1 Test

口语 Part 1 的话题都是生活中常见的，ideas 并不难想。但如果一边想思路，一边又想英语怎么表达，就可能导致 fluency 严重下降。其实正反两方面都说一说是个不错的选择，肯定比只说一方面内容多点。因此本章里的话题都按照正反两方面给大家提供思路，把它们串起来的方式可以参考本书前面的 Day 4 和 Day 5。不过实战的时候也没必要太机械，如果一方面已经够了也就没必要再正反都说。

请充分熟悉下面素材库里的句子，不要 100% 照背，多看看就行。时间紧的同学按照 Pat 在博客 blog.sina.com.cn/ieltsguru 里贴的最新口语预测题进行准备就够了。

Topic 1: Studies（including learning English）
学习（含学习英语）

★ I'm sure my hard work will **pay off**（会有回报）.	
AFFIRMATIVE（正方）	**NEGATIVE（反方）**
My university has a great reputation（名誉）. 注：IELTS 口语中也经常可以用 excellent 来代替 great	The curriculum（课程）is too hard for me. 注：hard 在地道口语中也经常可以用 tough 或 difficult 代替
★ This is a pretty promising field（有前途的领域）. 注："领域"在口语里还可说 erea 或者 sphere	I guess I will have a hard time finding a job when I graduate. 注：地道英文中"找到工作"也经常会用 land a job 这一固定表达
★ It enables me to fulfill my potential.（让我发挥我的潜力）注：enable sb. to do sth. 让某人可以去做某事 例：The new student loan will enable the undergrads as well as grad students to continue their studies. undergrads 是国外大学校园里对本科生	We are not encouraged to exchange（交换）ideas with other students.
	I hate the force-feeding approach to teaching.（填鸭式教学）

（续表）

(undergraduates) 的更常见说法，而研究生（graduate students）在实际校园生活里则通常被简称为 grad students	
My professors are really thoughtful and considerate（关心人的）.	But sometimes what they teach in class is over my head（听不懂）. 注："听不懂"在地道口语里也常会说成 It's beyond me.
My teachers are pretty lenient（要求不是很严的）. 注：在国外一般私立学校 private school 的老师要求得严一些（strict/ demanding）而公立学校 public school 的老师相对比较 lenient	My teachers are so strict. It seems very few Chinese teachers encourage their students to explore（探索）areas that are beyond academic boundaries（超出学术课程界限的）.
★ On top of that, there's a wide variety of extracurricular activities（课外活动），like the debate club, the chess club, the school newspaper, the basketball team, the choir（合唱团）and even a rock band. 注："学校的社团"在地道英文中一般就叫做某某 club，这里并非指俱乐部	But extracurricular activities can be time consuming（很耗时间的）. 注：time-consuming 是"很耗时间的"意思，它在地道英文中的反义词有两个：一个是 efficient（高效率的），另一个则是 rewarding（回报丰厚的）
I volunteer at the university library/school library. 注：其实做 volunteer work 是 LW 考官们相当喜欢听到的一种经历；而且 volunteer 的用法很灵活，可以用做 verb, adjective 和 noun	I have a heavy class load this term. 这学期课业负担很重。 注：在学校里当你听到别人说 workload 时其实也是指课业负担
★ The canteen / cafeteria（食堂）serves great food. 注："好吃的"，如果你已经厌烦了 delicious，那么请和考官说 scrumptious 或者 tasty 中的一个，但 yummy 在国外成年人说时一般都是半带开玩笑的口气，考试时说未必就显得可爱	The canteen / cafeteria food is atrocious（差得出奇的）. 注：说食物极其难吃还可以用 gross，但雅思口试时请不要用 yucky ☒

It's important to be **bilingual**（双语）today.	
AFFIRMATIVE（正方）	**NEGATIVE（反方）**
★ Understanding English enables you to understand the English-speaking cultures better. 注："双语的"bilingual 很多考生认识，但口试时却往往会忘记你自己其实就是bilingual	You are considered "left behind" if you can't speak English. 英语读写能力的真正地道表达不是 English writing and reading skills，而是叫 English literacy
Reading English novels and online magazines is an excellent way to boost your vocabulary（扩大词汇量）.	Learning a foreign language takes time and energy. 注：地道英文中还有 an arduous process（是一个艰苦的过程）的说法
English abilities give you a competitive edge and improve your chances of employment.	There're plenty of test-taking techniques（应试技巧）. But as a matter of fact, there're no shortcuts（捷径）to learning a foreign language.
★ We can travel the world with few language barriers（语言障碍）if we speak good English. 注：travel the world 是地道英文里的一个固定短语，这里 travel 后面不一定要加介词	中文字幕则叫做Chinese subtitles，中文配音的电影叫做movies dubbed in Chinese。

★ **Singing along to** English songs can help you **acquire**（获得）this language as well.

注：acquire 是教育类的地道加分词，后面可以跟某种知识或技能，比如 acquire languages skills

Topic 2: Work
工作

FOR（正方）	**AGAINST（反方）**
It's well-paid. 注：同义表达是 The pay is good. 请国内同学注意这里的 pay 不要说成 payment	I'm really tired of working for peanuts（挣钱少）.

（续表）

★ My boss treats everyone equally. .	I have to work overtime（加班）practically every day. 注：practically 在口语中经常代替 almost
The working environment is pretty friendly.	It doesn't offer the opportunity for quick promotion（提升）.
★ It offers me a whole lot of benefits（这里不是好处，而是福利），like paid vacation, a pension（养老金）plan and, on top of all that, a company car.	My boss is a slave driver（真不把员工当人）. "同事"英语怎么说呢？在多数公司里叫做 colleagues 或者 co-workers，而在车间或者工地工作的人员则可能管自己的同事叫 workmates
I'm learning new skills to help my career prospects（事业的前景）.	It's a dead-end job（没有前途的工作）。
Sometimes I have to take charge of the whole team. 注：下次当您下意识地想到 be respon-sible for 的时候，请考虑是否可以用 be in charge of 去替换	I'm constantly on the go. 注：constantly 这个副词在地道口语中经常代替 always
★ Employees are paid time-and-a-quarter（125%）if they work on weekends. time-and-a-half（150%） double time（200%）	This job is back-breaking work.

Pat指南

☆ 请已经工作的朋友们注意：你回答的工作并不一定是你的真实工作，只要英文正确就很好了。绝不用担心后面会问和你的工作相关的技术（specialized）问题。

☆ 下面几种工作回答起来更有特色：

I'm a freelancer（自由职业者）.（freelance writer, a freelance photographer...）

I'm self-employed.（自己有 business）

a surgeon（外科医生），a photographer（摄影师），a pastry chef（面点师），

a veterinarian（兽医），a biologist（生物学家），geologist（地质学家）

但如果您对自己的口语没有足够的自信，就请不要说自己是一位 translator（翻译）或者 interpreter（口译员）。原因？It's plain as the nose on your face. ☺

☆ 在国外工作中凡是可以给员工带来动力的东西都可以称为 an incentive。

Topic 3: Hometown（Including Traffic & Pollution）
家乡（含交通和污染）

AFFIRMATIVE（正方）	NEGATIVE（反方）
★ My hometown is a coastal city（沿海城市）. It offers some of the best beaches in China. 请一定注意 beach 中的 ea 是长音，绝不要说成短音，否则会把考官惹"毛"）	The air is so smoggy（烟雾重的）.
	Lots of people there suffer from respiratory diseases（呼吸系统疾病）.
★ My hometown is an inland（内陆的）city best-known for the gentle, rolling hills surrounding it.	The traffic is always bumper-to-bumper（= tied up）during the rush hour. 注：表示在……期间时 during 在地道英文中用得极多，但国内考生都不太爱用，遗憾
This city is steeped in（沉浸在）time-honored（历史悠久的）traditions.	The cost of living is sky-high.
It's prosperous（繁荣的）.	"经济不景气"英文：The economy is in a slump.
★ There's a real sense of community（社区）.	There's no sense of community.（邻居间缺少交流）
★ This city is well-known for its architectural heritage（建筑遗产）.	I can't stand the hustle and bustle（拥挤，喧闹）there. 注：can't stand... 无法忍受……
The cityscape（城市景观）is gorgeous and there are tons of towering skyscrapers（摩天楼）there.	Most of the buildings there are two to three storeys（层）high.

（续表）

★ High-rise buildings **are** sprouting up all over the city.	Some areas are pretty run-down（破旧的）.
It's pretty sprawling.（宽阔的，建筑分散的，比如美国的 Arizona 州）	It's densely-populated.（人口密集的，比如中国的香港）
★ I enjoy the peace and quiet there. · 在这里 quiet 是名词	The noise here was so disturbing（烦人的）I didn't sleep a wink last night.（一夜没睡）
This city is like a magnet（磁铁）for the tourists.	It's not so well-known , not even in China.
★ town→small city→**medium-sized city**→ big city→**metropolis**（规模越来越大） ★ 城市里的 **leisure facilities**（休闲设施）： **concert halls**, **opera houses**, movie theaters, **art galleries**, **coffee shops**, **sports stadiums**, **gyms**	
★ The sky is always crystal-clear. = The sky's clear as a bell.	The car exhaust fumes（汽车尾气）are poisonous（有毒的）.
★ We enjoy a great climate（气候）all year round.	The climate is harsh.（气候恶劣） 注：有个稍大的词 inclement 也经常被受过良好教育的英国人用来形容天气恶劣：inclement weather
My hometown has a dynamic and vibrant（有活力的）nightlife with countless bars and clubs. Young folks（= young people）often go partying, clubbing and bar-hopping（体验不同的酒吧）at night. 注：请注意本句里的 nightlife 其实是特指一种生活方式，所以前面需要加 a 家乡适合年轻人居住的理由除这些之外还可以有 It's a university town/ college town（是一所大学城）. The economy is thriving.（经济发展快）和 There're plenty of job opportunities around.（就业机会多）	The rising unemployment rate is driving up the crime rate. 注：家乡如果不适合年轻人生活的另一个重要原因则可能是 It lacks variety.（生活缺乏变化）

（续表）

★ At night, it's tranquil and serene（宁静的 = peaceful）.	It's close to an airport（机场）and the noise is so disturbing（烦人的）. At night, we have a hard time falling asleep and wake up tired in the morning because of the noise.
★ People there are pretty laid-back（放松的）.	The pace of life（生活节奏）is fast and stressful（压力大的）.
★ Going to concerts is a popular pastime there.	People in this city don't have much leisure time（休闲时间）.
In many cities, a driver's license（驾照）is a necessity for finding a job. 注：a necessity 是指必要条件或必需品。 在英国、美国和加拿大的不同地区驾照的说法略有不同，Pat 至少见到过 driving license, driver's license 和语法上并不正确的 driver license，但它们都是在实际生活中被使用的地道英文。	There're an awful lot of reckless drivers out there. 注：reckless drivers 指开车完全不考虑后果的危险司机，也可以说 They drive like crazy. 或者 They're offensive drivers. 它的反义词则是 defensive drivers（善于自我保护的司机）。不过今年年初在美国最新公布的一项民意调查则显示大家一致认为最可怕的司机其实是 slow drivers
Driving makes life much easier for me and for my family members. 注：除了上班可以开车 drive to work 之外，当然也可以为了休闲而开车 drive for pleasure	Driving is not a right. It's a privilege（特权）. 注：这是在欧美极为有名的一句话，意思就是必须要符合法律对驾驶的规定你才能有权开车。 形容某事"有风险的"可以使用 risky 或者 hazardous，不过在国内城市里让 Pat 感到最恐惧的并不是 cars，而是 mopeds（电动自行车），每次都是悄没声息地就杀出来了（very sneaky）

（续表）

It's vital for us to **drive safely**. 注：这三个词的重要程度依次递增： important→essential→vital	Drunk driving **can kill**. 注：酒后驾车也经常被简称为 DUI （Driving under Influence）
The written test was just a piece of cake and then I passed the road test without a hitch. 注：a piece of cake 大家应该很熟悉，就是"小菜一碟"，而 do sth. without a hitch 则是对轻松过关的地道说法，出国后您在学校里则常会听到人说 I passed the test with flying colours！	I failed my road test twice before I finally passed it.
I don't have a car so I'm free of all the burdens of car ownership: having to keep the car maintained and filled with gas, the parking fees and of course the insurance ☺ 注：the burdens of car ownership 作为车主的负担；maintain 在说到车时是维护、保养的意思；而 insurance 当然就是保险了	I frequently find myself sitting in my car stuck in traffic for hours. 注：get stuck in… 国外生活中相当常用的一个短语：被……困住 有关 biking 的英文知识请看本章中的 Topic 12

Even public transport is not so **dependable**（不是很可靠的）these days.

AFFIRMATIVE（正方）	**NEGATIVE ↑（反方）**
It's fun to ride around on a bus coz you get to see many interesting people.	I take the bus so I can take a nap（睡一小觉）.
When I'm in a hurry, I take the subway（= the underground / the Tube）.	I often get stuck in traffic.
比较拿分的交通工具（即使你可能从来没有乘坐过也放心说吧）： minibus（中巴）；shuttle bus（班车和机场巴士）；ferry（轮渡）；light-trail（轻轨）	Sometimes the traffic can be obnoxious（= terrible）. The cab fare（打车费）is expensive in Beijing and Shanghai.（任何车费都叫 fare）

Pat指南 🔊

☆ "打车"除了 take a taxi 在国外生活中还经常有人会说 flag down a cab / hail a

cab / grab a cab。

Topic 4: Entertainment（including the movies，TV，the radio，and other leisure activities） 娱乐（含电影、电视、广播以及其他休闲活动）

All work and no play makes Jack a **dull boy**	
Just **escape reality** for **a couple of** hours and watch a movie.（逃避现实几个小时去看场电影）	
FOR（正方）	**AGAINST**（反方）
★ I'm into animated movies（动画片＝cartoons）. I'm a movie buff.（影迷，你是不是又想到了 fans？那至少也得改成单数）	The plot of that movie was too far-fetched.（情节太牵强）
I enjoy movies with a fun plot（情节＝storyline）. 注：当形容词时，fun 是有趣的而 funny 则是搞笑的	你一定已经知道 comedy 是喜剧，但是你有没有试过用 slap-stick 这个词代替 comedy 呢？
Suspense movies（悬念片）keep me on the edge of my seat.	I dislike gangster movies（警匪片），'cause they are so violent. 英雄当然是 heroes，反派是叫 villains
★ I prefer movies with great acting（演技）.	I hate movies with a predictable storyline.（看了开头知道结尾的那种）
In that movie, Angelina Jolie（安吉丽娜·朱莉，认真听录音，Jolie 的发音超级容易错）played the lead（演主角）. And Brad Pitt played opposite of her.（演对手戏）	The soundtrack（电影音乐）from that movie was just mediocre（比较一般的）. 注：如果想把欧美名星一网打尽就要熟记一个网址：www. people. com/people/celebrities
★ I like movies with a happy ending.	I can't stand romantic movies cuz they are so corny（没创意的）.
Good movies are always thought-provoking（引人深思的）.	The special effects（特效）in that movie were not very impressive.

（续表）

★ That movie has **a strong cast**. （演员阵容强大）
My favourite star had a cameo role （客串） **in it.** （也可以说 **He / She just had** a bit part （小角色） **in it.** ）替身演员叫 stuntman / stuntwoman

Good movies can be really entertaining （娱乐性强的）.	That movie was too serious. It was a drag （ = it was boring）.
That movie was a blockbuster. Its box office take was incredible （让人难以置信的）.	I adore （喜欢） movie stars with a "bad boy" or "bad girl" appeal （吸引力）. 注：adore就是like的加强版，跟LW们谈电影时尽管多用

★ 低成本电影地道英文叫做 **low-budget movies**，而上座率很高的电影则叫 **a smash / a box-office hit**

THE MOVIE THEATER / THE CINEMA （电影院）	HOME （家里）
It has a better atmosphere （气氛）. 注：better 在雅思口语中可以用 more desirable 这个常用表达代替	You have more choices. 注：choices 也常用 options 代替
★ You watch a movie on an enormous （巨大的） screen.	Pirated DVDs are dirt-cheap. （盗版碟超便宜）
The sound and visual effects are way better. （视听效果好多了） ★ You share the viewing experience with a large audience.	比 sound effects 更大的说法叫 acoustic effects 或者 audio effects，但后两个在口语里都不如第一个常用
★ Watching TV is fun, no doubt about it.	But on the other hand, it can be totally time consuming （消耗时间的）.
Some TV programs are educational while others tend to be more entertaining	Some TV series are not all they're cracked up to be. （有些电视剧并不像宣传的那么好） I'm tired of watching the boob tube（TV 的通俗说法） every night. 注：厌烦在地道英语里也可以说成 I'm fed up with… 或者语气更强的 I'm sick and tired of…

（续表）

★ Sometimes I just flick through the channels coz there're too many channels to choose from.	Actually, televisions are barriers to strengthening families.（是增进亲情的障碍）
TV programs 的常见种类（genre）有：TV series（连续剧），reality show（真人秀），quiz show（问答节目），variety show（综艺节目），sports show，news show，sitcoms（情景喜剧），game show，documentaries（记录片，在 Discovery Channel 和 National Geographic Channel 上经常放的那些），脱口秀（这个英文自己说吧，嘿嘿）	Watching too much TV gives you square eyes.（在英美有一种说法：看电视太多眼睛会变方）
	★ Many people eat their evening meals sitting in front of the TV set, which is very unhealthy. 这种现象在国外太普遍了，以至于英文里已经出现了一个极为常用的词叫 TV dinner，说不健康的生活方式时也别忘了跟考官说这个词
	I'm a bit of a couch potato on Sundays.
	There're too many commercials（电视广告）during prime-time（黄金时段）viewing.

Pat 指南 🔊

☆ 以下这些闪光的人名都是 Pat 发现国内同学们最容易念错的明星名字，请仔细听光盘：

Leonardo DiCaprio《盗梦空间》男主角莱昂纳多的名字稳居读错榜榜首

Beyoncé Knowles 其实这位美女的名字准确发音并不是"碧昂斯"

Anne Hathaway 她演的公主日记很多同学应该都看过

Avril Lavigne 这位太火了应该不用解释大家也知道是谁，但她的名字却经常被人读错

Nicole Kidman 妮可·基德曼这么简单的英文名字其实也很容易读错

Cameron Diaz 连影坛大姐大的名字都有人敢说错

Keanu Reeves 基努·里维斯有 1/8 的印第安人血统所以有一个原住民的名字

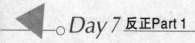
Miley Cyrus 去年如果谁生活在欧美却没听说过 Hannah Montana 那这人真的很难再混下去了

Matt Damon 拯救大兵瑞恩里的男主角，最近两年更火了

Halle Berry 黑珍珠哈里·贝瑞的名字同样是一个考验

David Beckham 小贝虽然不是影星，但他的姓总是被国内同学念错，也放进来吧

说来说去，最不容易发错音的还是超模 Kate Moss 和影后 Natalie Portman 的名字，所以她们一定会红。

☆ 恐怖片叫 horror movies，动作片叫 action movies，Titanic 那种就叫 romance/romantic movies，sci-fi 就是科幻，外星人地道英文叫 aliens。

☆ 另外，和考官聊的时候如果说到电影，一定别忘了 flick 是口语里经常用来代替 movie 或 film 的拿分表达。

☆ 电视剧的一集叫一个 episode。

☆ 电视节目中间插播的广告除了叫 TV ads，也经常被称为 TV commercials，专门播放广告的时段叫 ad slot / commercial slot，"黄金时段"是 prime time，而"让人很烦"最拿分的词则是 disturbing。

Topic 5: Reading & Writing
报纸、杂志、阅读和写作

★ I'm always **on the lookout for** a good book. （我总是在寻找好书）	
AFFIRMATIVE（正方）	**NEGATIVE**（反方）
★ When you read a good book, you communicate（交流）with a great mind.	I can't stand motivational books（励志书）cuz essentially（本质上），they're pretty much the same.
Reading English novels is an excellent way to boost your vocabulary（扩大词汇量）.	Some biographies（传记）are false.
★ Reading expands your thoughts.（开阔思路）	I don't put pen to paper very often.（很少用笔写东西）
Many coffee shops and restaurants offer free wi-fi（无线上网）now.	

（续表）

Children can improve their handwriting（笔迹）by imitating（模仿）nice examples of hand-writing online before developing their own style.	Practice makes perfect.（熟能生巧，虽然俗但确实地道，忍了吧）So kids should try not to type everything.
★ Email is much more convenient and much faster than regular（常规的）mail.	I hate writing letters coz, you know, my handwriting is pretty messy（混乱的）.
★ And it's cost-efficient（= economical）. 也可以说 cost-effective 这个词	But letters convey our feelings more effectively.（更有效地表达情感）
The information highway has put a wealth of information at your fingertips.（考试时请体验一下用 information highway 代替 the Internet 的感人效果）	But kids often get addicted to online games.（对网络游戏上瘾）
★ On the information highway, everything is just a click away from you.（距离你只有点击一下鼠标的距离）	Lack of computer skills is a handicap（严重的缺陷）today. 注："精通电脑的"最常用的表达是 computer-savvy
Reading newspapers helps us keep up with the world around us.	
★ Newspapers get us updated on daily events. 注："时事"则叫 current events/current affairs	Compared with newspapers, magazines tend to specialize in certain subject matters.
★ Local newspapers focus on the local happen-ings. 注：如果您对不停地重复使用 events 感到厌倦，那么 happenings / occurrences 就是不错的选择	Local newspapers tend to be somewhat biased.（有偏见的）
★ International newspapers are more comprehensive, which means they deal with a wide range of issues.	报纸的头版叫 the front page，头条叫 the headline
As I see it, magazines make you more knowledgeable while newspapers make you more worldly（精通世事的）.	
The articles（文章）are well-written.	But the layout（排版）is kind of messy.

（续表）

Some magazines are geared towards an adult audience while others cater to the teenage readership.	When I feel bored, I just flip through some magazines. （随便翻翻）

Pat指南

☆ 说"一本书好看"在地道英文里有个说法，国内同学很少用，因为觉得语法貌似是错的，但其实它是很常用的英文。话说 Pat 上学时曾在图书馆找到了一本 *On the Road*（在路上），拿给图书管理员准备 check out 时，librarian 突然就来了句：It's a good read.

☆ 请注意"书虫"bookworm 这个词在地道英文里并没有贬义。

【剑桥例句】Bookworms spend most of their spare time reading and are interested in collecting books.

☆ 有几种书值得一说（虽然并不一定值得一看）：

best-sellers（畅销书，可以是任何种类的）

literary classics（文学经典）

motivational books（励志书）

fiction books（大致就等于中文里的小说）

suspense novels（悬念小说）

cookbooks（菜谱，注意单词 recipe 是指一个菜的做法，而不是一类书）

travel guides（旅行指南）

☆ newspapers 常见的栏目（sections）

business section（贸易栏目）

financial section（金融栏目）

international news（国际新闻）

national news/domestic news（国内新闻）

local news（地方新闻）

cultural section（文化栏目）

classified ads（分类广告）

☆ 不止是音乐会的听众，报纸和杂志的读者群其实也可以叫做 audience，或者叫 readership，报纸和杂志的销量则叫做 circulation。

e. g. The newspaper has a daily circulation of 60,000.

☆ 如果说某种媒体"面向"某种群体，有三种表达，大家至少应该掌握一种，而且说到 TV 和 advertising 也经常用到：be geared towards ＝ cater to ＝ target（v.）

☆ 杂志的出版时间可以这样介绍：

It comes out once a week. 或者 It's published monthly.

☆ 订阅杂志英文叫 subscribe to a magazine，失望地取消订阅则是 cancel the subscription 或者 unsubscribe to a magazine。

Topic 6: Clothing
服装

Clothes make the man.	
FOR（正方）	**AGAINST（反方）**
These days, baggy clothes（肥大的服装，就跟面口袋似的那种）are really "in"（＝popular）.	I'm into stylish stuff. 注：stylish ＝ fashionable ＝ trendy
★ Nice clothing enhances appearance.（美化形象）	A poor taste in clothing spoils the impression that you make.（破坏你给别人的印象）
I prefer a classy, mature style, like suits.（有品味的成熟的风格） 注：suit 就是套装，比如 business suit 就是"西服"	Half of my clothes are out of style（过时了）.
I prefer a youthful, casual style, like tees and jeans.（青春休闲的风格） 注：T-shirt 很多时候在地道英语中会被年轻人用 tee 这个词代替	They look pretty outdated（过时的）.
★ I prefer the athletic（运动的）look, you know, just like a baseball tee, gym pants and sneakers（运动鞋）.	说服装有一个词请一定记得和考官用一下：outfit，复数是 outfits，其实就是 clothes 的意思，这个词在国外年轻人中用得极多，几乎已经过多
★ Fashion has become an important way for us to express ourselves.	
These days fashion is very diverse（多样化的）. ／There are different styles to match our	I'm a fashion victim.（一心追随时尚的人）

（续表）

individuality（意思是个性，而不是性格 personality）.	
Name-brand clothing is often considered a status symbol.（名牌服装经常被看做是身份的象征）	Some people just prefer to go against the norm and don't pay any attention to the trends.（不走寻常路，美特斯·邦威……）
I just stick to（坚持）my own style. 注：如果说一个人很有个性，地道英文可以说：He/She has character.	Some folks are just conformists（盲从的人）.
★ We should follow our own paths.	Some people prefer fashion over comfort.
卖服装的小店叫什么？国外生活里最常用的是 boutique，请您一定仔细听 CD 中这个单词的发音	

Pat 指南

☆ 虚荣心的地道英文是叫 vanity。比如：Vanity makes a person unrealistic.（不现实的）

☆ 如果真考到 fashion 话题不妨跟考官提一下 *The Devil Wears Prada*（穿普拉达的恶魔）这部 flick。

☆ casual clothing 的反义词是 formal clothing 或者有时也说 dressy clothing。

Topic 7: Weather & Seasons
天气与季节

Weather affects our mood.	
AFFIRMATIVE（正方）	**NEGATIVE（反方）**
I really enjoy the glistening snowflakes（闪亮的雪片）in winter.	The monsoon season（梅雨季节）in Shanghai is pretty long.
The winter is pretty mild（温和的）.	The summer is scorching（热得不行的）. 您要是夏天去过美国的菲尼克斯就能最深刻地领会 scorching 的本质含义。
Hong Kong is pretty warm all year around.	I can't stand the muggy weather.（闷热的天气）

（续表）

★ I like autumn best coz we can see the colourful foliage （树叶，不要加复数）.	Overcast weather （阴天）gives us a bad mood. 注：考试时"阴天"不一定非要再用 cloudy weather
I feel comfortable when it drizzles in summer.	But I feel upset when it pours. （drizzle 下小雨，pour 下大雨） 注：描述心情不好时 upset 极为常用，很像中文里的"郁闷"
The rain washes away the pollution. 注：wash away 不是洗走而是冲走	Heavy rain often results in flooding. 注：雨下得大也可以说 It often rains heavily during the summer months.
Everything feels so fresh in the spring. 注：地道口语中还经常可以用 refreshing 这个词来形容事物让人感觉焕然一新的	还可以说 Many plants bloom in the spring. 注：bloom 在这里是动词：开花
My birthday is in the spring / summer/ autumn winter. That's exactly why it's my favourite season. 注：That's exactly why… 正因为如此……，同样的意思有时也可以改说 That's precisely why…	Autumn is the back-to-school time for students. That's why I kind of dislike it… 注：kind of 是常用的副词短语，有点儿……的意思。dislike 的语气没有 hate 那么强，还算比较客气
Christmas is my favourite time of the year and that's during the winter. 注：during 是地道英文中表示"在……期间"时极为常用的介词，可惜国内的同学用得过少	The long and harsh winter makes me feel miserable. 注：harsh 是"严酷的"，而 miserable 在口语中则经常用来形容一切可怜兮兮的人或者东西，连《悲惨世界》的英文版标题都叫 *The Miserable World*
关于冬天有几个词提示大家一下： 中文里的"雪花"在地道英语里不能说 snowflower，而要说 snowflakes 建筑物都被大雪覆盖了英文可以讲 Buildings	The winter there is not necessarily very snowy. But when it snows, the snow is blown around by strong winds, which makes things inconvenient for people.

133

（续表）

are buried in snowdrifts. 而超大的暴风雪则是 blizzard	注：is not necessarily… 是一个颇为常用的口语句型，表示"不一定是……"的意思
对于夏天那种湿热的天气，瞄准机会还可以用这句地道的英文跟考官抱怨一下：It's not the heat. It's the humidity（潮湿）that feels unbearable. 注：unbearable 是令人无法忍受的常用说法	The winter is like, … freezing, or…, you know, frigid.（这两个词可一个比一个冷） Pat 在国内时注意到有的老师教学生用 chilly 这个词表示"很冷的"，其实在地道英文里 chilly 只是"凉嗖嗖的"，而不是严寒。 例：In October, the days will still be warm but the evenings will get chilly.

Topic 8: Arts（including Music, Painting, Drawing and Photography）艺术（含音乐、绘画与摄影）

Beauty is in the eye of the beholder.
有些人说这句话是中文的"情人眼里出西施"，其实在地道的英文中这句话完全可以用来说 artwork，意思是每个人对艺术的理解都不尽相同

FOR（正方）	AGAINST（反方）
★ Music makes us more imaginative and it molds our temperament as well.（也塑造我们的性格）	Downloading music off the Internet for free is a very controversial issue today. 免费下载音乐现在是一个很有争议的话题。
Nice music infuses our lives with joy.（让我们的生活充满乐趣）	The lyrics（歌词）of her songs are too mushy for me（太肉麻了）.
Good music makes everything around us come to life.（让生活活跃起来）	Pop music doesn't have much depth.（没深度）
Classical music tends to calm you down.	Most pop songs get us excited. Sometimes wild.

（续表）

★ I like Beethoven, Mozart and Tchaikovsky. 其实地道英文就是用音乐家的名字表示他们的音乐，猜猜这三人是谁？	I'm into music with a strong beat（强烈的节奏感）.
★ Research has proved that playing musical instruments makes kids / babies more intelligent（聪明的偏正常说法）.	Learning to play a musical instrument（乐器）takes time and energy, and... lots of money, for that matter（ =as well）
★ Some music makes us feel inspired（受到激励的）. 英文里有种很地道的说法还算比较常用：Music is a mood enhancer（是调节情绪的好方法）. 从没听国内的朋友们用，不妨学起来	Some catchy songs（一听就会的那种歌）are actually pretty annoying（烦人的）
Nice music calms the nerves and restores the soul（放松精神）.	说 music 对精神的影响还有一个更好记的短语叫 lift our spirits，它的形容词 uplifting 也较为常用，意思很像中文"给力的" 例：For Olivia, this was an uplifting concert.
Some paintings make us feel calm and peaceful.	Honestly, I can't understand abstract paintings（抽象画）.
★ Painting skills give us a better appreciation（欣赏）of art.	
Some other paintings are thought-provoking（令人深思的）.	
Photos bring back memories.	
★ Lighting, composition and a good subject are important to taking good photos（对一张好照片来说，光线、构图和所拍摄的内容都非常重要）	People in the background can really ruin a photo. 注：ruin 表示"破坏"在口语里很常用
You can just slip a compact camera（卡片机）into your pocket.	
★ Photos capture（捕捉）precious（珍贵的）moments for us.	Some people are camera-shy（不喜欢照相的）.

（续表）

★ Photos record memorable（值得回忆的） experiences.	portrait, landscape and still life 分别是人像、风景和静物。我们随时随地拍的"快照"地道英文叫做 snapshots
Going through a photo album is like a trip down the memory lane. 看相册就像回到了过去的一次旅行。	I'm not so photogenic（上镜的）.
Some people look better in photos.	Others look better in person.
★ Some photos are candid（真实的）.	Some pictures are very flattering（比真人好看的）.
★ We can use Photoshop to touch up（改善）digital photos.	So these days, photos can really lie about their subjects.
Twilight（黄昏，去年大红特红的《暮光之城》当然也是这个词）and sunrise are the best times for photography coz the light is gentle.	

Pat 指南

☆ 在国外说音乐的种类除了 kinds/ types，还有一个超酷的词叫做 genre，在地道英文里这个词其实可以用来说任何艺术品的种类，相当拿分，但它的发音请您仔细听 CD，如果发音不准那可就没有震撼力（overpowering effect）了。

☆ 一首歌的歌词叫做 lyrics / words，曲子则叫做 melody / music。

☆ Part 1 里描述音乐只要记住三个形容词 touching（感人的），mushy（肉麻的）和 corny（老掉牙的）就已经挺厉害了。

☆ 关于音乐的种类如 country, classical, rhythm & blues 考生们说得都太多了，或许还剩下点新鲜感的是 heavy metal 和 Latin music。

☆ 令人放松的音乐，除了 relaxing music，还可以说 soothing music。

☆ Beethoven, Mozart and Tchaikovsky.（英文里就用音乐家的名字来指代他们创作的音乐，请仔细听光盘，这几个人是谁应该没什么悬念吧）

☆ 乐器的英文名称千变万化，真不知道为什么大家都要口径一致地告诉考官自己会 piano 和 violin。其实 flute（长笛），saxophone（萨克斯）和 keyboard（电子琴）不是更好记吗？而 violin 的近亲 viola（BrE /vaiˈəʊlə/；AmE /viˈəʊlə/）中提琴和 cello（/ˈtʃeləʊ/）大提琴也是简单易记却被受过良好教育的英美人士所偏爱的 instruments。

☆ 如果你实在记不住 LW 音乐家们的人名那就说 Lang Lang 吧，用汉语拼音就行而且还特地道，但同时要知道他是 an award-winning pianist。

☆ 谈到 paintings 应该知道三个形容词：realistic（真实的），representational（具体的）和 abstract（抽象的）。

Topic 9: People (including Family, Friends and Meeting New People) 人（含家庭、朋友、邻居与新认识的人）

AFFIRMATIVE（正方）	NEGATIVE（反方）
★ I grew up in a very close, loving family. And I still keep in touch with my family regularly（定期的）.	
★ China has a one-child policy.	Overpopulation（人口过多）led to this policy.
My family consists of my parents and me. (consists of = is made up of)	Sometimes I feel lonely coz I have no siblings（兄弟姐妹的总称）.
★ I'm the/an only child.	Sometimes I wish I had a bunch of (= some) siblings.
My parents are pretty lenient（不是很严厉的）.	Just like most other Chinese parents, my parents are really strict.
★ I had a very strict upbringing（家教很严）.	Some kids never do housework at home. 常见的 housework：do the dishes / do the laundry（洗衣服）/ take out the trash（倒垃圾）
★ My folks can always give me good advice when I need it from them.	We shouldn't take our parents for granted.（不要把父母的爱当成无所谓的事）
Eating together as a family has a particular significance（重要性）in children's lives.	We're so busy these days even eating together as a family seems like a challenge for us.
★ Sometimes a good neighbour can make a house a home.	
When we moved in, they respected our privacy and didn't ask us any question that would be too personal for us.	Our neighbours never return things that they borrow from us. 注：如果打算说这个那就要满腔悲愤的

（续表）

注：欧美人多数都不喜欢 nosy people（喜欢打听事儿的人），跟考官说这个他/她会很认同的	
Sometimes we invite our neighbours over for a get-together. 注：get-together 小型的聚会	They make an awful lot of noise. 注：在地道英文里表示不好的东西很多经常会用 an awful lot of... 来形容
Knowing our neighbours well brings us a sense of security（安全感）.	邻居发出的噪音可能有 loud music, blaring TV sets 或者 The couple fight every day.
We often invite our neighbours over for dinner.	I hardly know my neighbours. 注：hardly 几乎不，类似的意思也可以说成 I rarely（极少）see my neighbours.
There's a strong sense of community among us. 注：谈邻居时 community 是一个很常用的词，它不仅指所居住的小区，也指邻居之间的良好关系	We rarely see each other. 注：rarely，很少，表示频率低的常用副词

★ How do you meet **new people**, besides people you already know?

Some people do volunteer work to meet new people. 注：很多国内同学误以为 volunteer 就等于中文的"志愿者"，其实这个词在地道英语里除了作名词"志愿者"之外，也还经常会用作形容词或者动词，比如：Max volunteers in the school library.	I didn't really like reading. I joined that book club just to meet new people. But when I realized I didn't share any common interests with other members, I just quit. 注：不再干某种工作地道英文叫 quit，退出某个社团也是 quit，而戒烟当然也是 quit smoking
It's popular to meet new people online through chatrooms and social networking websites. 注：社交网站的英文是 social networking websites，例如国外的 Facebook, Twitter, Myspace 和国内的 Renren 网络社区则叫做 online community	I tend to feel nervous when I meet new people. 注："社交恐惧症"的英文则是 social anxiety disorder

（续表）

★ Friends are people you can **count on** (= depend on). A friend in need is a friend indeed.	
All friends of mine are intelligent, amusing, sincere and trustworthy（聪明的，有幽默感的，真诚的而且值得信任的）. 日常生活里 amusing 这个词比 humorous 常用得多	They are just fair-weather friends（这个就像中文的酒肉朋友）.
We share a lot of interests with each other.	I hate back-stabbers（出卖朋友的人）.
We hit it off right away.（这个就是中文的"一拍即合"）	We drifted apart（逐渐疏远了）. =We just went our separate ways.
We really enjoy each other's company.（这里是"陪伴"）	
Share and share alike. 这是个 proverb（谚语），意思很像中文的"有福同享"	很忠实的朋友叫 loyal friends，不忠诚的则是 disloyal friends。朋友除了 friends，也可以说 companions 或者更口语化的 buddies
★ We're really tight = We're really close.（说两个人关系很"铁"）	I've lost touch with most of my childhood friends. 注：lose touch with 意思是"失去联系"，它的反义词组当然就是您熟悉的 keep in touch with
I have long-distance friends as well, like friends living in France and Finland.	We meet up in chatrooms and play online games against each other. But… we've never met in person. That's a shame.（太可惜了，That's a shame. 是固定用法，与"羞耻"无关）

Pat 指南 🔊

☆ 中文名可能带有的特殊含义：

It represents prosperity.（代表繁荣）

It means strength and loyalty.（力量与忠诚）

139

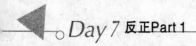
It's ^{associated with} purity and nobility. (和纯洁与高贵相关)

It ^{signifies} good luck. (意味着好运)

^{stand for} 这个词组在地道英文里通常指 "是……的缩写",所以这里如果你的名字并不是任何中文词汇的缩写,就不要说 stand for。

☆ 介绍家庭的时候,如果你能够正确地区分下述两组词汇,考官将会非常惊讶 (a nice surprise)。

☆ ^{immediate family} 就是指中文的家人,而 ^{relatives} 一般是指家人之外的亲戚;^{nuclear family} 是指父母和孩子两代一起的家庭,而 ^{extended family} 是很多代人一起住的大家庭 (three or even more generations ^{live together under the same roof})。

☆ 如果说 "孩子像父母",英文怎么讲呢? 最地道的说法就是用词组 ^{take after},如 They ^{take after} their parents/folks.

Topic 10: Collection
收藏

It's ^{my greatest passion} in life. (……是我人生当中的最爱)	
AFFIRMATIVE (正方)	**NEGATIVE (反方)**
★ Some folks collect ^{antiques and old coins} (古董和老钱币) while others collect new things like ^{toys and souvenirs} (纪念品).	Collecting things can be an ^{expensive habit}.
People who collect ^{antique furniture} (古董家具) have ^{exquisite taste}. (高雅的品味)	Different strokes for different folks. 这个是 proverb (谚语),意思非常像中文的 "萝卜白菜,各有所爱。"
★ Collecting stamps can be ^{a lifetime hobby}.	Some people collect ^{artworks} as ^{investors}. (投资者)
Some people collect things for personal pleasure.	Others collect stuff in order to increase their wealth (财富).
Some people collect ^{precious stones}. (宝石)	
关于 collection 还有两个词很酷,一个是 ^{valuable artifacts} 基本上等于中文的 "工艺品",另一个是 ^{connoisseur},就是 "鉴赏家"。	

Topic 11: Buildings（including Museums，Libraries，Hotels，Houses，Flats 英式英语／Apartments 美式英语）
建筑（含住所、博物馆、图书馆和宾馆）

Home sweet home.	
HOUSE / FLAT（住所）	**ITS SURROUNDINGS（周围环境）**
★ The rooms feel pretty spacious（宽敞的）. 注：狭小的叫 cramped	It's not in a really convenient location.
★ The big windows let plenty of natural light in.	It's hard to get around if you don't have a car.
The whole place feels light and airy（通风好的）.	There's a wonderful view outside the window.
I decorated（装饰或者装修，这两个意思这个单词都可以表示）my flat all by myself.	
AFFIRMATIVE（正方）	**NEGATIVE（反方）**
★ There're some Chinese ink paintings（水墨画）and a family photo on the wall.	My flat / apartment looks pretty cluttered（乱糟糟的）.
★ It has a roomy kitchen.（宽敞的厨房）	My flat has a balcony（阳台）. But it's pretty messy as well. 注：messy 的反义词是 organised
The hardwood floors are in good condition.	The floors are worn-out（陈旧的）.
☆ 对于打算说自己住在 house 里的孩子们，不妨试试这两句然后看考官的反应： I grow organic（有机的）vegetables in the yard. ／ I can almost taste the freshness of the air.	

Pat 指南

☆ 常见 housework 的地道英文表达：wash the dishes/do the dishes（洗碗），do the laundry（洗衣服，在生活里较少有人说 wash the clothes），take out the rubbish（倒垃圾，这是英式英语，在美国则叫 take out the trash），vacuum the floor（用吸尘器吸地板，英美的多数家庭都铺地毯所以 vaccum 很重要），mop the floor（擦地板），change the bed linen（换床单、被套），cook（meals），而 spring cleaning（春季大扫除）也是

141

三、四月间经常能听到的说法。

Libraries hold **a wealth of** knowledge.	
Some people think of libraries as a haven, a place where they can get away from the busy city life. （haven 是避风港）	There's plenty of parking around.
★ I enjoy the quiet atmosphere there. （安静的气氛）	But there's a limit on the number of books you can check out. 注：check out（books）借阅，也有些借书人会说 sign out books，意思相近
★ Libraries offer you a wealth of books. Good libraries put tons of resources at your disposal. （任你支配） 注：一个设施完备的图书馆叫 a well-equipped library	

Museums are buildings where **historical**, **cultural** or **scientific** stuff is kept and shown to the public.	
★ There're tons of fossils on display （展出） in that paleontological museum. （这个要好好听 CD，古生物博物馆）	比较少有考生说但是很拿分的 museums: folk art museum 民俗艺术博物馆 marine museum 海洋博物馆 wax museum 蜡像馆 planetarium 天文馆
★ There are many hands-on exhibits in children's museums. 注：也可以很形象地说 Visiting a museum brings history, science and arts alive for the children.	
★ I just enjoy wandering around in this museum. （到处走走） Coz... the tickets are free.	"大饱眼福" 的地道英文是 It's a feast for my eyes.
★ In 5-star hotels, there're usually tons of entertainment facilities. （娱乐设施） Each room has Internet access, which is commonplace （= very common） today.	高档的宾馆叫 posh/luxurious/upscale hotels；经济性宾馆叫 motels 或者 B&B （bed and breakfast），motel 国内翻译成汽车旅馆很不合适，因为其实你不开车去一样可以住

（续表）

★ 服务很完美怎么说呢？ he service is perfect. 是个一般的答案 The service is flawless. 是个有意思的答案 The service is impeccable. 是个很棒的答案	"拆老房子" 英语有很多说法，IELTS 口试里面推荐：knock down old buildings /demolish old buildings 和更口语化的 raze those buildings

Pat 指南

☆ 有两个词要分清，一个是 exhibition 展览，另一个是 exhibit，这个词也可以表示展览 = exhibition，但是它也可以表示单独的一件展品。

☆ 宾馆的类型很多，按星级有 three-star，four-star，five-star 甚至 7-star，比如逐渐没落的迪拜（Dubai）Burj Al Arab。

☆ 注意地道英文里住宾馆动词不用 live，而是用 stay in a hotel。

☆ 关于 libraries 我们在 Day 8 还将会有进一步的发掘。

Topic 12: Sports，Other Outdoor Activities，biking & Games
运动、其他户外活动、骑自行车以及游戏

It's important to **balance** our time **wisely** between our work/studies and **leisure.**	
FOR（正方）	**AGAINST（反方）**
Jogging（慢跑）and swimming are excellent ways to get fit.	Some sports, like marathon and hurdle-race（跨栏），are too strenuous（累人的）for average people.
★ Exercise gives me a feeling of accomplishment（成就感）	Some sports require months of training.
Many elderly folks（= people）in China practice tai-chi（太极）in the morning.	average people 在口语里面比 ordinary people 更常用
★ I work out regularly（经常锻炼）at a gym, which helps me lose weight.	Jogging every day is too hard on my knees.
Individual sports boost our confidence in ourselves（增加我们的自信）.	关于 sports，有两个形容词请一定记清：strenuous（消耗体力的）和 laid-back

（续表）

★ Individual sports train self-discipline. （训练自制力）	（放松的）。如果能再记住三个名词就更好了：strength （力量），flexibility （柔韧性）和endurance （耐力）。
★ Individual sports help us discover our own worth and potential. （潜力）	
☆ Team sports require （需要） team spirit （团队精神）.	
★ Extreme sports can be really adventurous / risky （冒险的）.	表达"需要"，主语如果是人还要说need，如果主语是事物就可以用一次require 了
I can soak up （吸收） some Vitamin D when I do outdoor activities.	It seems sunbathing （日光浴） is not very popular in China.

★ You feel the wind in your face when you go hiking （徒步旅行）.

★ At/On weekends, we often have a picnic （野餐） out in the open air. （注：at weekends 是英式的表达）

Riding a roller coaster （过山车） can be totally thrilling （非常刺激的） and you can hear passengers （乘客） scream at the top of their lungs （尖叫）.

I'm into a variety of outdoor activities, like hiking （徒步旅行）, biking, camping, walking dogs （遛狗）, going to amusement parks （游乐场） and rafting （漂流）.

★ You know, I just love the Great Outdoors. （就是nature，大自然）

I'm quite the outdoorsman/outdoorswomen. At weekends, I often spend hours watching wildlife.

★ We can enjoy the beauty of nature by doing outdoor activities like camping, biking, hiking and fishing. （注意nature 作大自然的意思讲时前面不加the）

PLUSES （喜欢的理由）	MINUSES （不喜欢的理由）
★ Kite flying （放风筝） is great fun.	Some games, like chess and card games, challenge your intelligence. （智力）
Biking: I just appreciate the simple pleasures in life.	
★ Good games give you a youthful heart and positive attitude （年轻的心和积极的人生态度）.	Some people like to gamble （赌博） when they play mahjong and card games. （麻将和扑克）

（续表）

★ Biking is very eco-friendly. （有益环保的）	But in big cities, biking can be risky（冒险的）
In the West, people ride a bike for pleasure and recreation（= leisure）.	In China, biking is more like a mode of transport.（交通方式） 注：大家爱说的 transportation 其实是美式英语，而在英式英语中 transport 的名词和动词形式都是 transport
I love the feel of the breeze（微风）on my face.	
★ You can see more when you **pedal**（蹬）a bike.	
I use my bike every day, though not for long distances.	As a student, I can't afford to take taxis often.
When riding my bike through the city, I always enjoyed stopping to taste the snacks cooked and sold by the roadside vendors. 注：roadside vendors 就是地道英文里对"路边小贩"的说法	I really hate it that cars spew fumes that I have to breathe in. 注：spew fumes 是拟人化的"喷尾气"说法
The bike doesn't pollute or cause traffic jams. It just helps people stay fit. 注：Pat 发现很多考生误以为 stay / keep fit 是指保持身材苗条，其实它在地道英文里的真实含义是"保持良好的身体状态"，而不仅指身材	But my hometown is not very biker-friendly. Bikes must share the road with cars and buses. 注：类似的合成词还有 user-friendly

Pat 指南 🔊

☆ 要说好 sports，我们应该知道：

什么是 individual sports（个人运动），比如 jogging，skating，swimming，skiing 和 sports car racing；什么是 team sports（团体运动）比如 basketball，American football （橄榄球）和 baseball（棒球）；什么是 extreme sports（极限运动，也可以叫 X-sports），比如 bungee jumping，white-water rafting（漂流）和 skateboarding（滑板）。

在 www. buzzle. com/articles/list-of-extreme-sports. html 上有对十几种极限运动的

详细解释。

☆ 常见中国传统游戏的英文表达：

tug of war，也可以叫做 rope-pulling（拔河） mahjong（麻将）

rubber-band jumping（跳橡皮筋）kite-flying（放风筝）

hide-and-seek（捉迷藏）

☆ 近期的国内游戏

Killers of Three Kingdoms（三国杀），Grows Vegetables and Steals Vegetables（种菜、偷菜），West Illusion Swims（梦幻西游），Dungeon and Warrior（地下城与勇士），Plants vs.（发音/ˈvɜːsəs/）Zombies 植物大战僵尸

☆ 英语国家的常见游戏：

card games，tag（基本就是国内小朋友玩的"捉人"游戏）

I-spy-with-my-little-eye（这个游戏可是 Pat 小时候的最爱，但国内孩子似乎不太爱玩，请看 Day 8 的详细解释），spelling bee（拼字游戏），math games and hide-and-seek（捉迷藏）。

关于游戏，我们会在 Day 8 中分享更多的地道英文。

Topic 13: Shopping
购物

People go shopping for different things, like clothing, toys, tools, books and **groceries**.

AFFIRMATIVE（正方）	NEGATIVE（反方）
★ Shopping is my favourite pastime（业余爱好，经常可以用来代替 hobby）	It's a pricey（＝expensive）habit.
	I tend to buy things on impulse.（冲动的）
Shop till I drop.（生命不息，购物不止）你甚至还可以说 It's my motto.（它是我的座右铭）	I'm a real shopholic（购物狂）.
★ I do a lot of comparison shopping（这句完全等于中文的"货比三家"）	Actually, I'm a last minute shopper. You know, I go shopping only when I really need something.

（续表）

It's dirt-cheap.（便宜到极点了）	It cost me an arm and a leg = It cost me a fortune = it was really pricey = It was very expensive. （注意 cost 的过去时还是 cost）
I love name-brand stuff.（名牌儿） 英语里还有一个词叫 brand name，两个词用法很像，如果非要区分，brand name 是指品牌，但是不是所有品牌都能叫 namebrand products 名牌货	shop assistants 就是"售货员"
★ Window shopping doesn't cost me anything.	scam artists 是从事哪种艺术的人呢？哪种也不是，这种人叫"奸商"，在国内还有个网名叫 JS 而骗局就叫 a scam

Pat 指南

☆ 说购物有两个非常拿分的词一定记得用一下，一个是 item，复数是 items，就是指商店里的东西，还有一个是 boutique，就是大家去的那些小服装店儿。

Topic 14: Pets
宠物

To some people, their pet is their constant companion（从不离开的伙伴）。	
AFFIRMATIVE（正方）	**NEGATIVE（反方）**
A dog is man's best friend. 请注意这里的 man 是人类的意思，前面不用加 a，是个 idiom	Pets may take up too much of your attention, at the expense of（以……为代价，牺牲）your family members.
★ Pets are good for our emotional health.	Sometimes pets wet the floor or chew up your shoes. 注：这里 wet 作动词，chew up 是咬碎的意思

（续表）

Raising pets can boost our confidence and self-esteem（增进自信和自尊）.	In cities, we need to make sure our pets are ____ or they would be in trouble.
★ I brush my puppy every day.	Some owners ____（虐待）their pets.
Pets **drive off** our **loneliness**.	

Pat指南

☆ 常见的 pets 包括 puppies 小狗，kittens 小猫，parrots 鹦鹉，tropical fish 热带鱼和 rabbits 兔子。

☆ 更有创意的答案包括 lizard 蜥蜴，pony 小马和 hamster，最后一种是胖胖的比老鼠大点的动物，Pat 本人可是不太喜欢（They rub me the wrong way.）。

Topic 15: Age
年龄

YES	NO
I grew up in… = I was raised in…	I'm not a person who ____ .（总留恋过去） I prefer to look to the future.
I go back home during winter break and summer vacation.	I wish I could do so but I ____ .
It has been a year since I left home.	I'm reaaaaaally ____ .（这个可不是在家养病，而是形容词，想家的）
I'm from / I come from…（这里如果只是介绍自己就不要说 came）	I'm ____ adapting to the way of life here. = Getting used to the way of life here is ____ .

Pat指南

☆ 说年龄，咱们要知道这几个词的分别：

baby / infants（大致是 1~2 岁的小朋友，不过在国外有时候 7、8 岁的孩子了还能听

到有 adults 指着这些孩子说 babies)

toddlers（走路摇摇晃晃的那种孩子，也就是差不多 2 岁的样子吧）

teens / teenagers（准确地说是 13~19 岁的孩子，不过也没有人算得那么清楚）

kids / children，这两个其实每个人的定义都可能不一样，在美国经常听到人说 college kids，基本上也就是未成年人了（法律上叫 minors）

people in their 20s / 30s / 40s…（这个应该一看就能明白，还可以更具体地说 people in their early 20s / mid 30s / late 40s）

middle-aged people（差不多就是中文的"中年人"，大概 40 多到 50 多）

pensioners / retired people /seniors / the elderly（这 4 个词其实概念不一样，不过从考试角度看，也没必要区分太细了，基本都是老年人了）

Topic 16: Travel
旅行

Traveling can be especially **fun** when you feel sick and tired of **the daily grind**（日常琐事）and want to **get away from** it all.

AFFIRMATIVE（正方）	NEGATIVE（反方）
★ We can explore（探索）new places and meet new people.	跟团旅行叫 take group package tours，旅行社叫 travel agency，自助旅行叫 independent travel，背包族则是 backpackers
★ Most importantly, we can try new foods（表示不同种类的 food 可以用复数）.	
I prefer to travel light（少带行李）.	Luggage（行李）can be really cumbersome.（不方便携带的）
Travel **frees** us **from** the grind of **daily routine**（日常琐事）.	
People from all walks of life enjoy traveling. 注：这是一个英文里的固定短语，但并不是指各行各业的人，其实就等于中文"各种各样的人"	跟年轻人 travel 最密切相关的三个名词是：exploration 探索，discovery 发现和 adventure 探险。说旅行带来的好处时还可以用到一个词组叫"充电"recharge our batteries，但要注意这个词在地道英文里一般指对体力或者精神的恢复，而不是周末上辅导班

（续表）

Traveling is my favourite pastime. 注：favourite pastime 就是指最喜欢的业余爱好，生活里没有 hobby 用得多，但在 IELTS 口试中却可以用来代替 favourite hobby	**Time and money are** two major factors that will determine **where we travel**, **when and for how long.** major 在这里不是专业，而是主要的；determine 是一个口试常用动词，确定、决定的意思，接近 decide
I was fascinated by the villages, the islands, the deserts, the forests and the valleys that I visited. valley 是山谷的意思，be fascinated by 是指被……彻底迷住了，比如 She was fascinated by Brother Sharp (*Xi Li Ge*).	旅行时的行程英文叫做 itinerary，安排行程就叫 plan the itinerary，跨越国界的友谊叫 friendship across borders

Topic 17: Food（including Restaurants, Meals, Healthy Eating and Cooking）食品（含餐馆、三餐、健康饮食与做饭）

You're what you eat. (This means if you want to be **fit** and healthy, you need to eat good food)

AFFIRMATIVE（正方）	**NEGATIVE（反方）**
★ I'm a vegetarian, so I'm really into things like tomatoes, carrots, cucumbers and broccoli.	
★ It's essential to have a healthy diet.（健康的饮食）	
Fish dishes are high in protein（蛋白质）and low in fat.	Junk food is very fattening.（让人发胖的）
★ Steaming（清蒸）is healthy coz no vitamins are lost.	
Grilling（烤）is healthy too 'cause no extra oil is used.	
★ I love Chinese cuisine.	
Our staple（主食）is rice.	

（续表）

★ I like to start my day with a hearty（丰盛的）breakfast.	I often skip（略去，不吃）breakfast.
I always eat three square meals（丰盛的三餐）a day.	When I've had a big breakfast, I just skip lunch.
We all need some **variety** in our **diets**.（饮食应该多样化）	
★ **People** socialize（社交）**at restaurants.**	
Sometimes we have corporate（公司的）dinners at restaurants.	The food that restaurants serve can be very unhealthy, no matter how good it tastes. unhealthy = unwholesome
★ They offer a wide selection of foods.（表示种类时 food 可以加复数）.	It's so greasy and fattening（油腻的，让人发胖的）
★ In Shanghai, classy, upscale（高档的）restaurants are always packed（挤满了人）on Friday nights.	餐馆的客人叫 customers，餐馆里的气氛叫 atmosphere 或者学着餐饮业的内行们更专业地说 ambience 这个词吧。
The portions are so big.（菜量给的多）	Sometimes you have to wait for ages（等很长时间）for your food.

Pat 指南

☆ 说一种食物"有营养的"最常用的英文词就是 nutritious。

☆ I'm a vegetarian, so I'm really into things like tomatoes, bamboo shoots, carrots, cucumbers and broccoli. 说自己是素食主义者是个挺拿分的选择，毕竟考官不能跟着你去看你晚餐吃什么，五种蔬菜分别是西红柿、竹笋、胡萝卜、黄瓜和西兰花，broccoli 的复数还是 broccoli，不需要加 s。

☆ 除了 pears（梨），grapes（葡萄）和 peaches（桃子）之外，雅思口试中更拿分的水果（fruit）名称包括：watermelon（西瓜），mango（芒果），kiwifruit（猕猴桃），papaya（木瓜发音挺逗的，请注意听 CD），还有很多种梅子，比如 raspberries（这个不知道中文怎么讲，是一种暗红色的梅子）和 blueberries（蓝莓），有个性的人也可以说 durian（榴莲）。说水果还经常会用到 juicy（多汁的）这个词。

☆ 蔬菜和水果的营养价值类似，基本也就是 rich in Vitamin C, minerals and fiber

（富含维生素 C，矿物质与纤维），如果偏偏要说得特别高深那可以试试They give us a wide range of valuable nutrients （营养物）.

☆ 指 food 的时候，healthy 这个词还有一个很棒的替换形容词叫wholesome。organic food （有机食品）一般都被认为更 wholesome。

另外，在谈到健康的 diet 时，well-balanced 这个词在国外生活中也相当常用。

我考过一些国内同学 "买菜" 的英文是什么，回答无一例外都是 buy vegetables。但 "买菜" 应该也不是只能买 vegetables 吧？其实get groceries 才是真正最接近于中文 "买菜" 的地道表达。

要说好 food，要知道三个词：

一个是cuisine，指一个地方所有菜的总称。在国外经常吃到的 cuisines 有 Scandina-vian （北欧的），Italian，Indian，Mexican，Thai，Japanese，Korean，Vietnamese… 各种风味都有的餐馆叫 fusion-style restaurants。其实在美国基本都是 fusion-style，因为太不正宗 （unauthentic），去尝尝美式中餐馆的 Kung Pao Chicken 或者 Ma Po Tofu 吧… Yuck！

另一个是recipe，指一个菜的做法，比如 Many people have secret recipes that they don't share with others.

最后一个是 ingredient （原料），比如 Fresh ingredients make meals healthier.

☆ 英文里的酸甜苦辣咸分别是sour，sweet，bitter，hot （英文经常把hot and spicy 放在一起说）and salty。如果太淡了根本没味儿，就说 It's too bland for me.

☆ 在国外住久了，多数人都深感西餐要吃的其实根本就不是菜本身的味道，而是各种各样的sauce/seasoning （调味酱） 的味儿。

☆ 下面三个词汇好吃的程度越来越强：mouth-watering ＜ scrumptious ＜ out of this world。

☆ 跟考官谈到你的日常习惯的时候，有两个地道的英文句子会非常拿分：

I rise and retire early. （早睡早起）

I usually turn in at midnight. （晚上 12 点才睡）

☆ 一顿丰富的饭还可以很地道地称为a hearty meal。

☆ 现在在英美人们开始越来越多地使用TV dinner 这个有意思的表达，但它并不一定要看电视才能吃，而是用来泛指一切 frozen food（速冻食品）和 prepackaged food（即食食品）这类怎么吃不健康就怎么吃的食品。

☆ a good selection of... 是说服务行业，比如商店和餐馆等地方极其常用的一个句型，e. g. That store has a good selection of stuff.

Topic 18: Colours
颜色与数字

Colours tell a lot about your **personality** and they affect your **mood** as well.	
FOR（正方）	**AGAINST（反方）**
I prefer catchy colours（抢眼的颜色）like bright orange, silver and black.	I hate loud colours. 我这个人就讨厌抢眼的颜色
★ Bright colours are considered outgoing and friendly.	Dark colours convey authority（体现一种权威）
★ Soft colours like cream（淡黄色），and brown are gentle and graceful（优雅的）.	鲜明的色彩叫 vibrant colours / vivid colours
There's truth in numbers.	
We tend to think of 6，8 and 9 as lucky numbers because they sound similar to some Chinese words that have positive meanings. 注：similar to（相似的），请注意介词用 to	Some numbers can be really tough to remember. Normally, I just make up a sentence with words that sound similar to these numbers to help me remember them. 注：tough 在地道口语里经常用来代替 difficult，normally 是口语里相当常用的一个副词，口试时可以用来替换现身过度的 usually。而 make up 则是"编故事"。例：The "millennium winter"（千年极寒）was made up.

Pat 指南 🔊

☆ 有些颜色说起来比 red/ blue 之类有意思多了，比如说 cream（淡黄色），lilac（淡紫色），maroon（一种比较暗的红色），或者 navy（深蓝色）。

Topic 19: Nature（including Gardens，Parks，Birds and Flowers）
自然（含花、花园、公园、鸟类）

I love **the Great Outdoors.** (= nature)
★ I prefer parks that have their own **unique atmosphere**（独特的氛围）.
You can almost taste **the freshness** of the air.

AFFIRMATIVE（正方）	**NEGATIVE**（反方）
★ I love the feeling of having my own garden and watching the plants grow.	Having your own garden is a luxury（奢望）in Beijing.
★ Gardens look **gorgeous** with all the **flowerbeds**（花坛），**lawns**（绿地）and **rockery**.（假山）	

I like to watch the **sunrise** in the park.

★ **Flowers** give off a sweet fragrance in that park.（fragrance 香气，可以用做可数名词）	更拿分的英文植物表达： daffodil　水仙花 sunflower　向日葵 tulip　郁金香 violet　紫罗兰 orchid　兰花 lilac　丁香花 （P233 还有更全面的植物名称）
★ When all the flowers are in bloom，（开花）the park is totally gorgeous.	
Sometimes we give bouquets（花束）to our loved ones.	
I decorate my living room with fresh flowers. 注；decorate 是动词"装饰"，名词则是 decoration，而 décor 则是泛指一个商店或者餐馆的总体装修风格，请认真听 CD 里对这个词的发音	
★ You can hear birds chirping（鸟叫）in the morning.	The serious pollution is driving birds away from this city.
Some birds have gorgeous feathers.（非常漂亮的羽毛）	Some other birds are hideous.（ = extremely ugly）
★ Magpies（喜鹊）are considered to be lucky birds in China.	Crows are often associated with（和……联系到一起）bad luck.

That's **kind of** a **widely-held superstition.**（迷信，kind of 是"有点像……"）

Pat 指南 🔊

☆ 一些花在中国的文化中所代表的意义：

Lotuses（莲花）symbolize（是……的象征）purity（纯洁）and integrity（正直）.

The plum blossom（梅花）is a symbol of arduous efforts（艰苦的努力）and outstand achievements.

The peony（牡丹花）embodies（体现）wealth and a high social status（地位）.

Lilies（百合花）represent one hundred years of love and devotion（love and devotion 是英文里的极常用固定搭配，爱与奉献的意思）.

Chrysanthemums（菊花）signify（代表）happiness and good luck.

☆ floral design 或者 floral arrangement 是插花，而花店除了可以直接叫 flower shop 外，也常会被更文雅地称为 florist's shop

Topic 20: Festivals, Holidays & Parties（including Birthday, Gifts and Dancing）节日、假期与派对（含生日、礼物与跳舞）

We **socialize** on these **occasions**（场合）.	
★ Chinese New Year is a nice time for family bonding.（家人增进感情的好机会）	地道英文里的焰火表演称为 fireworks display；放鞭炮则叫 set off firecrackers。如果非要跟考官说"中央电视台元旦联欢晚会"，下面这个表达会让他/她听得很舒服，虽然你自己会说得比较累：the nationally-televised gala on New Year's Eve
On Chinese New Year, people get together and catch up（叙旧）.	
★ On New Year's Eve, people watch New Year's specials on TV.（这里 special 是名词，特别节目）	
★ Chinese New Year is a festive time.	"喜气洋洋"的这个词英文怎么说？并不是 happy 或者 exciting，而是 festival 的形容词形式 festive 最地道，贴春联是叫做 stick couplets on doors
We visit relatives and exchange new year greetings.（互相问候）	

Pat 指南 🔊

☆ 中国全年中最重要的 public holidays 的英文说法：

the New Year holiday, the Spring Festival holiday（也可以说 the Lunar New Year holiday）, the Qingming Festival holiday（也可以说 the Tomb Sweeping Day holiday）, the Labour Day holiday, the Duanwu Festival holiday（也可以叫 the Dragon Boat Festival holiday）, the Mid-Autumn Festival holiday 和 the National Day holiday

☆ 英国人最熟悉的 public holidays：

New Year's Day

Saint Patrick's Day 相当惊讶地发现很多学生误以为这个节日和 Pat 有关，让我受宠若惊，但其实这是传统的爱尔兰节日，现在在美国和加拿大也都相当重要，3 月 17 号这一天出门最好身上穿点带绿色的东西，否则朋友们 will pinch you 没商量。

Good Friday, Easter Monday 这两个假日分别在 Easter（复活节）Sunday 之前的周五和之后的周一，而 Easter Sunday 这天在大城市经常会有 Easter Parade 花车游行，而且满街都是真人扮的大兔子，相当好玩。

Christmas Day

Boxing Day 这个节在加拿大也有，圣诞节之后的第二天大家集体去超市疯狂抢购的"打包节"，全民总动员凌晨就到商店门口排队的盛况不亚于春运。

此外，当您在英国听人说 bank holidays，别去银行，乖乖放假休息就好了☺

It's always better to **give** than to **receive**.	
FOR（正方）	AGAINST（反方）
★ **Parents give their kids gifts to** celebrate major **festivals.** 注：major 在这里作形容词：主要的	It's not uncommon for **people give their boss** pricey（= expensive）**gifts** to develop guanxi（这个其实已经是地道的英文词了，"搞关系"）.
★ **On Valentine's Day, people give their lovers gifts to express their love and** emotions.	注：It's not uncommon for sb. to do sth. 意思就是：It's common for sb. to…
★ It's **the thought that** counts. 重要的是心意 注："给人印象深刻的礼物"的地道英文叫 unforgettable gift 或 memorable gift	常见的礼物可以准备一下，但最好不要只是很 general 地讲 toys 或者 flowers，可以试一试 a model car bouquets（花束）, a detective novel（侦探小说）, a necklace（项链）, candies, fashion magazines 或者 the Harry Potter Series

（续表）

At parties, we **get rid of stress** and meet new people.	
The more, **the merrier**！（人越多越好玩！）这句是国外有人说要开 **party** 时一句极度常用的话，记得也让考官听到你说	
FOR（正方）	**AGAINST（反方）**
★ Some people are naturally the life of the party.	Some people just go wild and do silly things at parties.
★ Party games are often organized.	I'm NOT really into parties. They make me feel like a fish out of water.（感到很不适应）
Throw yourself right into it.	而非常喜欢参加 party 的人英文叫 party animal：I'm a real party animal.
There are different types of parties, like birthday parties, beach parties, housewarming parties, farewell parties…最后这个是送别的 party，非常 sentimental（伤感的）	如果 party 不成功有一个很棒的中文词"尴尬的"，但它的英文怎么说呢？请记住 awkward 这个词不管在任何时候都完全等同于中文的"尴尬的"
At birthday parties, people can really **let their hair down**.（完全放松）	
★ We'll throw a surprise birthday party for the birthday boy / birthday girl.	Sometimes people get drunk at parties.
Sometimes presents are exchanged.	And this often leads to unwanted sex or drunk driving, which can be disastrous.（灾难性的）
★ Nice parties are fun, exciting and … memorable.（值得回忆的）	开 party 英文怎么说呢？你可能选择 hold a party，但考试时请一定记得用一下 throw a party 这个说法，看看 examiner 的反应
★ It's always fun to **get wrapped up** in（陶醉在）the exciting atmosphere.（气氛）	
We had **a blast**！（玩得非常开心！）这句是开完 party 后经常说的话	
★ We love attending dances（舞会）. ★ Some dances have a theme（主题）.	

（续表）

> Teens really enjoy costume dances（化装舞会）.
>
> I enjoy dancing to exciting music.
>
> ★ Dancing to slow music is more graceful, though.（更优雅的）

Pat 指南

☆ 想说好 festival / party 有关的话题，请一定记住用一个词：reunion（团聚），比如 class reunion（同学聚会），family reunion（家庭聚会），catch up（叙旧），和动词 celebrate 大家应该都认识了，在这个话题也很常用。

☆ 唱卡拉 OK 英文叫 sing karaoke，请仔细听 CD，注意英语里面的日文词最后一个 e 全都是要发音的。

☆ 小型聚会在口语里也经常被称为 a get-together。

☆ 关于 birthday，在西方有一个生日特别重要，就是 the 21st birthday，因为这天之后 adults 能享受的所有权利你都有了，再去酒吧也不用总被查 ID 了。地道英文里还有一个词组叫 paint the town red，经常用来形容庆祝生日时的疯狂活动。

对于备考时间有限的同学来说，先集中准备好最可能出现的题目仍然是重中之重。可以先把 Pat 博客 blog. sina. com. cn/ieltsguru 里本月口语预测中的 Part 1 考题结合本章语言点讲解准备好，如果还有时间再考虑系统学习相关词汇和句型。

Day

剑 8 时代的 Part 2 真题全集
The Entire Spectrum of Part 2 Topics

Pat's Guide
To the Speaking Test

How many roads must a man walk down
Before they call him a man
How many seas must a white dove sail
Before she sleeps in the sand
How many times must the cannon balls fly
Before they're forever banned
The answer, my friend, is blowing in the wind
The answer is blowing in the wind

IELTS 口试 Part 2 真题库全集索引

口语 Part 2 话题指南

对于您考试当月最新出现的话题，您还可以在我的博客 blog. sina. com. cn/ieltsguru 的本月口语预测中看到。

考官给你的 Part 2 一分钟思考时间里你应该做的事

好消息是：在 Part 2 考官将会给你纸和笔（如果他/她居然很不敬业地忘了你就说 Could I have a pen and a sheet of paper?）。在六十秒的思考时间里，考官是允许你在纸上写一些 notes 的。除了今天要学的 ideas 之外，还有几件事特别提醒口语基础不太好的考生朋友们注意：

☆ 卡片题必须注意时态，对于过去的内容一定一定一定要用过去时。

在思考的一分钟里干脆直接在纸上写上 -ed 这个符号，确保自己在描述的时候不要忘记时态。

☆ 卡片题名词的复数和谓语动词的单数很容易忘记加 -s。

基础不太好的童鞋也可以在纸上写出一个大 S 的标记提示自己说的时候不要忘了。

☆ 如果是描述 a person 的题，必然会有考生将 he/she 不分。

如果对这方面真的没有把握，甚至可以把 he/she 也写在纸上……

☆ 记录 ideas 的 notes 时一定要清晰，字可以写得大一点，在这方面考官管不着你，你也不用替剑桥省纸。但如果你在描述之后因为看不清纸上的字而一再停下来"阅读"就可能导致"杯具"甚至"餐具"。

★　　★　　★

Part 2 要说多难？

对于绝大多数中国考生来说，口语卡片题是 IELTS 口试里最难斩将的一关，因为是"独白"，开始之后全程都要自己说，而且还得面对考官，不能扭着脸儿说。更恶心的是很多雅思卡片题的 topic 在中国孩子的眼里压根儿就"不可理喻"。相当多考生的最后一道心理防线在怪异的话题、漫长的自言自语和考官的审视联合夹击下轰然倒塌。

例如《剑8》Test 1 的卡片题就是一道怪题中的怪题：

> Describe a time when you were asked to give your opinion in a questionnaire or survey.
>
> You should say:
>
> what the questionnaire/survey was about
>
> why you were asked to give your opinions
>
> what opinions you gave
>
> and explain how you felt about giving your opinions in this questionnaire/survey.

问卷调查？多数考生用中文都将难以下"嘴"。但其实如果胆儿大、敢想的话用相当浅易的英文就足以把这个题讲清楚了。请看 Pat 怎样描述我自己上周刚寄出的一个问卷调查（同时请仔细听光盘里的外教朗读）：

A couple of weeks ago, I bought a laptop at Best Buy（北美最大的电子产品连锁店）. Then last Friday, I got an email from Best Buy, asking me if I could fill out their customer satisfaction questionnaire and send it back to help them improve their service. The questionnaire was attached to the email. As I felt pretty happy with the purchase, I decided to take some time to answer the questions.

The questionnaire was a PDF file… uh… not a scanned one. It was divided into three sections. The first one was about the customer's personal information, like age, gender, address, phone number and email address. The second part was about the product, you know, questions like what I bought and whether I was satisfied with it. The longest section was the third one, which focused on the service I received at Best Buy. This section alone contained more than twenty questions, such as how I would rate the friendliness of the staff, what my overall rating was this shopping experience with Best Buy and if I would recommend their service to others.

It took me about half an hour to complete the form. From the well-designed questionnaire, I could tell Best Buy tried really hard to further improve their service. So next time I need electronic stuff, it'll still be the place for me to go.

而且不仅是这道题，事实上是所有的雅思卡片话题，对用词的难度要求其实并不高。卡片题的真正难点并不是词汇，而是思路。本章给出的全部答案和关键词全都是为了说明这个道理。请积极体会 Pat 的思路，但坚决放弃把你的卡片题答案武装到牙齿的幻想。对于 native speakers 考官来说，充满只有韦式字典里才有的单词的答案是令人费解的甚至令人痛苦的。请对考官"嘴下留情"。

本章中的真题请您充分结合 Pat 在博客里贴出的本月预测来准备，把卡片题库在考前全看一遍没有可能也没有必要。

A 建筑与城市

Pat 解题　Pat's Decryption

建筑师（architects）在西方社会的地位从历史上到今天一直是比较高的，属于"professionals"（这个词在地道英文里有时是特指像 lawyers，doctors，accountants，architects 这样高收入的专业人士）。有些 architects 甚至已经成了文化明星，地位已经跟摇滚巨星差不多了（They have even attained the status of cultural heroes or superstars with their own followers.）。比如 Frank Gehry 就是其中的一个，下面这张照片是 Pat 本人在世界顶级的 MIT 校园拍摄的 Frank Gehry 作品，够另类（funky）的吧？

关于 建筑 ，有两个单词大家经常弄混：即 building 和 architecture。building 指的是一栋一栋的房子，而 architecture 一般作不可数名词，很少用复数，除非指很多不同种类的建筑风格，它其实指的是一个城市或者地区建筑的总称，而不是某一个单独的建筑。

关于 城市 ，也有两个词经常被用混：即 city 和 urban，其实 urban 不是"城市"，而是形容词"城市的"，如果要用 urban 表示城市，就一定要说 the urban area。

本节我们会学到各种不同类型建筑的英语表达，包括商场、宾馆、图书馆、别墅、四合院儿、寺庙等。此外还有对三个重要中国城市——北京、上海和香港的描述。

On top of all that，我们还将选出全球 beauties 最多的六大城市，严重期待 ing...

展开本类话题思路的线索　Brainstorming Techniques
（熟悉下面的表格可以确保你在拿到任何本类卡片题时都能有话说）

Buildings	Cities
Location	Location
History	History
Users/Visitors	People
Exterior	Food
Interior	Cityscape
Atmosphere	Entertainment
Service	Movies
My own feeling /	Music
Other "rounding off" remarks	Sports
	My own feeling /
	Other "rounding off" remarks

本类话题最新完整真题库　The Complete Question Pool on This Topic

❋ Describe a modern building.

❋ Describe a hotel.

❋ Describe your favourite shop/store.

❋ Describe a school/library you studied at before.

❋ Describe a building in your school / college / university.

❋ Describe your ideal house.

❋ Describe an old building.

❋ Describe how you spent the last weekend.

❋ Describe an important building.

❋ Describe a historical building/place.

❋ Describe a quiet place.

❋ Describe a place in your city that you know well.

❋ Describe an important city in China.

❋ Describe a city you would like to visit.

❋ Describe a long-distance trip you took before.

❋ Describe an interesting trip.

❋ Describe a three-day holiday.

❋ Describe a childhood experience.

❋ Describe a school holiday.

分级演示 A Spectrum of Sample Answers

1. 建筑（building）

☆ 一个有水的地方

Pat 指南

这个其实不是 building，但是最近也总出现，不好分类，放在这里吧。如果您想描述自然界中有水的地方，还可以参考 C 类话题里的第 1，2 题

> Describe a place where there is water.
>
> You should say:
>   where the place is
>   what this place is like
>   what kinds of people go there
> and explain why people choose to go to this place.

难度指数：★★★★☆

Pat 的答案

Our neighborhood has a community swimming pool. Lots of people go there during hot summer days. Some of them just go to the pool to cool off Others go there to work

out. You know, swimming is probably one of the best all-around exercises coz it keeps you fit and keeps your body in shape.

But frankly, not all the people there can swim well. Yes, there are folks who can swim like fish but I would say many others just splash water around or even have a hard time doing the doggy-paddle.

On any hot day in summer, the pool is buzzing with kids. And there're instructors giving swimming lessons to them. Enjoying the sun and getting paid is a pretty good deal, huh?

And, you know, I don't have a girlfriend (for girls: boyfriend). So who knows? Maybe this pool'll give me a chance.

轮到你了   It's Your Turn.

▶ **Word Bank on This Topic**

社区   neighborhood / community   放松，休闲   hang out

[剑桥例句] Sophie is well-known in the local community.

健身   work out

[剑桥例句] Andrew works out in the gym two or three times a week.

坦白地说   frankly   完全的初学者   absolute beginners

溅起水花   splash water around   狗刨   doggy-paddle

教练   instructor   救生员   lifeguard

男式游泳裤   trunks   女式游泳衣   swimsuits / bikinis

拥挤的   crowded   热身运动   warm-up exercises

[剑桥例句] Warm-up exercises are important before a run so as not to strain any muscles.

蛙泳   breast-stroke   仰泳   back-stroke

蝶泳   butterfly-stroke   自由泳   freestyle

来回游   swim lengths   游泳好   swim like a fish

彻底不会游泳   swim like a brick   浅水区   the shallow end

全面的   all-around

[剑桥例句] Eleanor's an all-round sportswoman.

请参考Pat的思路，并适当借鉴这个词汇表里的单词，思考如果是您会怎么说

Pat 的海外生活英语实录

上面这个工具箱里的词都挺不错的，但也没必要全搬。可下面的这个词要是考到这个话题您还存着不用那就将是"一不说成千古恨"的结果——spot。这个单词作名词时在地道口语里完全等于中文的"地儿"。例如：

【剑桥例句】

(1) This park looks like a nice spot for a picnic.

相应地，下次说到"有水的地儿"，您就可以理直气壮地对考官说：This is a nice spot for swimming and playing water games.

(2) This museum is one of the region's best-known tourist spots.

☆ 一个现代建筑

(A) 酒店

> Describe a hotel you have stayed in or visited.
>
> You should say:
>> where the hotel is located
>>
>> when you stayed there
>>
>> why you went there
>>
> and explain what you liked about it.

难度指数：★★★★☆

Pat 的答案

I stayed at the Yong-Fan Hotel while visiting Shanghai last July.

It was situated on the southeast corner of the city and was renowned for its guests, you know, coz I was told many celebrities stayed there before, like Daniel Wu（吴彦祖）and Takeshi Jin（金城武）.

It offered comfort, convenience, great service and ... luxury! The rooms were pretty spacious and they all could be temperature-controlled by the guest, which I found really convenient.

Actually, the hotel had a variety of rooms, from single rooms including microwave and fridge to luxurious Presidential Suites, which all had wireless Internet connection. The restaurants were open for breakfast, lunch and dinner. They featured great Italian and French food. And the enormous ballroom had an upscale Bohemian feel. I spotted lots of famous people there...

轮到你了   It's Your Turn.

▶ Word Bank on This Topic

著名的　renowned（在 IELTS 口试里用它代替 famous 很棒）　　　名人　celebrities

[剑桥例句] The region is renowned for its outstanding natural beauty.

奢侈的　luxurious（luxury 名词）　　　　有……的特色　feature（这里作动词）

[剑桥例句] This week's broadcast features a report on Internet fraud.

总统套房　Presidential suite　　　　　　高档的　classy / chic / upscale

舞厅　ballroom　　　　　　　　　　　　看见　spot＝see

波西米亚风格的　Bohemian　　　　　　　精美的　exquisite

[剑桥例句] Their house is exquisitely furnished.

入口大厅　lobby / hall　　　　　　　　　装饰　decorations

无可挑剔的　impeccable　　　　　　　　问候　greet

地标性建筑　landmark　　　　　　　　　巨大的　enormous / vast

扶梯　escalators　　　　　　　　　　　　壮观的　spectacular

[剑桥例句] There was a spectacular sunset last night.

高档的　upscale / classy / chic　　　　　无线上网　wireless Internet connection

口碑好　enjoy a superb reputation　　　　位于　be situated

豪华的　posh　　　　　　　　　　　　　客房服务员　room attendants

房价　rates　　　　　　　　　　　　　　桑拿　sauna

门童 bellhop/ bellboy   上流社会 the upper crust

鸡尾酒吧提供鸡尾酒、葡萄酒和啤酒 The cocktail lounge offers cocktails, wines and beer.

提供洗衣和待客泊车服务 Laundry and valet service are also available.

热情的 helpful/go out of their way to help you/be willing to go the extra mile for the guests

告诉客人关于景点的信息 help the guests discover the exciting attractions

可以乘地铁直接到达那里 You can take the Metro directly there.

请参考Pat的思路，并适当借鉴这个词汇表里的单词，思考如果是您会怎么说

Pat 的海外生活英语实录

如果要用英语说"宾馆的服务设施"，基础不错的同学可能会想到 hotel facilities。但在地道英文中还有个更地道的 hotel amenities 才是表达这个意思的最佳选择：

【剑桥例句】The council has spare cash which it proposes to spend on public amenities, such as swimmings pools, gardens and parks.

Time to Branch Out.
推而广之

Describe a modern building in your city.

补充弹药

office complex	写字楼	administration building	行政大楼
glass-wrapped	用玻璃包裹起来的	reinforced concrete	钢筋混凝土
commercial building	商业建筑	residential building	居住建筑

Extra Ammo

（B）购物中心

> Describe a shopping center that you like.
>
> You should say:
>
>   where it is
>
>   what it is like
>
>   how often you visit this shopping center
>
> and explain why you like this shopping center.

难度指数：★★★★☆

Pat 的答案

    Let me talk about my favourite mall, Oriental Plaza. It's located right in the heart of downtown Beijing and is just a stone's throw away from the Tian'an Men Square.

The mall is huge... enormous, you know. It's 20 storeys high and looks reaaaaaally exquisite coz it's wrapped by a bunch of shiny glass curtain walls.

The interior is amazing as well: very spacious and all the equipment is brand-new.

    I'm fascinated by this mall coz all the stuff there is top-notch and reasonably priced. And the service is impeccable. When we get to the store, we are treated as honored guests. The shop assistants greet customers warmly and always try to help us find what we want, which really makes shopping a breeze. The service counter provides a variety of services including gift-wrapping, coupons and information on sales.

    This mall is like a landmark in Beijing, not just because of its size, but because it's good in any possible aspect that you can imagine...

轮到你了   It's Your Turn.

▶ **Word Bank on This Topic**

距离……近在咫尺（地道英文习语） just a stone's throw away from…

[剑桥例句] We were staying in a small flat just a stone's throw away from **the beach.**

容易去的	easily accessible	精美的	exquisite
建筑的外观	exterior	把……包起来	wrap
几层高……	storeys high	玻璃幕墙	glass curtain walls
室内	interior	宽敞的	spacious
入口大厅	lobby / hall	装饰	decorations
顶级的	top-notch	无可挑剔的	impeccable

[剑桥例句] Chloe was impeccably **dressed.**

顾客	customers	售货员	shop assistants/salesclerks
问候	greet	很轻松的事	a breeze
优惠券	coupon	地标性建筑	landmark

[剑桥例句] The Rock of Gibraltar is one of Europe's most renowned landmarks.

巨大的	enormous / vast	电梯	lifts（BrE）/ elevators（AmE）
扶梯	escalators	灯光	lighting
壮观的	spectacular	室内装饰	interior décor（请注意听录音）
高档的	classy / chic	全额退款	full refund
地铁线	Metro line	口碑好	enjoy a superb reputation
受到追捧	enjoy a large following	服装店	boutiques

[剑桥例句] Rebecca has attracted a large following **among the rich and famous.**

化妆品专柜	cosmetics section	美食街	food court
特价	special offers	全场打折	store-wide sales
百货店	department store	便利店	convenience store
花店	florist's（shop）	面包房	bakery
售后服务	after-sale service	收据	receipt
特别热情	go out of their way to help you / be willing to go the extra mile for the customers		

请参考Pat的思路，并适当借鉴这个词汇表里的单词，思考如果是您会怎么说

Pat 的海外生活英语实录

在商场里"闲逛"的最准确英文表达不是 walk in the mall，甚至都不是 browse through the stores 而是 hang out in the mall 这个地道的说法:

【剑桥例句】

(1) You still hang out at the pool hall?

(2) Who's Jonathon hanging out with these days?

Time to Branch Out.
推而广之

Describe a famous building in your city.

补充弹药

flock to （*v.*）涌向

celebrity 名人

packed 挤满人的

Extra Ammo

（C）别墅

> Describe your idea of an ideal house（理想的别墅）.
>
> You should say:
>
> what type of house it would be
>
> why you would like to live there
>
> what special features it would have
>
> and explain whether you think you will ever live in a house like this.

Pat指南

在这道题里您可以向考官尽情地展示您会用虚拟语气这种貌似高深其实没什么的句式。

难度指数： ★ ★ ★ ☆ ☆

Pat 的答案

Actually, my ideal house would be just like an average house, nothing too fancy, you know. It would be in a convenient location, have a couple of cozy bedrooms with balconies on each, a spacious living room, a roomy kitchen, some bathrooms and a garage where my cars could be locked for the night. Most importantly, it should have a big backyard for flowers and vegetables. I love the feeling of watching the plants grow. And hopefully, there would be a fish pond in the yard.

There should be plenty of appliances in the kitchen, like a gas stove, a microwave, a fridge and a dishwasher. Then next to the kitchen there would be a dining area, pretty small but very convenient, with a dining table and some chairs.

The living room must have high ceilings, a sofa, some armchairs, a rocking chair and a coffee table. I would have a few vases on the mantelpiece and some family photos on the wall. As for the TV set, it should be a high-definition TV set with a large screen. And the big windows would let lots of natural light in.

What else? ... Oh, the bathrooms! There must be a bathtub in each bathroom so my family members and I can relax in warm water.

The garage is for the cars, bikes and tools. Such a house would cost like 3 million Renminbi in cities like Beijing and Shanghai. So I guess it's nothing more than a dream for me...

轮到你了　　　　　　　　　　　　　　　　　　　　　　It's Your Turn.

▶ **Word Bank on This Topic**

几个　a couple of　　　　　　　　普通的　average（这里不是"平均"的意思）

[剑桥例句] The food was fairl average（ =not excellent, althought not bad.）

阳台　balcony　　　　　　　　　　　　　新奇的　fancy

[剑桥例句] Caroline wanted a simple black dress, nothing fancy.

家庭用具（比如家用电器）　household appliance

舒适的　cozy　　　　　　　　　　　　　天花板　ceiling

宽敞的　spacious / roomy　　　　　　　长沙发　sofa / couch

单人沙发或者单人座椅　armchair　　　　花瓶　vase

摇椅　rocking chair　　　　　　　　　　壁炉　mantelpiece

高清晰电视　high-definition TV set　　　浴缸　(bath) tub

车库　garage　　　　　　　　　　　　储藏室　closet

还房贷　pay a mortgage　　　　　　　　郊区　the suburbs

乡村　the countryside　　　　　　　　市中心　the city center

社区　community / neighborhood　　　秋千　a swing set

自己装饰它　I'll decorate it all by myself.　烧烤　barbecue

花坛　flowerbed　　　　　　　　　　　草坪　lawn

鱼塘　fish pond

生活和休闲设施　amenities (such as stores, sports centers and parks)

非常近　It's right around the corner.　（地道英文里面也经常用来形容一件事情
　　　　很快要发生了，比如 The IELTS Test is right around the corner!）

这只是个幻想　It's just (a) fantasy.

[剑桥例句] Steve's favourite fantasy was to own a big house and a
flashy（很抢眼的）car.

请参考Pat的思路，并适当借鉴这个词汇表里的单词，思考如果是您会怎么说

Pat 的海外生活英语实录

地板上铺的大地毯叫 **carpet**，小方毯叫 **rug**，床上盖的毛毯叫 **blanket**，但墙上挂的挂毯叫什么呢？跟考官说 **a tapestry**，他/她将对你刮目相看。

【剑桥例句】It was hard to hang the tapestry on this curved wall.

☆ 一个历史建筑

(A) 民居（四合院儿）

难度指数：★★★★☆

Pat 的答案

As far as I know （国内孩子说卡片的一大问题就是口气总是像该领域的权威似的，但其实听起来挺假的，因为没有人会是所有问题上的专家），most Beijingers used to live in courtyard buildings called "Siheyuan". But now living in a courtyard building is kind of a status symbol in Beijing coz it's spacious and super comfy.

A small or medium-sized Siheyuan usually has its main gate built at the southeastern corner of the courtyard with a screen wall just inside. Such a residence offers space, comfort and privacy. It is also good for protection against dust storms. With all plants and flowers, the court is also a sort of garden.

In the past, from the size and style, one could tell whether it belonged to average individuals or the powerful and rich. Siheyuans are delightful buildings to live and work in. The courtyard itself can be a thing of beauty coz it can serve as a "light-well" for daylight to come in.

These days, Siheyuans are pretty much private oases from the noise of urban life...

轮到你了   It's Your Turn.

▶ **Word Bank on This Topic**

据我所知	As far as I know, ... / To my knowledge, ...	风俗习惯	custom
过去曾经	used to...	宽敞的	spacious

[剑桥例句] Jason used to live in Glasgow.

四合院建筑 courtyard buildings （courtyard 就是围起来的院子）

属于	belong to	民居	ethnic houses / vernacular dwellings
简朴的	spartan	中等规模的	medium-sized

住所	residence	隐私	privacy
沙尘暴	dust storm	身份的标志	a status symbol

[剑桥例句] Among young people, this brand of designer clothing is the ultimate status symbol.

| 天井 | light-well | 令人愉快的 | enjoyable / delightful |

[剑桥例句] Our new neighbours are delightful.

沙漠中的绿洲 oasis 可以说是 are pretty much…

[剑桥例句] Audrey knows pretty much everything there is to know on the subject.

| 破旧的 | run-down | 超级舒服的 | super comfy |

[剑桥例句] The building looks run-down.

阳台	balcony	修补，翻新	renovate (v.)
鱼塘	fish pond	宽敞的	spacious / roomy
天花板	ceiling	社区	community / neighborhood
郊区	the suburbs	乡村	the countryside
舒适的	cozy	自己装饰它	I'll decorate it all by myself.

请参考Pat的思路，并适当借鉴这个词汇表里的单词，思考如果是您会怎么说

Pat 的海外生活英语实录

要说四合院里的房间有明确的"等级"，不能用 levels，更不能说 grades，而得用个有点偏大但对于这个意思是唯一正确的词 hierarchy.

【剑桥例句】He rose quickly through the hierarchy to become the CEO.

Time to Branch Out.
推而广之

Describe your childhood home.

补充弹药

childhood memory / childhood memories　童年的记忆

childhood buddies　童年时的玩伴

recall　(*vt.*) 回忆

Extra Ammo

（B）庙

难度指数：★★★★☆

Pat 的答案

In my hometown, there's a famous temple, which dates back to the 15th century. Even though it's a holy place, it's located on the busiest street of my hometown. But from the moment you enter the temple, you feel calm and peaceful.

The temple, like many other Chinese structures, faces south and the front gate is guarded by two stone lions. Entering the front hall, you'll see four huge sculptures made of wood, two on each side. They are the Four Heavenly Kings.

The Great Hall is separated from the front hall with a courtyard. There are lots of trees in the courtyard, which makes the yard very pleasant.

The Great Hall stands on a set of plinth and its roof is supported by enormous pillars. The main altar can be found there. You'll see a Buddha seated between two of his students. On the east and west sides of the walls of this Great Hall, you will see a variety of statues and paintings.

There is also an eight-sided pagoda with inscriptions on its walls.

This temple offers cultural services as well, including classes about Chinese paintings and antiques. So you see, it's not only religious, it's also educational and fun.

轮到你了

It's Your Turn.

▶ Word Bank on This Topic

雕塑	sculpture	雕像	statue	庭院	courtyard
基座	plinth	屋顶	roof	巨大的	enormous / vast
柱子	pillar / column	神坛	altar	佛祖	Buddha
塔	pagoda	雕刻的文字	inscription	古董	antique

[剑桥例句] You can't give away Granny's old bookcase — it's a valuable antique.

教育的	educational		宗教的	religious
从……隔开	be separated from...		历史开始于……	dates back to...

[剑桥例句] They found a large collection of records dating back to the 1950s.

许愿	pray and make a wish		烧香	burn incense sticks
尼姑	nuns		和尚	monks
虔诚的	devout			

预言很准确 Their predictions are very accurate.

让人顿悟的	enlightening		佛教徒	Buddhist

[剑桥例句] That was a very enlightening programme.

> 请参考Pat的思路，并适当借鉴这个词汇表里的单词，思考如果是您会怎么说

Pat 的海外生活英语实录

谈寺庙时很可能会用到"信仰"这个意思，很简短的一个小词 faith，当对考官说出来的时候震撼力可一点都不小。

【剑桥例句】Britain is a multi-faith society.

Time to Branch Out.
推而广之

Describe a peaceful place.

补充弹药

worship   崇拜，敬仰

faithful   忠实的

followers   信徒

calm one's nerves   放松精神

2. 城市

> Describe a famous city in China.
>
> You should say:
>   where the city is
>   why it is important
>   whether you visited it before
> and explain whether you think it will be better in
> the future.

☆ 城市之 北京

难度指数：★★★☆☆

Pat 的答案

I guess all people, regardless of（不论，这是一个特棒的短语，可以代替被考生用滥的 no matter what）their background, have heard something about Beijing, not just because of its long history, but also because of the Olympics three years ago.

Apparently, Beijing is best known for its brilliant history. It's the capital city of China, not just now, but in five dynasties in the Chinese history as well. Beijing is also renowned for its cultural diversity. Over 1 million foreign people from over 150 countries are living in Beijing now, which is absolutely amazing. And as you probably know, Beijing is politically important to China coz most of the national leaders live here.

What fascinates me most is the interaction between modernity and tradition here. You know, glass-wrapped buildings are sprouting up all over this 3000-year-old city…

轮到你了 ///   It's Your Turn.

▶ Word Bank on This Topic

不论	regardless of	显然	apparently / obviously
辉煌的	brilliant	朝代	dynasty
著名的	renowned	文化多样性	cultural diversity
互动	interaction	让某人着迷	fascinate someone
现代生活	modernity	传统	tradition

[剑桥例句] There is a stark contrast between tradition and modernity on the streets of the city.

大量出现	sprout up	玻璃围起来的	glass-wrapped
天际线	skyline	柔和的	gentle
小吃	snacks	庙会	temple fair
豌豆黄儿	pea paste	直率的	frank / candid / straightforward

[剑桥例句] Just following the signs to Bradford — it's very straightfoward.

热情好客的	hospitable	胡同儿	narrow alley

[剑桥例句] The villagers were very hospitable to anyone who passed through.

文物   ancient relics

豆汁儿   bean juice（在北美其实只有 soy milk，很少听到有人说 bean juice，不过我觉得北京的豆汁儿叫 bean juice 更准确）

请参考Pat的思路，并适当借鉴这个词汇表里的单词，思考如果是您会怎么说

Pat 的海外生活英语实录

要说某城市是一个"文化中心"，您一定会脱口而出：a cultural center！而且还自我感觉超好……唉，瞧你，一不小心又俗了不是？跟考官试试 It's a cultural hub，看他/她可爱的蓝眼睛是怎么"变绿"的：

【剑桥例句】

(1) The City of London is the hub of Britain's financial world.

(2) Chicago is a major transport hub, with the busiest airport in North America.

☆ 城市之 上海

难度指数：★★★★☆

Pat 的答案

Shanghai is the largest city of China in terms of population.

In terms of area though, I guess the largest one should be Beijing coz Beijing is so sprawling while Shanghai is dense.

Shanghai is definitely a world-class city and an economic powerhouse.

The history of Shanghai is actually, kind of short, like… I'm not sure, 200 years maybe. In many ways, Shanghai was a Western invention. The Bund is the best spot to see its colonial past.

Now the city is a popular tourist destination, famous for attractions like the classy Xintiandi, the bustling City God Temple, the peaceful Century Parks, the gorgeous gardens and lawns, and the breath-taking Pudong skyline.

Every time I went there, I could spot something new. It's so dynamic. And the bar and club scene in Shanghai is incredible.

By the way, the Shanghai dialect sounds pretty cute. I enjoyed mimicking it when I was there…

轮到你了　　　　　　　　　　　　　　　　　　It's Your Turn.

▶ Word Bank on This Topic

在某方面	in terms of	面积	area
分散的	sprawling	密集的	dense

[剑桥例句] There's a dense network of towns and cities in this region.

经济中心	economic powerhouse	有点儿……	kind of
创造	invention	外滩	the Bund
地点	spot (*n.*) = place	看见	spot (*v.*) = see

殖民地的历史	colonial past	旅游的目的地	tourist destination
旅游景点	(tourist) attractions	繁华的	bustling
高档的	classy / chic	特漂亮的	breathtaking / gorgeous
城隍庙	City God Temple	有活力的	dynamic / vibrant

[剑桥例句] We need a dynamic expansion of trade with other countries.

模仿着说	mimic	超好的	incredible / marvelous

[剑桥例句] She was mimicking the various peoplle in our office.

精致的（形容人）	refined	精致的（形容物）	exquisite / refined
有品位的	have exquisite taste	聪明的	bright / intelligent / smart (AmE)

"小资" bobos (Bourgeois Bohemians) 这个词的意思很像中文的"小资"

迪斯尼乐园 Disneyland　　大城市的地铁系统 Metro

请参考Pat的思路，并适当借鉴这个词汇表里的单词，思考如果是您会怎么说

Pat 的海外生活英语实录

　　如果要说"上海迪斯尼已经开始建设了"，一种很普通的说法是 The Shanghai Disney Project has started. 一种有点意思的说法是 Disney has broken ground on its Shanghai Disneyland Project. 一种让考官"耳"前一亮的说法是 Construction of Shanghai Disneyland is underway（已在进行中）。

【剑桥例句】

(1) The film festival gets underway on 11th July.

(2) British economic recovery is already underway.

(3) The conference will get underway tommorrow in London.

☆ 城市之　香港

难度指数：★★★☆☆

Pat 的答案

In my view, the most striking thing about Hong Kong is... the people. No doubt about it. So many talented people work in this city. Not just the movie stars and the super singers, but gifted people in almost every area. Finance, business, arts, fashion... you name it.

Another thing that's really amazing about this metropolis is, of course, the skyscrapers. It's fascinating how such a tiny island accommodates so many vast buildings. Hong Kong has the most beautiful skyline in the world, hands down (is + 形容词最高级 + hands down 不是 "举手投降"，而是 "最……" 很地道的强调表达形式). And the view of Hong Kong Island is breathtaking, especially when you take the Star Ferry across the Victorian Harbor.

Hong Kong is a mecca for fashion lovers like me coz there's always name-brand stuff on sale.

Actually I just returned from Hong Kong last week. Its economy was kind of in a slump and people were complaining about that. But it's still one of the best places to live in the world...

轮到你了　　　　　　　　　　　　　　　　　　　　It's Your Turn.

▶ Word Bank on This Topic

惊人的　striking / amazing　　　　　有才华的　talented / gifted

[剑桥例句] Schools often fail to satisfy the needs of gifted children.

应有尽有……　you name it.　　　　大都市　metropolis

[剑桥例句] Everglades Camp offers horseback riding, tennis, water sports, you name it.

[剑桥例句] Soon afterwards he left to begin his career in the metropolis.

容纳　accommodate　　　　　　　巨大的　enormous / vast

轻松胜出　the best..., hands down　　渡轮　ferry

维多利亚湾 Victorian Harbor　……的圣地 a mecca for...

[剑桥例句] His own bookstore became a mecca for writers and artists.

名牌货	name-brand stuff	经济在衰退	The economy is in a slump.
抱怨	complain	密集的（建筑）	dense
经济中心	economic powerhouse	殖民地的历史	colonial past
旅游目的地	tourist destination	名望	fame

[剑桥例句] She moved to London in search of fame and fortune.

东西方相遇（英文固定习语） East meets West.

中药 Chinese herbs / Chinese medicine

爱尔兰酒吧	Irish-style pubs	大片儿	blockbusters
娱乐业	entertainment industry	叉烧包	barbecue pork buns / roast pork bun
成龙	Jackie Chan	周润发	Chow Yun-Fat
吴宇森	John Woo	刘德华	Andy Lau
财富	wealth	王家卫	Wong Kar-wai
繁华的	bustling	高档的	classy / chic
天际线	skyline	特漂亮的	breathtaking / gorgeous
旅游景点	(tourist) attractions	有活力的	dynamic / vibrant

请参考Pat的思路，并适当借鉴这个词汇表里的单词，思考如果是您会怎么说

Pat 的海外生活英语实录

要介绍城市很有"活力"，国内考生立刻会想到名词 energy，power 或者形容词 lively 等，但查尔斯王子（Prince Charles）在香港回归时却偏偏赴港说了这样一句话：HK has shown to the world how **dynamism** and stability（稳定）can be defining characteristics（关键特征）of a successful society. 这个 **dynamism** 其实才是考官在听你描述城市或区域的"活力"时最期待的那个词。

【剑桥例句】They felt greatly encouraged by the **dynamism** of the local market.

Time to Branch Out.
推而广之

Describe a trip you took recently.

补充弹药

itinerary	行程安排	destination	目的地
hospitable	好客的	check out...	体验……
delicacies	美食	uneventful	（旅行）顺利的

3. 一个图书馆（双语感悟）**Random Bilingual Reflections on Libraries**

Describe a library that you have visited.

You should say:

where the library is located

what you use it for

how often you visit this place

and what people think of this library.

校园里可说的建筑很多，比如 cafeteria/canteen 食堂，dorm/dormitory/hall of residence 学生宿舍楼，gym 体育馆或健身房，administration building 行政楼，student union building 学生会大楼，recreation center 休闲活动中心（在有的国外学校里是和 student union building 放在一起的）。至于教学楼，在英语里一般不叫 teaching building ⊠，而是叫某某 Hall 或者 faculty building。

国内学校里的 library 多数是近乎四方的，英语可以讲 looks blocky 或者 foursquare。近年来欧美的图书馆有盖得越来越怪异的趋势，我个人最喜欢的是 Seattle Public Library（右图），真正的 the Information Age 的建筑。

很多图书馆有大面积的玻璃墙面，英文叫 glass curtain wall。如果还有曲线墙面，就是 curved wall。外观漂亮可以说 The exterior is gorgeous，室内也好看则说 The interior is neat as well。入口处的门厅是 entrance hall 或者 lobby，更专业的说法则是 vestibule。大厅里的大柱子叫 enormous pillars / massive columns。借书柜台是 circulation desk，还书直接扔进 drop box 就好了。阅览室，说 reading room 考官就能听懂。还有一种 group study room 是可以进行集体学习和讨论的，但是一般要预订（reserve）。有些图书馆还设置了一些 study carrels，是木板的小隔间，可以自己坐在那里看书。

图书馆的书库分两种：一种叫 closed stacks，另一种是 open stacks。目录室叫 catalog room，复印室叫 photocopy room，计算机房是 computer lab，多媒体室可以叫 multi-media classrooms，图书管理员当然是 librarians，借书说 check out books，还书就是 return books，过期不还要罚 late fee，有些图书馆还有 self-access center，也是类似多媒体教室的功能。如果你说图书馆里的气氛很让人放松，即是 The atmosphere there is really refreshing. 如果说它是智慧的宝库 It is a fount of wisdom，提供很多书籍 provide a wealth of books，是求知者的乐园 It is a mecca for knowledge-craving students！

更多本类相关句型　Bonus Sentences（高分内容）

It dates back to the 1950s.

This has been a time-honored tradition in this city.

It's a mecca（必去之处）for international tourists.

It's like a magnet for international travelers.

It's a must-see.

It's steeped（沉浸在）in history and culture.

The locals are warm-hearted and good-natured（善良的，在拿分方面，比 nice 更加 nice）.

The architecture there is spectacular and the local snacks are absolutely tasty.

This building looks very imposing（壮观的）.

The layout（布局）of this building is very organized（规则）.

It's kind of a landmark（标志性建筑）in my hometown.

It enables people to live more comfortably.

There are many folktales (传说) about this building.

The service there is impeccable (谈服务时可以用来代替 perfect).

I'm a regular (常客) there.

It's totally spacious.

It's kind of cramped.

It has very high ceilings.

The whole place is light and airy (通透的).

It's a place that really lifts your spirits.

临时抱佛脚

我们可以把下面这个不按常理出牌的卡片题也放在本节一起准备：

Describe a famous architect (建筑师).

让孩子们用中文描述一个建筑师都是难上加难，更别说用非母语了。

别急，其实你完全可以用几分钟就解决它。分两步走：

（a）牢记说艺术家的几个英文必备词：talented / gifted 不是"有礼物的"而是有才华的，prolific 高产的，作品源源不断的，creative / original designs 有创意的作品，trendsetter 引领潮流的人，be passionate about 对……满腔热忱的和 masterpiece 杰作；

（b）适当了解一个建筑师的大概生平，比如有个网站是世界顶级建筑师大全 www.greatbuildings. com/architects. html。人名都按照英文姓氏的首字母排列，点击其中一个然后下拉到 Biography 板块就成了。比如找找咱们华人的骄傲 I. M. Pei（贝聿铭）或者试试目前在国内也挺有名的 Tadao Ando（安藤忠雄）吧。

更棒的是，有了这道题我们就一起把最近常考的难题 Describe an artist 也轻松搞定了。

architects 在西方的社会地位很高，了解一些相关知识还是挺有必要的，重要性绝不低于参加"公测"（open beta testing）。

另类话题　Off-the-Wall Topics

我的"驴友"杂志最爱 *Travelers' Digest* 今年评选出了全球美女最多的六大城市，可惜都不是英联邦国家的城市，雅思考生可能暂时还去不了。不过你会发现：这本著名的旅游杂志（但请注意它绝对不是一本黄色杂志!）在描述这么让人流鼻血的城市时用的竟然都是这么简单的小词。

☆ Top 6. Moscow, Russia

Mother Russia is home to some of the world's most beautiful women. The Moscow subway alone has more beauties than most of the states in America. It's not only the tall, blonde hair, blue eyed girls that make it so great, it's also the amazing level of friendliness that you will find. It's a definitely unique experience when what seems the world's most beautiful woman is looking your way, it leaves you wondering whether you have something on your shirt. But you in fact probably don't, they could very well think you're attractive.

☆ Top 5. Los Angeles, California

How much can be said about L. A. girls? Well I think you will find upon arrival that so much can be said you'll find yourself at a lost of words. The women of L. A. are on a level unlike most any other kind you may have ever seen. All the beautiful people from across the United States flock to this mecca, this is where the cool people come to live, to work, & to try to "make it" (=become successful). This is what the Beach Boys had in mind when they wrote the song *California Girls*.

☆ Top 4. Varna, Bulgaria

Many of you may not have heard of Bulgaria, some of you may not know where to find it on a map, but you have all been there, in your dreams at night when you sleep. It's the land of sunbathing. But more importantly, it's the land of the world's most beautiful, charming & affable women, oh how I love them so.

☆ Top 3. Buenos Aires, Argentina

Buenos Aires should be the capital of the Western Hemisphere, not only for it's wealth of beautiful women on a scale unlike any other Latin Country, but for being the best city this side of Paris. Where else can an average person get invited to model scout competitions, invited to Fashion TV parties, & kiss a 6″4 supermodel, well not too many other places let me tell you.

☆ Top 2. Copenhagen, Denmark

Copenhagen has surely got some of the world's most beautiful ladies, & also some of the friendliest. For instance, I had just arrived at the Copenhagen train station; it was late, I was tired, but I must've been looking good, coz I noticed a gorgeous Danish girl looking my way, so I looked hers, then I smiled, then she pointed me out to her friend. This alone is why I say Copenhagen is one of the best.

☆ Top 1. Stockholm, Sweden

Stockholm is a city filled with the best-looking women in the world, women so good looking that when you walk into a 7-11 you will swear that you have just walked into a reality TV set, What Happens When Supermodels Work at a Convenience Store? Yes I know it's a long name, but hey it's true. Better yet, the women are super friendly, & extremely educated, they speak English with English accents, they start making you wonder whether England in fact had good-looking women but they're all on working vacations in Sweden, turns out they're not, in fact they're all really well studied Swedish girls.

描述建筑与城市的网址

下面的网址对骨灰级 DIYers 准备有关 buildings 和 cities 的卡片都"灰肠"有用：

现代建筑：

www. guardian. co. uk/artanddesign/series/greatmodernbuildings（It's a website that features a whole lot of world-renowned modern structures...）

老建筑：

http://art. eserver. org/（This is a website that offers tons of info on Western architecture）

城市：

http://www. lonelyplanet. com/destinations（This is a leading website that is specifically geared towards travel info）

B 组织与个人

Pat 解题 Pat's Decryption

讲到关于人物的话题，我经常会想到 Akon 的那首 *Mr. Lonely*

Lonely I'm so lonely,

I have nobody,

To call my own...

其实人生有一半的时间是很孤独的，而另一半时间，是爱我们的人（those who genuinely care about you）和我们爱的人（our loved ones），让这个世界变得不再空旷（Love makes the world go around.）。

这一节我们学习 organization 和 individuals 的描述。

经常有学生问我，到底什么是 organization？给大家一个权威的英语答案吧，根据 *Longman Dictionary of Contemporary English*: An organization is a group of people with a special purpose, such as a club or business. 所以应该说 organization 的选择还是很多的。

其实最好说的 organisation 就是一个 English learning club 了，说说大家最熟悉的 English lectures，English corner 和 the importance of English 就够了。不过这种内容确实有点"鸡肋"（mediocre）。我想中国孩子们最感兴趣的 organization 应该是 the NBA，所以今天我们会好好看看这个组织。

至于 individuals，意思当然就是"个人"。每天咱们都和个人打交道，但其实描述个人并不容易。比如一个"胖"英语就有很多词，除了 fat（很贬义），还有 overweight（口气客气一点），chubby（胖乎乎的，很可爱的），pudgy（又矮又胖的），stout（粗壮的），buff =muscular（健美的），blimp（名词，胖子）……

再比如"外向的"，"内向的"，经常听到国内的孩子们用 extroverted 和 introverted，但这两个词有点大，在国外生活中确实偶有听到但用得不算频繁。口语"外向的"其实可以说 He's really sociable. / He likes to socialize.（= outgoing）而"内向的"则可以说

He tends to be quiet around people. (= not so outgoing)

本节咱们要研究很多种不同的人。

OK. Here we go.

展开本类话题思路的线索　Brainstorming Techniques
（熟悉下面的表格可以确保你在拿到任何本类卡片题时都能有话说）

Organizations	Individuals
History	Appearance
Members	Personality
Location	Hobbies
Responsibility/Duty	Past experience
Influence	Relationship with others
My own feeling/	My own feeling/
Other "rounding off" remarks	Other "rounding off" remarks

本类话题最新完整真题库　The Complete Question Pool on This Topic

❋ Describe an organisation.

❋ Describe a workplace.

❋ Describe a famous person who you admire.

❋ Describe an artist.

❋ Describe an adventurous person.

❋ Describe a wealthy / rich person.

❋ Describe an old person who you admire.

❋ Describe an international celebrity / a famous person in a foreign country.

❋ Describe an intelligent person.

❋ Describe a family that is not yours.

✴ Describe a teacher who helped you before.

✴ Describe an ideal job.

✴ Describe a neighbour.

✴ Describe a musician/singer.

✴ Describe a business leader.

✴ Describe a historical person.

✴ Describe a movie star.

✴ Describe a family member.

✴ Describe a childhood teacher.

✴ Describe a friend.

✴ Describe an architect.

✴ Describe a happy person who you know.

✴ Describe a successful leader who you admire.

✴ Describe someone you know who speaks another language.

✴ Describe a person who helped you before.

分级演示 A Spectrum of Sample Answers

1. 组织 (**organization**)

Describe an organisation.

You should say:
>   which organization it is
>   what kind of organization it is
>   what people think of it
> and whether it is popular.

☆ 一个组织之 NBA

难度指数：★★★☆☆

Pat 的答案

I'm most interested in the NBA, which stands for the National Basketball Association. It's probably the most renowned sports organization in the entire world（entire 在口试里代替 whole 很不错，副词形式 entirely 则经常用来代替 completely）.

As far as I know, currently the NBA is made up of 30 teams from America and Canada. The organization was founded in New York like 60 years ago. At first, things were kind of tough, but these days, it's one of the most influential sports organizations in the world.

There are tons of basketball buffs in China and that's why NBA has such a huge following here. Some NBA games are even played in China and the tickets always sell out in like 20 minutes.

I don't know why but sometimes in China, live broadcasts of the regular season or playoffs stop being aired all of a sudden. The TV station just doesn't give us any explanation. And that really bothers me. Well, it's good we still have the Internet.

My favourite basketball players are Yao Ming and Kobe Bryant. They are really cool. I admire them not just for their successes, but also for their spirit, you know, their sportsmanship. They have been named the MVP many times, which made them real legends in my eyes.

The NBA is a legend, too. No doubt about it. Coz it's so successful in terms of making money. And more importantly, it's so entertaining. I hope more NBA players will come over to China and show us their amazing basketball tricks.

轮到你了　　　　　　　　　　　　　　　　　　　　It's Your Turn.

▶ **Word Bank on This Topic**

现在　currently / now / at present / at the moment

是……的缩写　stand for...　　　　　著名的　renowned

艰难的　tough

……迷　buffs / nuts = fans

有影响力的　influential

（门票）卖光　sell out（这里不需要用被动）

[剑桥例句] The first issue of the magazine sold out within two days.

常规赛　regular season

受到追捧　enjoy a huge following

现场直播　live broadcast

播放　air

[剑桥例句] The game will be aired live on CBS at 7. 00 tonight

季后赛　playoffs

让人很烦　bother sb.

解释　explanation

MVP　（这个不用解释了吧……）

运动精神　sportsmanship

传奇　legend

在……方面　in terms of/as for

娱乐性强的　entertaining

鼓舞人的精神　lift our spirits

关注他们最喜欢的球队　keep track of theirfavourite teams

激励人的　inspiring

热情　passion

[剑桥例句] Tennis arouses（激发）a good deal of passion among its supporters.

组织、管理得很好的　well-run

队伍很团结　There's real team spirit.

达拉斯小牛队　Dallas Mavericks（地道英文里也经常简称为 the Mavs）

迈阿密热火队　Miami Heat

休斯顿火箭队　Houston Rockets

波士顿凯尔特人队　Boston Celtics

洛杉矶湖人队　L. A. Lakers

克里夫兰骑士队　Cleveland Cavaliers

奥兰多魔术队　Orlando Magic

底特律活塞队　Detroit Pistons

由……组成　be made up of... = consist of（后面这个不要用被动语态）请参考Pat的思路，并适当借鉴这个词汇表里的单词，思考如果是您会怎么说

俄克拉荷马雷霆队　Oklahoma City Thunder

菲尼克斯太阳队　Phoenix Suns（这个州的夏天超热，这大概也锻炼了球员的顽强精神）

Pat 的海外生活英语实录

两支球队"棋逢对手"怎样表达呢？跟 chess 或者 opponents 都没关系，而应该用 evenly-matched 这个简单却地道的合成词。

【剑桥例句】 The two teams were fairly evenly-matched.

请仔细听光盘中这些 NBA 球星的名字怎么发音（并且猜一猜他们是谁）：

Tim. Duncan

Derrick Rose

Vince Carter

Dwyane Wade

Russell Westbrook

Kevin Durant

Chris Bosh

Steve Nash

Kobe Bryant

Allen Iverson

Tracy McGrady

LeBron James

Kevin Garnett

Shaquille O'Neal（frequently referred to as "Shaq"）

Rasheed Wallace

Dirk Nowitzki

顺着这道题的思路，我们把下面这道题一起快速准备一下，这个题在去年考过，但后来一直没有再出现，所以只要有个大致印象就已经足够了。

☞ **Describe an athlete / sports team you admire.**

Fast facts about Yao:

He's a giant, you know, a seven-footer.（*1 foot = 30. 5cm*）

He was born and raised in Shanghai.

Both his parents played for the Chinese National Basketball Team.

Yao played for the Shanghai Sharks until 2002.

The Rockets made him the top pick in the NBA draft that year.

When Yao first arrived in Houston, his English was pretty limited.

But he shot the ball extremely well.

Now his English has improved a lot.

And he's one of the best centers in the NBA today.

He took China into the Olympic quarter-finals.

He's smart, tough and most importantly, he loves his home country.

He raised lots of money for the Chinese charity (=money or help given because of kindness).

His wife gave birth *to a baby girl in May 2010.*

He's my idol and my role model (= a person whose behavior is copied by others).

您还可以在 www. worldathletes. com/athlete_biographies. htm 看到更多在英美大家都熟知的体育明星。

☆ **一个组织之　健身俱乐部**

难度指数：★★★★☆

Pat 的答案

Let me talk about a fitness club. It's next to my place. Last month, I felt really out of shape. A friend of mine told me some exercise would get me back in shape. So I went to this fitness club.

The club was open from 9 a. m. to 10 p. m. It offered a variety of membership types with different rates to meet different needs. They also had a three-day guest pass for first-timers. I'd never been to a gym before so they recommended their "two-week membership plan". I could try the classes and facilities there for two weeks.

It turned out that this club was pretty cool. It had lots of good machines like the treadmills, bikes and steppers. All the equipment was brand-new. This club also offered Pilates and yoga classes so the members could tone up without building up too many muscles. And now, since I've joined the club, I can use the swimming pool for free.

When I first started working out there, my body hurt all over. But then I got used to the exercise and now I'm feeling pretty good. And sometimes I ask the trainers for some advice. They are real experts and they show me a lot of new exercises. And on top of that, they also advise me on my diet and my fitness plan.

My one-year membership cost me 1,500 renminbi, kind of pricey, right? But I'm sure I'm getting my money's worth...

轮到你了 /// It's Your Turn.

▶ Word Bank on This Topic

……的家　　……'s place（其实地道英文里面经常不说 my home，而说 my place，或者干脆直接说一个人的名字加 's，比如 Patrick's 就是 Patrick 的家）

状态不好　　out of shape（这个跟体型没关系，而是指身体状态，如果身体状态好就是 in shape）

坚持 stick to...		会员资格 membership	

[剑桥例句] You have to apply for membership of the sports club.

价格 rates		会员卡，通行证 pass	
健身房 gym		推荐 recommend	
设施 facilities		设备 equipment	
跑步机 treadmill		举重 lift weights	
踏步机 steppers		普拉提 Pilates	
崭新的 brand-new		改善形体 tone up	
瑜伽 yoga		锻炼 work out	
肌肉 muscles		饮食 diet	
专家 experts		钱花得值 get your money's worth	
贵的 pricey		改善 improvement (n.)	

[剑桥例句] It's a bit pricey but the food is excellent.

体型 physique		尊巴舞 Zumba dance	

[剑桥例句] Joseph has a very powerful, muscular physique.

请参考Pat的思路，并适当借鉴这个词汇表里的单词，思考如果是您会怎么说

Pat 的海外生活英语实录

　　您出国之后立马会发现：健身对于年轻白人来说实在是生活里太重要的一个部分了，我的很多朋友都是可以不要命，但是不能不去 gym，而且有几天没去健身就开始 feeling guilty（有负罪感）。参加健身俱乐部的目标多半是为了让自己变得"更有形"。用地道英语介绍这种健身目的绝不能说 give myself more shape.

☒ 而应该说 get toned 或者 tone my body. 假如你的 IELTS 考官正好也是一年轻白人，

考试时你能在扣题的前提下用出这两个表达将立刻让他/她"心有戚戚焉"，不信你就试试。

【剑桥例句】

(1) Leo is exercising regularly to get toned / tone his body.

(2) This is a good exercise for toning up the arms.

2. 个人

> Describe a famous person.
>
> You should say:
>> who the person is
>>
>> why he/she is famous
>>
>> why you admire this person
>
> and explain what others think of him/her.

☆　娱乐人物之　歌手 a

难度指数：★★★☆☆

Pat 的答案

Faye Wong is my idol. She was born and raised in Beijing. Her father took her to Hong Kong when she was 18.

At first, Faye went to modeling classes there coz she looked gorgeous: tall, slim and had sparkling eyes. But she soon lost interest in modeling. Faye enjoyed humming tunes because it was relaxing. A songwriter was so impressed by her voice and he encouraged her to sign a record contract. She released her first album at the age of 19. Then, a very important album was produced. Several songs in this album became big hits and won awards for her. So far practically all her albums have been really well-liked.

Unlike other singers in Hong Kong, Faye ignores the press. And that gives her some bad-girl appeal, which I find reaaaaaaaally attractive.

Faye is not only a talented singer but also a great actress. A couple of years ago, she even won a best-actress award.

I like her so much coz she's multi-talented. And I adore her "rebel" image. She never treats the press well but the press has to respect her for her incredible talent...

轮到你了   It's Your Turn.

▶ **Word Bank on This Topic**

王　Wong（大家出国之后经常可以看到一些香港或者广东移民的 last name 是 Wong，而不是 Wang）

苗条的　slim　　　　　　　　　有神的眼睛　sparkling eyes

哼歌儿　hum（songs），在表示歌曲的时候除了说 songs，很多时候地道表达中也可以用 tunes 这个词

签约　sign a contract　　　　　出专辑　release an album

几乎　practically（代替 almost 很棒）　成功的作品　big hit

新闻界　the press　　　　　　　忽视　ignore

有魅力的　attractive / appealing　吸引力　appeal

[剑桥例句] Spielberg's films have a wide appeal.

多才多艺的　multi-talented / versatile　有才华的　talented / gifted

叛逆　rebel　　　　　　　　　特喜欢　adore

[剑桥例句] Don't you just adore lying in a hot bath?

模特班　modeling class　非常棒的　incredible / amazing / marvelous

请参考Pat的思路，并适当借鉴这个词汇表里的单词，思考如果是您会怎么说

Pat 的海外生活英语实录

　　95% 以上的国内考生都知道 idol 是 "偶像" 的意思，但在地道英语里其实还有一个比偶像地位更高的词：icon，是指文化、艺术、娱乐、体育等领域里最具代表性的人。它在英美文化里是个非常地道的词，谈明星时使用将会给考官带来 "心灵

的撞击"。

【剑桥例句】、Kobe Bryant is a basketball icon and role model（榜样）to a lot of young athletes.

☆ 娱乐人物之　歌手 b

难度指数：★★★☆☆

Pat 的答案

I guess you heard a lot about Jay Chou too coz he's so incredibly famous in China.

He grew up in a single-parent family. When he was little, Jay didn't get good grades at school. His mother was really concerned about him, but he just looked on the bright side. When he felt lonely, he looked for nice music to cheer him up.

He was kind of average-looking so no one really expected him to make it as a singer. He wrote songs for many popular singers like Karen Mok（莫文蔚）and Vivian Hsu（徐若瑄）.

Jay released his first album "Jay" eleven years ago. His soft voice was so unique and this album turned out to be an instant hit.

His music is always original. That's why so many young folks simply adore him. His latest album "Volume 10"（Kua Shi Dai）is, again, a smash hit.

Jay's music blends many elements, like R&B, hip-hop, and folk music. Recently, it seemed like he was really into giving his songs some traditional Chinese appeal, like "The Porcelain"（Ching Hua Tzi）.

Young folks are just crazy about him and tickets to his concerts always sell out in just a couple of hours…

轮到你了　　　　　　　　　　　　　　　　　It's Your Turn.

▶ Word Bank on This Topic

极度…… incredibly（后面加形容词）	担心 be concerned about
看到积极的一面 look on the bright side	让人开心 cheer sb. up
外表普通 average-looking	成功 make it
出专辑 release an album	独特的 unique
刚出现就立刻热卖的作品 instant hit	原创的 original
非常喜欢 adore	结合 blend

［剑桥例句］Then you should blend the ingredients（原料）into a smooth paste.

元素 element	民俗音乐 folk music
很喜欢 be really into…	刚出来就卖光了 sell out（不需要用被动）
巨大的商业成功 smash hit	

（Jay 的 squinted eyes 有很多美国和加拿大女孩特喜欢，韩国的歌手 Rain 也是这种类型的眼睛）

请参考Pat的思路，并适当借鉴这个词汇表里的单词，思考如果是您会怎么说

Pat 的海外生活英语实录

　　周董的音乐已经不知不觉地火了十多年，而且始终保持着很高的质量，影响了整整一代人，堪称是音乐界的传奇人物。"音乐界"的地道英文叫做 the music scene，而"传奇人物"则是 a legend 或者 a legendary figure。

【剑桥例句】Jazz legend, Ella Fitzgerald, once sang in this bar.

☆ *网络歌手之* 许嵩（Vae）

Pat指南

　　Pat 生活工作在海外，但却仍然能领略到许嵩的多才多艺，这可就是 modern technology 的神奇之处。请您特别注意听光盘里英国外教对于 Xu 这个拼音的发音，是不是觉得有点怪怪的？因为英文里并没有 Xu 所对应的发音，所以外教播音员就只能打"擦边球"了☺

难度指数 ★★★☆☆

[Pat 的答案]

Xu Song, also known as Vae, is one of the most talked-about singers in China now.  Actually he's much more than a singer. Vae is a singer-songwriter, composer, arranger, producer, pianist, mixer and website designer. What's even more amazing is that he went to medical school before he started to do music full-time!

Vae is unique not just because he's so multi-talented, also because he used to be an indie music maker who was extremely popular on the Internet for quite a few years. He has made three albums so far and he sung, wrote, composed, recorded and produced them all by himself. I particularly like the lyrics of his songs. Really flow like poetry.

I heard that Vae signed a contract with a record company recently and released a new album, so more nice music from him...

轮到你了 // // //   It's Your Turn.

▶ **Word Bank on This Topic**

又被称为 otherwise known as / also known as

最常被人们谈论的 most talked-about （你把它当个词组记下来在描述任何名人时都会很有用）

作曲 compose （作曲人则是 composer）   编曲 arrange （编曲者则是 arranger）

独特的 unique   多才多艺的 multi-talented/versatile

[剑桥例句] Chris is a versatile young actor who's as happy in action films as he is in TV comedies.

独立音乐人 indie music maker   专辑 album

单曲 single

歌词 lyrics （请注意这个词在地道英文里一般被当成复数名词来使用）

曲　music / melody　　　　诗歌　poetry

[剑桥例句] Tony started writing poetry at a young age.

签约　sign a contract　　　发行新专辑　release a new album

乐器　instrument　　　　　有才华的，有天赋的　talented / gifted

制作出畅销曲目　score a hit（注意这个短语里的 score 作动词）

请参考Pat的思路，并适当借鉴这个词汇表里的单词，思考如果是您会怎么说

Pat 的海外生活英语实录

　　许嵩是一个相对比较低调的歌手。"低调的"用地道英文怎么来表达呢？最准确的英文词就是 **low-key**，另外还有个 **low-profile** 也是近似的意思，出国之后您也会时有耳闻。

【剑桥例句】

（1）The reception itself was surprisingly low-key.

（2）It's been a low-profile campaign.

☆ **娱乐人物之　乐手马友友**（instrumentalists Yo-Yo Ma）

难度指数：★★☆☆☆

[Pat 的答案]

　　Yo-Yo Ma（马友友）is one of the most renowned cellists in the world. His father gave him lessons on the cello when he was just four. When Yo-Yo was nine he had the opportunity to study at the famous Juilliard School of Music in New York.

　　Now he's considered to be one of the greatest cellists in the world. He tours the world playing his cello. When he plays by himself, he likes to play classical music. But Yo-Yo plays more than that. He has recorded country music, traditional Chinese music and African music as well and

actually he's always looking for new ways to express himself. He also likes to perform on stage with other artists. Wherever he performs, audiences are moved by his music. Sometimes the effect is so great they don't even want to applaud.

He's a reaaaaaaaally talented guy...

轮到你了   It's Your Turn.

▶ **Word Bank on This Topic**

著名的 renowned（"举世闻名"的则是 world-renowned）/ celebrated（在这里不是 "庆祝的"）

[剑桥例句] Celia is a celebrated opera singer.

大提琴手 cellist   长号 trombone

在舞台上演出 perform on stage   深受感动 be moved by

长笛 flute   鼓掌 applaud

熟练的 adept / skillful   竖琴 harp

[剑桥例句] Tamsin Palmer gave an impressive and technically adept performance on the piano.

独奏 solo performance

请参考Pat的思路，并适当借鉴这个词汇表里的单词，思考如果是您会怎么说

Pat指南

guy 这个词似乎经常被英汉字典翻译成中文的 "家伙"，但其实单独这个词就是口语里面的 man，并没有任何坏的意思，除非你非要明确地说 a bad guy。而且虽然它的单数只能指男性，但是在地道英语里它的复数 guys 却不一定只是指男性，男女都有的群体也可以叫 guys，比如很多时候在校园里一群男女学生相互打招呼就会说 Hi, guys！

Pat 的海外生活英语实录

Yo-Yo Ma 五岁就开始登台演奏大提琴了，无论如何也得算是个 "神童"（prodigy）。很多成功的国外乐手都是从小就被人们称为 prodigy，有趣的是剑8 Test 3 的 Reading 题里也出现了 There has always been an interest in geniuses and

prodigies. 这样的句子。所以请记住"神童"这个词，在 IELTS 口试中被考到 artist 的话题时你就可以做到"与狼共舞"了。

【剑桥例句】He read in the paper about a math prodigy who was attending university at the age of 12.

Time to Branch Out.
推而广之

Describe your favourite book.

补充弹药

biography   传记   autobiography   自传

entertaining   娱乐性强的   informative   信息量大的

I found it almost impossible to put this book down. 书实在太吸引人了。

Extra Ammo

☆ 娱乐人物之　影星（英美观众熟知的刘玉玲）

难度指数：★★★☆☆

Pat 的答案

Let me talk about my favourite Chinese-American actress, Lucy Liu. Having experienced some ups and downs in her career, now Lucy is one of the most successful Chinese-American actresses in Hollywood.

Her straight black hair makes her so different from the blonde actresses. I think she really knows what she looks good in and wears clothing with so much confidence. For instance, she often wears slim pants to accentuate her long legs.

Lucy's most famous role was in *Charlie's Angels* as a confident and stylish angel who looked so graceful fighting bad guys. Her style expresses a clear "Don't mess with me!" look. I like it!

The 21st century is often called the Chinese Century and I'm sure even more Chinese stars will break through Hollywood in the future...

轮到你了　　　　　　　　　　　　　　　　　　　　It's Your Turn.

▶ **Word Bank on This Topic**

ups and downs　　　　　起起落落（这么复杂的概念，英文就这么简单）

事业　career　　　　　金发的　blonde（男性金发的是 blond，少一个 e）

自信的　confident（confidence *n.*）　　　瘦的　slim

时尚的　fashionable / stylish / trendy　　　强调，凸显　accentuate

[剑桥例句] The singer's dress was tightly belted, accentuating the slimness of her waist.

优雅的　graceful　　　　　海报　posters

狗仔队　paparazzi（注意这个词本身就是复数概念，所以口语里不要再加-s）

[剑桥例句] Paparazzi follow famous people everywhere they go in order to take photographs of them for newspapers and magazines.

请参考Pat的思路，并适当借鉴这个词汇表里的单词，思考如果是您会怎么说

访谈　interview　　　　　魅力四射的　glamorous

名人　celebrity

Pat 的海外生活英语实录

　　在 Hollywood，Lucy Liu 是能够出演高上座率电影（box-office hits）的少数华裔演员之一，这种显赫身份（prominent status）真够让人羡慕的。其实不仅是明星，对任何让你"羡慕"的人，比如拿到 LSE 全奖的大牛或者复议之后单科提高了 1.5 的幸运儿，你都可以发自内心地说，"I really envy him / her!" 不过请注意 IELTS 口试里一般是用不到 jealousy 那个词的，反倒是出国以后在真实的海外生活里你将会有更多的机会听到甚至感受到 jealousy ☺.

【剑桥例句】

(1) I envy her ability to talk to people she's never met before.

(2) Lucy was eaten up with jealousy when she heard that James had been given a promotion.

☆ 艺术家之 梵高

难度指数：★★☆☆☆

Pat 的答案

Vincent Van Gogh（梵高）is now considered to be one of the greatest painters because of his profound influence modern art. His most famous masterpieces were the Sunfowers and the Starry Night.

Van Gogh was born and grew up in the Netherlands. He was a compassionate person and loved the poor people there. He even gave away most of his own things to the poor, but then got fired by his boss and had to rely on his brother for money.

Van Gough painted farmers and workers. He was incredibly talented and creative. Instead of trying to copy what he had before his eyes, he just used colours freely in order to express himself with more power.

Later he moved to Paris, where he sold no pictures. Van Gogh was totally poor and had serious illnesses. In the end, he suffered so much from his illnesses that he took his own life with a gun.

As a painter, he sold only one painting during his lifetime and was little known to the art world at the time of his death. But his fame grew fast after his death. I admire him not just because of his talent. Actually he's much more than a great painter. He is one of the greatest cultural heroes of modern times…

轮到你了 ////　　　　　　　　　　　　　　　　　　It's Your Turn.

▶ **Word Bank on This Topic**

深刻的影响　profound influence　　　　荷兰　the Netherlands（形容词：Dutch）

有同情心的　compassionate　　　　　　名誉　fame

（绘画的）笔触　brushstroke / brushwork　　抽象的　abstract

具象的　representational（艺术家）　　多产的　prolific

[剑桥例句] He was probably the most prolific songwriter of his generation.

受到好评的　receive rave reviews　　　　名人　celebrity

一夜成名　an overnight success　　　　叛逆的　rebellious（发音是/rɪˈbelɪəs/）

[剑桥例句] Julia's teachers regard her as a rebellious trouble-making girl.

天才　genius　　　　　　　　　　　　珍贵的　precious

杰作　masterpiece

> 请参考Pat的思路，并适当借鉴这个词汇表里的单词，思考如果是您会怎么说

Pat 的海外生活英语实录

　　最成功的艺术家通常都会有独特的风格。基础一般的国内同学会用 He/She has a very special style. 来表达这个意思，而基础好的同学则多半会讲 He/She has a unique style.（请注意 very unique ☒ 是中式英语，因为 unique 本身就不能再比较程度了）但其实在海外英文里还有 *an instantly recognisable style*（一眼就能辨认出来的风格）这样更加形象而且地道的说法。

　　【剑桥例句】The Eiffel Tower in Paris is an instantly recognisable landmark.

Pat 指南 🔊

　　关于艺术家，这个网站最大的优点是内容相当专业，但英文却简单得跟玩儿似的：library. thinkquest. org/J001159/famart. htm

　　☆ **中国历史人物之　政治伟人**

　　难度指数：★★★☆☆

[Pat 的答案]

I'd like to talk about the late Mr. Deng Xiaoping.

He was just average in terms of appearance, except that his sparkling eyes showed this must be a super intelligent gentleman.

As far as I know, he joined a "work study" program in France when he was young and learned a lot of new ideas about social development. Then he returned to China and became a military leader. Deng had his own ideas about education and economy, which was vastly different from most of other leaders' back then. Some of his ideas even landed him in jail. But he never gave up and he never stopped learning throughout the years.

Deng rose back to power again in the late 1970s. From then on, he used his knowledge and experience to finally become one of the most powerful men in China. His great thinking was obvious when he said, "To get rich is glorious.", which was, at that time, so different from all the other political thoughts in China.

Deng gave a billion people the chance to lift themselves out of poverty and showed us that a lot could actually be learned from studying other cultures.

I admire Deng because he was wise and successful. And most importantly, he showed us we should be tough and hold on to our own beliefs even when others laughed at us…

轮到你了　　　　　　　　　　　　　　　　　　　　It's Your Turn.

▶ **Word Bank on This Topic**

已经去世的……	the late…	普通的	average
			（口语里面说人普通，这个词比 ordinary 还常用）
外貌	appearance	有神的眼睛	sparkling eyes
军队	the military	男士	gentleman（口语里面这个词就是男士，不一定是"绅士"，其实就是 guy 的正式版说法）
勤工俭学	work study	非常不同的	vastly different
光荣的	glorious	贫穷	poverty
艰难的	tough	坚持	hold on to
正直	integrity	诚实	honesty

战略　strategy　　　　　有远见的　forward-looking

［剑桥例句］Timothy's a forward-looking leader who always plans for the funture.

权力　authority／power　　聪明的　intelligent／brilliant／smart（AmE）

好接近的　affable

［剑桥例句］Margaret was quite affable at the meeting.

请参考Pat的思路，并适当借鉴这个词汇表里的单词，思考如果是您会怎么说

Pat 的海外生活英语实录

　　邓小平先生是一位务实的政治家。"务实的"在英文里有很多不同的表达方式，大家很熟悉的如 practical，一般熟悉的如 down-to-earth，而大家最不熟悉但在地道英文里却经常会被 native speakers 用来形容政治家和企业家的一个词则是 pragmatic。

【剑桥例句】

（1）In business, the pragmatic approach to problems is often more successful than an idealistic one.

（2）While there may be a lack of clarity about a total railway system in the United Kingdom, local authorities are planning to use railways for purely pragmatic reasons.

☆ 历史人物之　军事人物（风靡欧美的孙武）

难度指数：★★★☆☆

Pat 的答案

Sun Wu was one of the greatest military theorists in ancient China. I don't know about you, but I have read *the Art of War* many, many times. His theories have profound influence on today's military and business leaders' decision-making.

He lived in an age of war about 3,000 years ago. Sun Wu wrote loads of books about military theories. When the ruler of the state Wu asked Sun Wu to show his theories by training ladies of his court, those beauties kept laughing at Sun Wu as he gave them orders. Sun Wu had two of them killed immediately, then none of the others dared to laugh again. Finally they were trained well enough to go into battle.

Sun Wu was appointed as a general because of this. From then on Sun Wu led his armies with great success. His military theories covered a lot of ground, including the factors that decided who would be the winner, how to defeat the enemy without even fighting a battle, making the best use of the situations and guiding the struggle to victory.

His theories were created thousands of years ago but they are still very useful today. Amazing, huh?

轮到你了   It's Your Turn.

▶ Word Bank on This Topic

军队	the military	理论家	theorist
深刻的影响	profound influence	宫廷	court
立刻	immediately = right away	战役	battle
任命	appoint (*v.*)	胜利	victory / triumph
光荣的	glorious	正直	integrity

[剑桥例句] No one doubted that the president was a man of the highest integrity.

战略	strategy	有远见的	forward-looking
权力	authority / power	勇敢的	courageous
无敌的	invincible / indomitable	非常不同的, 迥异的	vastly different

[剑桥例句] The indomitable lady said she would continue to flight for justice.

请参考Pat的思路，并适当借鉴这个词汇表里的单词，思考如果是您会怎么说

Pat 的海外生活英语实录

用英语说人"很聪明的"，有些同学爱用 clever，也有人喜欢说 smart，但仅就 IELTS 口试的 Part 2 而言，用这两个词的效果远不如用 intelligent 好。如果因为紧张突然想不起来这个词了那么也可以用 He/She has a high IQ. 对付过去。

【剑桥例句】

(1) Helen had a few intelligent things to say on the subject.

(2) Noah is highly intelligent , but dislikes studying.

☆ **人物之 企业家**（entrepreneur）/**有米的人**（a wealthy person）

Bill Gates

难度指数：★★☆☆☆

Pat 的答案

Let me talk about one of the richest guys in the world, Bill Gates. Actually, I guess you know more about him than I do. But... anyway, let me give it a try.

When Bill was little, sometimes when his mother asked him what he was doing, he simply replied he was thinking. An unusual answer for a little kid, huh?

At age 13, he started programming computers. Bill Gates went to Harvard, only to drop out in his junior year. He started a company called Microsoft coz he had the idea that a personal computer should be in every home. It would be a valuable tool in gathering information and in communication. His dream was to create software technology that would be inexpensive and easy for people to use. Bill Gates also wrote a famous book called *The Road Ahead*, which clearly explained the value of computer technology in modern life.

Microsoft has become the leading business in the world, which had made Bill and his wife the richest couple in the world. But they did much more than just becoming rich. They established a foundation to help people suffering from poor health...

轮到你了   It's Your Turn.

▶ **Word Bank on This Topic**

不平常的 unusual	辍学 drop out of school
编程序 programming	创业者 entrepreneur

[剑桥例句] Ramon was one of the entrepreneurs of the eighties who made their money in property.

便宜的 inexpensive（比 cheap 听起来客气一些）　建立 set up/ establish

基金会 foundation　　榜样 role-model

慈善事业 philanthropy　　慈善组织 charitable organisation

勤奋的，敬业的 industrious/conscientious　　激励人的 inspiring

完美主义者 perfectionist　　崇拜 worship（语气比 admire 强）

一个有远见的幻想家 a visionary　　反垄断法 antitrust law

官司 lawsuit　　垄断 monopoly

（相当地道的英文习语）某人从不停止思考 He / She has an inquiring mind.

请参考Pat的思路，并适当借鉴这个词汇表里的单词，思考如果是您会怎么说

☆ 苹果　CEO Steve Jobs：与病魔抗争

难度指数 ★★★☆☆

Pat 的答案

To many people, Steve Jobs, CEO of Apple, is the most creative businessman in the world. He co-founded Apple in the late 1970s and has served as its CEO since the late 1990s. Actually, he's also a large shareholder of Disney. So he must be like … super rich.

But to Apple buffs, myself included, Steve Jobs is much more than a successful businessman. He's more like an artist. Over the years, Apple has brought us loads of beautifully-designed high-tech gadgets such as iPod, iPhone and MacBook Pro.

He's a great public speaker as well and I recall him saying in a speech, "Don't waste time living someone else's life, or living the result of someone else's thinking."

Steve Jobs shows us the importance of the courage to follow our own heart and intuition. Many friends of mine totally worship him and study the way Steve Jobs does almost everything. They want to be just like him, you know. When he went on a medical leave from Apple recently because of a rare form of cancer, we were deeply shocked and worried. Really hope he can get well soon!

轮到你了 /////

It's Your Turn.

▶ Word Bank on This Topic

有创意的　creative / innovative　　　　共同建立　co-found

大股东　large shareholder　　　　　　迪斯尼　Disney

……迷，粉丝　fans / buffs（出国后您会发现后面这个"……迷"也相当常用，例如经
　　　　　　常能听到的 car buffs 和 movie buffs）

也包括我自己在内　myself included（常见的句中短语，一般它的前面会是复数名词）

大量的　loads of / tons of　　　　　　设计很优美的　beautifully-designed

高科技的　high-tech　　　　　　　　　好用的小型用品　gadget

苹果笔记本系列中的一款超轻薄机　MacBook Air

苹果笔记本系列里的一款高端机　MacBook Pro

记得　recall（觉得自己在考试时将会连用十几次 remember 的同学就必须得学会这个
　　　词）

[剑桥例句] Noah recalled seeing her outside the shop last Thursday.

公共演讲　public speech　　　　　　　勇气　courage / bravery

直觉　intuition

[剑桥例句] Often there's no clear evidence so you just have to base your judgment on
intuition.

崇拜　worship（这个动词的崇拜程度比 admire 还要强很多）

病假　medical leave　　　　　　　　　罕见的　rare

尽快好起来　Get well soon!（很多国内朋友们知道 Have a speedy recovery. 这样祝
　　　　　　病人痊愈的说法，但在国外生活里 Get well soon! 却更为常用）

精通的　savvy　　　　　　　　　　　　天才　genius

[剑桥例句] Matt bought the laptop on the advice of a computer-savvy
friend.

不走寻常路（英文习语）　go against the grain

请参考Pat的思路，并适当借鉴这个词汇表里的单词，思考如果是您会怎么说

Pat 的海外生活英语实录

Steve Jobs 无疑是产品定位（positioning）方面的天才，所以才导致会有人说，"Microsoft makes products we have to use, but Apple makes products we want to use." 成功的 business people 必然是有个人魅力的，但"魅力"一词如果用国内朋友们使用过度的 charm 来表达却实在是相当地没有"魅力"。请改用 **charisma** 来描述政治家、企业家甚至明星们的"范儿"吧，考官对这个词的反应绝不会让你后悔。

【剑桥例句】How did a man of so little personal charisma get to be the Prime Minister?

☆ **人物之　普通人（教师）**

难度指数：★★★☆☆

Pat 的答案

Let me talk about my favourite teacher — my mother. She's a high-school teacher, you know, a reaaaaally good one. Her classes are always well-liked and she's great at sharing knowledge with her students.

In terms of appearance, my mom is kind of average. She just looks like any other lady her age, with some wrinkles on her face and gray hair. But she always wears a friendly smile on her face, which makes her pretty approachable. I guess that's partly why her students are so crazy about her lectures. And... she's totally graceful, coz she has exquisite taste in clothing.

She's articulate, knowledgeable and most importantly, patient. I would say she's a teacher who's never cramped her students' style.

The most impressive thing about my mom as a teacher is, of course, how much knowledge she has. She read tons of books in her college years and has been always on the lookout for a good book. By the way, she often told me interesting and educational bedtime stories when I was little.

My mom has amazing cooking skills as well. The hot and sour soup she makes is second to none. And you know what? She often takes snacks she makes to class and shares them with her students.

My mom is not just a wonderful teacher, but a great wife and a great mother as well. And everyone says I take after her…

轮到你了　　　　　　　　　　　　　　　　　　　　　　　It's Your Turn.

▶ Word Bank on This Topic

皱纹　wrinkle

受欢迎的　well-liked（这个词并不是中式英语，恰恰相反，其实这个单词和 popular 一样地 popular）

[剑桥例句] A colleague（同事）described him as well-liked and respected by all.

好接近的　approachable

讲课　lecture（注意这个其实就是国外学校里的讲课，而不一定是"讲座"）

优雅的　graceful

口齿清晰的　articulate

知识丰富的　knowledgeable

阅读　read（注意过去时还是 read，但是发音变化了，请听录音）

有品味　has exquisite taste

限制某人的发挥　cramp one's style

睡前故事　bedtime stories

最好的　second to none / top-notch / the best

热情　passion

让学生们敢于发言　get students out of their shells

[剑桥例句] Kyle used to be very withdrawn but he has really come out of his shell since Leah took an interest in him.

态度　attitude

孩子像父母　take after（my mother / my father）

投入　commitment

不听讲的学生　unruly / disruptive students

激励　inspire

开阔眼界　expand one's outlook（是否可以不用 broaden one's horizons 那个表达了？）

很有启发的　enlightening

把学生分组　divide students into groups / pairs

鼓励　encourage

成绩　grades

表扬　praise / compliment（其实后面这个在国外生活里用得更多，但国内同学普遍只用第一个）

[剑桥例句] I must compliment you on your handling of a very difficult situation.

给老师的苹果　an apple for the teacher（国外的学生经常用一个苹果表示对某个老师的喜爱）

某种品质或者外表的特征在一个大家庭里一代代地延续。It runs in the family.

请参考Pat的思路，并适当借鉴这个词汇表里的单词，思考如果是您会怎么说

Pat 的海外生活英语实录

在英美文化里，大家公认的一个好老师应该具有的素质除了 patience, confidence, leadership skills / strong will power 与 full command over the knowledge 等等之外，"表达能力强" 也是必不可少的要求之一（事实上，不仅是对教师，英美教育从 nursery / junior kindergarten 阶段开始就极为重视对于学生 public speaking 能力的培养）。所以当准备 a teacher 这个题目的时候，请务必记牢 **articulate** 这个单词，因为它就是在国外生活英语里形容一个人口齿清晰、表达能力强最常用的那个词。

【剑桥例句】

(1) Daisy gave an entertaining and articulate speech.

(2) This lady was an intelligent and articulate spokeswoman for a lot of causes（公共事业）.

Time to Branch Out.
推而广之

Describe a person who helped you before.

Describe a person who speaks a foreign language.

Describe your ideal job.（理想的工作）

补充弹药

intelligent 聪明的	encouragement （n.）鼓励
creativity 创造力	cultivate 培养
expand our outlook 开阔我们的眼界（broaden our horizons 已经被用得太多了）	

Extra Ammo

3. 人物之　老人与孩子（双语感悟）Random Bilingual Reflections on Elderly Folks and Kids

对于老人身体很好，我们可以说 He/She's hale and hearty. 或者 He/She's healthy and active. "灰白的头发"除了说 gray hair，还可以叫 salt and pepper hair，皱纹如果实在不想再说 wrinkles，那么说 lines 也成。说老年人乐观除了大词 optimistic 之外，还可以简单地说 He/She always look on the bright side。老人下象棋是 play chess，打太极除了 practice taichi 之外比较难的说法可以叫 go through the tai-chi routines，"舞剑"叫 brandish swords，老太太舞扇子就说 wave fans。如果老年人走路有点摇摇晃晃的，可以说 He/She staggers a little. 如果去哪儿都要拄着拐棍儿，就是 never goes anywhere without his/her walking stick. 而要说老人"睿智"，那么仅仅用 smart 就不够了，应该说 wise 或者 intelligent and sophisticated。

对于孩子，如果长个儿快，就是 growing like a weed（野草）。小孩个子小有一个特别有趣的说法叫 knee-high to a grasshopper（只到蚂蚱膝盖那么高），小孩皮肤好，就是 His/Her skin is smooth as silk，小孩胖乎乎的叫 chubby，小孩肚子大叫 His belly sticks out，小孩特别好动，叫 hyperactive，或者说 is a perpetual motion machine（永动机），小孩安静，说 tends to be quiet around people，小孩不认真听讲，叫 unruly kids / disruptive kids，小孩成绩好就说 get good grades at school；小孩可爱除了 cute 还可以叫 adorable，小孩是父母的掌上明珠叫 the apple of his/her parents' eye（单数！），拧一下小孩子的脸叫 pinch his/ her face，不过需要注意，在国外如果跟家长不熟就去碰孩子的脸很容易被起诉（taken to the court），因为 It's a litigious society！（什么事情都要打官司的社会）

更多本类相关句型　Bonus Sentences（高分内容）

He/She's remarkable.

He/She's a household name.（酷似中文的"家喻户晓"）

She's capable and efficient.

He's been around. (阅历丰富的)

He's my role model.

She's a legend (传奇).

Wherever she goes, she's the center of attention.

He/She's very easy-going and can get along with anyone.

He's always quick on the draw (反应快).

He has an inquiring mind. (爱思考问题).

He's knowledgeable and well-read.

She can express herself fluently and clearly.

She's self-motivated (工作主动).

He's an eager beaver (工作积极).

She's a team player.

临时抱佛脚

最近在亚太区时常露一小脸儿的人物卡片话题是:

Describe an international celebrity / a famous person who is in a foreign country.

对于周六就要考了周一还没开始准备、根本没有可能系统学习本章关键词和句子的人来说,这道题也可以用一种很"寓教于乐"[※]的方法来准备:

▶ Sam Worthington

先牢记 4 个用来描述大腕儿的拿分好词: talented / gifted 有才华的, dedicated 全身心投入的, fame and wealth 财富与名望 ("淡泊名利" 可以叫 does not seek fame and wealth) 和 charisma (这个词特像北京话里说明星时常用的 "范儿", 比 charm 动人多了)。

※ 近年来在英美教育界出现了一个挺时髦的新词叫 edutainment, 等于 education + entertainment, 虽然在一些过时的英文词典里还不一定能查到, 但它确实已经是 "寓教于乐" 在当代英文里最地道的说法了。

然后您就去做雅思 L，R 或者 W 的练习吧，当实在累了的时候，抽空儿浏览一下这个娱乐性极强的网页：

www. celebritywonder. com/html/biography

这个网页的下方一网打尽了现在所有在欧美当红大牌明星的 Biography。明星人名都是按照姓氏的首字母排列的，比如你可以在 W 部很快找到去年在英美红得发紫的 *Avatar*（阿凡达）和 *Clash of the Titans*（诸神之战）的主演 Sam Worthington 以及在今年的 Oscar Night 出尽风头的 Natalie Portman。

▶ Natalie Portman

另类话题　Off-the-Wall Topics

大家都知道 idol 是偶像，估计很多朋友们也都听说过 *American Idols* 这个全世界最有名的选秀节目。但是你听说过 William Hung（孔庆祥）这个人吗？如果还没有，请看他的 success story。

William Hung came on American Idol, and sung Ricky Martin's " *she bangs*".

"You can't sing, you can't dance, so what are you going to say?"

Asked Simon Cowell, as Paula and Randy（these were the other judges）shook their heads in disbelief.

"I already gave my best, and thus I have no regrets at all." William Hung answered. "That's the best attitude." Paula praised him, as he further tried to explain everything,

"You know, I have no professional training of singing…"

He left the trial performance, thanking the judges, with a backpack on his shoulder, most likely headed to（=going to）the library.

So guys, you still think IELTS is so scary?　Give it your best shot, then you won't have any regrets at all.

C 人与自然

Pat 解题　Pat's Decryption

natural beauty 这个词在英文中其实有两个意思，一个是指自然景色，一个是指用天然的化妆品（cosmetics）。当然两个意思都挺好，不过这一节咱们只说第一个。

中国文化很强调"天人合一"（unity and one-ness of nature and humanity），但是由于自然资源长期被过度开发（overexploited），我们反而离自然越来越远了（more alienated from nature）。

北美的生活离自然还是挺近的。Pat 在 BC 开车时还见过一只灰熊（grizzly bear）妈妈带着小熊横穿马路，如果真的不小心撞到（run over）它们就要被动物权益主义者（animal rights activists）告上法庭（be taken to court）。

北美的生活中最重要的娱乐也是 fishing, camping, hiking, skiing, mountain biking 这些比较接近自然的活动。需要强调的是，如果你在北京爬香山，就一定不要说 climb the Xiang Shan Mountain，因为在地道英文里那是指全副武装地去香山攀岩，挑战会很大，正确的说法应该是 hike in the Xiang Shan Mountain。

雅思口语里近期有一道挺常考的卡片题是 Describe a walk with a friend。本节中的大量内容都可以用来准备这道题，只要再知道两个关键词：stroll（散步）和 scenery（风景），然后再和朋友谈学业（academic pursuits）或者谈事业（career）就行了。

北美的国家公园很多，我个人最喜欢 Alberta 的 Banff，那里的雪真的把人的呼吸都带走了（It took my breath away.）。

除了自然景色，在本节我们还会谈到动物。在北美，不仅野生动物、宠物很多样化，比较好玩的除了 dogs，还有 hamster, parakeet, tropical fish, pony 甚至 iguana。

展开本类话题思路的线索　Brainstorming Techniques
（熟悉下面的表格可以确保你在拿到任何本类卡片题时都能有话说）

Natural Beauty	Animals
Location	Appearance
History	Habits
Visitors	Their habitat
Activities	Food
(Equipment)	Relationship with humans
Atmosphere	My own feeling/
My own feeling/	Other "rounding off" remarks
Other "rounding off" remarks	

本类话题最新完整真题库　The Complete Question Pool on This Topic

❋ Describe a garden/park.

❋ Describe a meal/picnic in a park.

❋ Describe a place of natural beauty.

❋ Describe a walk with a friend.

❋ Describe a peaceful place.

❋ Describe a one-day trip.

❋ Describe a quiet place.

❋ Describe a river / lake / sea you have visited.

❋ Describe a place where there is a lot of water.

❋ Describe a trip that was not as good as you planned.

❋ Describe a place that has been polluted.

❋ Describe a place in your city that you know well.

❋ Describe a photo.

❋ Describe a place that comforts you.

❋ Describe a walk that you regularly take.

分级演示 A Spectrum of Sample Answers

1. 一个有水的地方

☆ **西湖**

> Describe a river, lake or sea you have visited.
>
> You should say:
>   why you went there
>   what you liked about this place
>   whether you would like to go there again
> and explain why it was nice.

难度指数：★ ★ ★ ★ ☆

Pat 的答案

It had long been a dream of mine to travel to the West Lake. This past spring I was fortunate to make that dream come true.

Unlike what I'd thought, the West Lake was actually not just one single lake. It consisted of five parts. The main part was a vast expanse of water. It was a breezy, shiny day and the water was shimmering and rippling gracefully. I could also see some gentle rolling hills within walking distance and feel the refreshing breeze on my face.

Obviously, the Hang Zhou government had spent tons of money developing the West Lake as a tourist attraction. The willows were well-trimmed and the grass was neatly-mowed. There were nice benches everywhere. Birds were chirping cheerfully around me as I strolled around.

I also checked out the "Ten Scenes of the West Lake", you know, the ten most famous scenic spots nearby, like the Lei Feng Pagoda. It offered a spectacular view...

轮到你了　　　　　　　　　　　　　　　　　　　　It's Your Turn.

▶ **Word Bank on This Topic**

由……组成　consist of / be made up of　　　巨大的　vast / enormous

闪亮的　shimmering /sparkling　　　　　　起波纹的　rippling

[剑桥例句] The breeze rippled the water.

优雅的　graceful　　　　　　　　　　　　让人振奋的　refreshing

[剑桥例句] It's refreshing to see a losing team shaking hands and still smiling after a match.

给人活力的　invigorating　　　　　　　　旅游景点　tourist attraction

柳树　willow（树枝）　　　　　　　　　　修剪整齐的　well-trimmed

（草坪）修剪整齐的　neatly-mowed　　　长椅　bench

漫步　stroll around　　　　　　　　　　体验　check out

[剑桥例句] Kevin's going to check out that new club.

风景点　scenic spot　　　　　　　　　　塔　pagoda

壮观的　spectacular　　非常美的　breathtaking / gorgeous

宁静的　tranquil and serene　　　　　　安静的　peaceful / quiet

微风　breeze　　　　　　　　　　　　　掠过　sweeps across

请参考Pat的思路，并适当借鉴这个词汇表里的单词，思考如果是您会怎么说

Pat 的海外生活英语实录

"风景如画的"，如果说 It looks like a picture. 并不准确，因为 picture 其实也可以很丑，但 picture 的形容词形式 picturesque 在地道口语中却是一个纯粹的褒义词。例如：

【剑桥例句】 It was a picturesque cottage on the edge of the Yorkshire Moors.

句子里的 cottage 在当代英美生活里是指度假用的小屋，中老年中产们如果有点闲钱的话往往就喜欢去海滨、湖滨或森林里买个比较便宜的 cottage 供度假时住。

Time to Branch Out.
推而广之

Describe a trip you took recently.

Describe a school holiday.

补充弹药

refreshing	让人焕然一新的	rewarding	有回报的
well-planned	计划充分的	tiring	让人疲惫的
have a blast	玩得很开心		

Extra Ammo

2. 公园/花园

> Describe a park/garden.
>
> You should say:
>
>   where it is located
>
>   what you do there
>
> and whether many other people go there.

☆ 一个公园之　瀑布

难度指数：★★★★☆

[Pat 的答案]

The Falls Park is one of the most renowned national parks in China, with over one million people visiting it each year.

The park lies in southwestern Guizhou and is best known for its natural beauty, especially its spectacular waterfalls. This park is also home to an amazing variety of wild plants and animals.

I went there last summer. The trees there reached so high into the air that they reminded me of the skyscrapers in Hong Kong. And as I strolled around the park, I saw a whole bunch of meadows, waterfalls, rivers, valleys and mountains. The scenery seemed to change every few feet. I even rode to the bottom of the valley on the back of a donkey … Some people just took the shuttle bus to go around the valley, which I thought was BORING.

When I felt tired, I just sat on a bench, stared into the sky and felt protected by nature.

Everything was good and the waterfalls were incredible.

It's absolutely a must-see for any nature lovers.

轮到你了   It's Your Turn.

▶ **Word Bank on This Topic**

著名的	renowned	位于	lie in / be located in / be situated in
壮观的	spectacular / magnificent	瀑布	waterfall

拥有…… be home to （注意这里不要加 the）

[剑桥例句] This region is home to many vineyards （葡萄园）.

摩天楼	skyscraper	漫步	stroll

[剑桥例句] The whole family was enjoying a leisurely stroll in the sunshine.

草地	meadow	山谷	valley
风景	scenery	毛驴	donkey
班车	shuttle bus	特别棒的	incredible
长椅	bench	非常美的	breathtaking / gorgeous
一定要看的地方	must-see	热爱自然的人	nature lover
宿营	camping	野餐	picnic
烧烤	have a barbecue	体验	check out
风景点	scenic spot	宁静的	tranquil and serene
壮观的	spectacular		

英尺 foot （复数 feet，在北美都还是用 foot, inch （长度）, pound （重量）, gallon 这些单位）

请参考Pat的思路，并适当借鉴这个词汇表里的单词，思考如果是您会怎么说

Pat 的海外生活英语实录

从多伦多开车两个小时就可以到举世闻名的 Niagra Falls. 瀑布当然壮观，但动静儿更大，从很远就能听到"隆隆的瀑布声"。用地道英文该怎么表达这个意思呢？绝不可以说 long long waterfall sound ☒，而要说 thundering waterfall。

【剑桥例句】The thundering waterfall plunges hundreds of metres to the river below.

Pat 指南

通过这道题目，我们完全可以把近期常考的一个题目 **Describe a place that has been polluted** 一起准备好。

这个题目首先就可以先说一下这个地方曾经很美……

It used to be a beautiful spot.

blah, blah, blah…

可以用前面学到过的内容说半分钟，然后就开始 complain 吧：

But now it has been seriously polluted. You know, when I went there this past January. I just couldn't believe how this place had been ruined by pollution. The air was totally smoggy, so smoggy I guess the locals probably suffer from respiratory diseases. And the water, which used to be crystal-clear, had become filthy because of the industrial waste dumped into the rivers. Plastic bags and disposable lunch boxes were scattered around neighborhoods or floating in the murky rivers.

The pollution was totally devastating to this place. Something must be done before the damage get irreversible…

轮到你了

It's Your Turn.

▶ Word Bank on This Topic

严重的破坏　ruin (v.)　　　　烟雾重的　smoggy

[剑桥例句] Mexico City is one of the world's smoggiest capitals.

漂浮	float	非常透明的	crystal-clear
脏的	filthy / dirty	工业废料	industrial waste
倾倒	dump	一次性的	disposable（一定不要说 one-time…）
社区	neighborhood	分散	scattered around

[剑桥例句] I scattered the whole lawn with grass seed.

浑浊的	murky	呼吸系统疾病	respiratory disease
不可逆转的	irreversible	灾难性的	devastating / disastrous

[剑桥例句] The drought（干旱）has had devastating effects.

喷（烟）	puff（v.）	烟囱	chimney
浓烟	dense smoke		

请参考Pat的思路，并适当借鉴这个词汇表里的单词，思考如果是您会怎么说

WARNING　很投入地一口气打完这段话之后才发现自己 went overboard（过头了），把自己能想到的所有污染都给堆进去了，就差说 desertification（沙漠化）了。这样的地方大概只有 expedition team（探险队）才敢去吧。您别说这么多了，就从里面挑几种比较好记的记一下吧。Pat 希望通过这个反例能让您真正明白这个道理：说成"高大全"其实更容易出问题 ☺。

☆ 一个公园之　海洋公园

难度指数：★★★★☆

Pat 的答案

The Ocean Park is like 20 minutes away from downtown Hong Kong by car. Or you can go on foot along the scenic Seawall Walk. The park is made up of many sections. There's a lot to see and do as you wander through these sections.

In the Strait, sharks and seahorses are just some of the thousands of creatures waiting for us. Turtles can be seen through the underwater

*D*o you know what amazes me more than anything else?
The impotence of force to organize anything.

—Napoleon Bonaqarte

windows. My favourite part is when divers feed the fish underwater every day. It's an amazing sight **coz you can see the whole thing so clearly without wearing the** diving gear.

In the outdoor **Wild Coast, you'll see the exciting** performance **of the high-flying dolphins and the** hyperactive otters. **Such shows** take place **several times each day. And the Amazon Rainforest is home to lots of exotic birds and fish.**

In Children's World, the play area, kids can even touch some of the sea animals they are interested in.

Trips to the Ocean Park are always eye-opening, even for those who already have a good understanding of the sea life...

轮到你了   It's Your Turn.

▶ Word Bank on This Topic

风景优美的	scenic / breathtaking	部分	parts / sections
漫步	wander / stroll	海峡	strait
鲨鱼	shark	海马	seahorse
海狮	sea lion	海龟	turtle
海象	walrus	海豚	dolphin
潜水员	diver	工具	gear
表演	performance	超级活跃的	hyperactive

[剑桥例句] Hyperactive children often have poor concentration（注意力）and require very little sleep.

水獭	otter	发生	take place
珍奇的，异国的	exotic	让人大开眼界的	eye-opening

[剑桥例句] Living in another country can be really eye-opening.

野生动物园	safari park	草地	meadow
山谷	valley	风景	scenery （请注意这个词不可以加复数）

一定要看的地方 must-see   对……来说是一个圣地 is a mecca for...

[剑桥例句] Historic Creek Street, lined with shops and restaurants, has become a tourist mecca.

请参考Pat的思路，并适当借鉴这个词汇表里的单词，思考如果是您会怎么说

Pat 的海外生活英语实录

"海洋生物"，大家一定会本能地想到 sealife 或者 sea animals。这些也是地道的英文，但不妨试试 marine life 吧，它会让考官冷峻的表情舒展开。

【剑桥例句】

(1) The oil slick threatened marine life around the islands.

(2) The kids were amazed by the enormous variety of marine life.

☆ 花园

难度指数：★ ★ ★ ☆ ☆

Pat 的答案

My favourite garden is the Classical Chinese Garden which is just a 10-minute walk away from my place. It's always a perfect place to visit. The covered walkways provide shelter so the beautiful views can be appreciated in any weather.

And the garden is breathtaking in every season. In spring, everything in the garden turns green and the flowers bloom. In summer, the trees are pretty shady so we can watch fish play in the sparkling ponds. The trees turn colours in autumn and the foliage looks absolutely fascinating. The garden is brilliant even in winter coz snow leaves the rocks neat and pure.

This place is so peaceful, almost like a window on another world. Many elementary-school teachers take their students there to discover the secrets of the Chinese culture and the garden is often rented for filming...

轮到你了   It's Your Turn.

▶ **Word Bank on This Topic**

我家　my place（其实日常口语真的很多时候不用说 my home）

遮风挡雨的地方　shelter   欣赏　appreciate

开花	bloom	阴凉的	shady
闪亮的	sparkling	池塘	pond
漫步	wander / stroll	树叶	foliage（不要加复数）

[剑桥例句] The dense foliage overhead almost blocked out（遮挡）the sun.

岩石	rock	发现	discover
小学教师	elementary-school teachers	水墨画	ink painting
学者	scholar		

诗歌 poetry（poetry 是泛指诗歌而 a poem 则是指一首具体的诗歌）

[剑桥例句] She started writing poetry at a young age.

让心灵平静	calm your nerves	抚慰人的精神	restore the soul
感觉很振奋	feel refreshed and invigorated	亭子	pavilion

请参考Pat的思路，并适当借鉴这个词汇表里的单词，思考如果是您会怎么说

Pat 的海外生活英语实录

"宁静的"，我知道你一定会想到 quiet，calm，peaceful 这些词，但估计您却想不到 serene 这个在地道口语里形容一个地方宁静相当常用的词，而且它还经常会被与另一个近义词 traquil 连在一起来构成词组 tranquil and serene.

【剑桥例句】The guest house is set in a tranquil and serene garden.

常见植物英文名称（发音都比较 tricky，请您认真听录音）

tulip	郁金香	lily	百合
chrysanthemum	菊花	peony	牡丹
daisy	雏菊	petunia	喇叭花
daffodil	水仙花	orchid	兰花
sunflower	向日葵	violet	紫罗兰
oak tree	橡树	palm（tree）	棕榈树
willow	柳树	holly	冬青
pine	松柏	maple tree	枫树

申请去加拿大的读者们去了之后一定要 check out the maple syrup，非常好喝！

poinsettia 一品红 很红很漂亮的一种花，Christmas 的时候经常作装饰用。

poplar 杨树 查字典中文是叫"杨树"，但我在国外看到过的 poplar 却都是树干上全部长满叶子，一排排（rows）的，装饰性很强（very decorative）。

Time to Branch Out.
推而广之

Describe a walk that you regularly take.

补充弹药

soothing　让人放松的

breeze　微风

stroll　漫步

feel refreshed and invigorated　感觉焕然一新的

Extra Ammo

3. 动物

Describe an animal.

You should say:

　　what the animal is

　　where it can be found

　　what is special about it

and explain how people feel about it.

☆ 野生动物之 大象

难度指数：★★★☆☆

Pat 的答案

Elephants are fascinating creatures.

*D*o you know what amazes me more than anything else?
The impotence of force to organize anything.

—Napoleon Bonaqarte

They are huge, gigantic, so you know. African elephant can stand as tall as **4 meters**. Actually, they are the largest four-footed animals in the world. But they are pretty gentle and slow-moving, so you know, they never "bully" other animals.

Elephants use their trunk to "grab" food and they use their tusks to dig for water.

They are social animals. The mothers lead the whole family group.

People say that elephants never forget. Trainers can even teach them to use signs and pictures. For thousands of years elephants have been trained to carry **heavy** loads and carry people through the jungle. They are like hard-working employees for their masters. But they ask for bananas instead of cash …

轮到你了
It's Your Turn.

▶ Word Bank on This Topic

巨大的	gigantic (= extremely large)	
森林	jungle	
濒危物种	endangered species	
交易	trade	
驯服的	tame (*adj.* & *v.*)	

大象的鼻子　trunk

现金　cash

偷猎　poaching (*n.*)

野生动物园　safari park

请参考Pat的思路，并适当借鉴这个词汇表里的单词，思考如果是您会怎么说

Pat 的海外生活英语实录

考到动物的话题，如果只是不停地说 animals 其实挺郁闷的。有两个办法：一是把动物分类，IELTS 口语里用到的三大类动物就是 **fish**, birds 和 mammals （哺乳动物），但更难的像 reptiles ☒（爬行类）和 amphibians ☒（两栖类）至少最近 7 年里还没考过，就没必要记了。口试里绕开 animal 这个单词的方法二则是用 creatures

这个词，或者可以叫 **living creatures**，这个词也经常用来指动物（但注意不要用来指 plants）。

【剑桥例句】Blue whales are the largest creatures ever to have lived.

☆ 野生动物之 狮子

难度指数：★★☆☆☆

Pat 的答案

Just like the tiger, the lion is also a member of the cat family and... in many ways lions are just huge cats. Humans have been so amazed by the lion's size and strength that we call them the king of beasts. A lion's roar can be heard by humans many kilometers away.

In Africa, lions live in groups. Adult females take good care of their cubs, hunt and eat together, and defend their hunting grounds together. But the males tend to be really lazy and some of them are even troublemakers. Some cubs even get hurt by adult males when the adult females are away.

I like lions not really because they are so strong, but because my girlfriend (for girls: boyfriend) is a Leo. So you know, it's kind of "love me, love my sign" ...

轮到你了

It's Your Turn.

▶ Word Bank on This Topic

猫科动物	the cat family	力量	strength
兽中之王	the king of beasts	吼叫	roar
小狮子	cub	捕食	hunt
保护	defend	狮子座	Leo

星座 sign   凶猛的 fierce / ferocious

猎物 prey

[剑桥例句] A hawk hovered in the air before swooping（俯冲）on its prey.

请参考Pat的思路，并适当借鉴这个词汇表里的单词，思考如果是您会怎么说

Pat 的海外生活英语实录

　　要表达"群居动物"，除了可以说 They live together. 之外，还有个很地道的说法：gregarious animals。而且这个词在口语里也经常用来形容某人"合群的"。例如：

【剑桥例句】

（1）Gregarious animals and birds live in groups.

（2）Emma's a gregarious, outgoing sort of person.

☆ *宠物之　鹦鹉*

难度指数：★★☆☆☆

Pat 的答案

Parrots have gorgeous feathers and a big tail. They are skilled at mimicking human sounds. When you visit a pet shop, you'll probably find some parrots repeating "Hello! Hello!" all day long. This ability to copy others serves parrots well. And parrot owners often notice that their birds say words like "goodnight" and "snack" at the right moment. And some parrots even have

the vocabulary of a two-year-old. But be careful! Sometimes parrots attack people around them. Most of the time, they are very friendly and adorable, though…

237

▶ Word Bank on This Topic

羽毛 feathers	模仿……说话 mimic
重复 repeat	对……很有好处 serve... well
攻击 attack	可爱的 adorable / cute
烦人的 annoying / disturbing	没创意的 uncreative / unoriginal

[剑桥例句] The programme contains scenes that may be disturbing to some viewers.

……岁的孩子 a...-year-old（地道英文在这里经常可以省略 child）

请参考Pat的思路，并适当借鉴这个词汇表里的单词，思考如果是您会怎么说

Pat 的海外生活英语实录

如果要用英文表达某人总是 "喋喋不休"，除了可以说 He's / She's very talkative. 之外，He / She is a windbag. 也是经常听到的说法。这个说法比较逗，考试时你的考官也将会心一笑。

【剑桥例句】 The TV show host is not really a windbag, but some of his guests are.

4. 公园（双语感悟）Random Bilingual Reflections on Parks

a park，这么美的话题，当然我们要用一点比较可爱的词，比如 This park is reaaaaaaaaally tranquil and serene. 就是说这个公园/花园真是很宁静。而如果你说 This park is pretty sprawling. 那就是说景点铺得很开，不是很密集的那种。

如果有一条小溪穿过公园，就可以说 A gurgling stream traverses this incredible park. 如果说喷泉，当然用 fountain（天然的用 spring）。说优美的雕塑，就说 graceful sculptures，或者更 "虚伪" 的说法叫做 breathtaking landscape designs。

要是 amusement park 游乐场一类的公园，那就可能有 Ferris wheel（摩天轮）和 roller coaster（过山车）了。小孩子们可以爬上去的铁架子叫 jungle gym，滑梯就简单地说 slide，旋转木马是 merry-go-round，沙坑叫 sandbox，秋千是 swing，跷跷板就叫 seesaw。公园里的 "小径" 可以称为 paths，但更长一些的要叫 trails。崭新的设备

叫 brand-new equipment，而陈旧的设备叫 worn-out equipment。如果要说一大片水面，就说 a vast expanse of water，如果说公园里点缀着一些湖泊，就说 The park is dotted with lakes. 而如果要说很多小孩子在草坪上跑跑跳跳的，那就是 Kids frolic on the lawns.

公园里空气新鲜，我们说 We can almost taste the freshness of the air. 如果要说你的朋友们也经常在这里休息放松，就说 Friends of mine like to hang out there. 而如果你自己也在这里休闲，那就是 I also like to just kick back and relax there! 了。

临时抱佛脚

近期在亚太区有一只卡片熊经常出没：

Describe a picnic / meal in a park.

这道题的 park 部分用本节前面的内容可以很容易就说到几十秒了，但关键是同学并不太了解如何用英文去描述野餐（picnic）。Pat 用下面的列表帮您瞬间掌握英文的野餐：

中文	地道英文表达
短途的郊外旅行	an excursion
景色	scenery
如诗如画的（当然也不一定非要说得这么酸，更多选择请看 Day 3 中的 Part 2 核心词）	picturesque
家庭聚会	family reunion
几家人一块儿聚餐（一般是每家都带些吃的，然后大家一起分享）	a potluck
公园里提供的野餐桌	picnic table
长椅	bench
小板凳儿	small stool
野餐时铺在地上的毯子（夏天则经常用 plaid sheet 格子布代替）	picnic blanket

（续表）

中文	地道英文表达
铺开	spread out
背包	backpack
纸盘／纸杯	paper plate / paper cup
装食品和餐具的篮子（这在国外野餐时是常用的，考官听到会觉得很亲切）	picnic basket
烧烤（注意 barbecue 既可以做名词也可以做动词）	have a barbecue
烧烤用的碳	coal
烧烤的（后面加上肉类或者海鲜就好了）	grilled / barbecued（chicken, shrimp…）
调味酱	sauce
沙拉	salad
糕点	pastry
甜点（注意它的发音和沙漠 desert 不同）	dessert
水果（比如草莓和葡萄）	fruit（like strawberries and grapes）
垃圾袋	garbage bag
宿营	camping

再加上对公园景色和心情的描述，早就够了……

更多本类相关句型　Bonus Sentences（高分内容）

There are lots of backpackers（背包族）there.

It's just located a stone's throw away from…（离……非常近）

There are huge grills（烤炉）at the picnic（野餐）area.

We can only have a barbecue inside the picnic area in the park.

After we pitch the tent（搭帐篷），we hike down to the lake.

I'm an active outdoorsman / outdoorswoman.

I was fascinated delighted by the scenery.

The well-maintained plants are fascinating.

The park equipment is brand-new.

They just hang out there, you know, kick back and relax.

You'll hear the birds chirping in the trees.

It's spacious.

The atmosphere there is very peaceful.

It's tranquil and serene.

But sometimes it becomes pretty dynamic.

The park is green with wide, plush lawns and artistically-tended shrubs.

It's a precious national treasure（国宝）.

It's very rare.

Now they are endangered animals.

They are an indispensable（不可缺少的）part of the ecosystem.

They are unique to China.

They help us keep the eco-balance.

Pets are good companions（伙伴）to have.

When he was little, he was pretty well-behaved.（地道英文里经常把宠物叫成 he/she）

It's really smart and adorable（可爱的，是口试时替换 cute 的好选择）.

另类话题 Off-the-Wall Topics

Nature, nature…

英文里面有个地道的说法叫 in your birthday suit，意思其实就是 not wearing any clothes。最接近自然的方式恐怕就是什么都不穿吧，这类人还专门有个名称叫 naturists。不爱穿衣服，跟 newborn babies 一样。很多学生好奇地问过我，国外的 nude beaches

（裸体海滩）是什么样儿。温哥华很棒的大学 UBC 旁边有个著名的 Wreck Beach，向大家隆重推荐（We proudly present the Wreck Beach.），但照片略去，未满 N 岁禁止观看。

Wreck Beach sits directly west of UBC. It enjoys its fame as one of the largest nude beaches in the world. For safety reasons, the "nude" section (=part) of the beach is clearly marked. For the fact that the surroundings are absolutely gorgeous, Wreck Beach continues to be a very popular place to visit in Vancouver. Family groups, seniors and young folks, anyone who want to be nude sunbathers in public goes there. It's a landmark, a very special, unique place in Canada. Yes, there are people who hate this beach and try to destroy it. But the community there just stick together to make their voice heard coz they feel they're so fortunate to have it. They just want to protect its naturalness and the nakedness, for that matter (=as well).

D 边玩边学

Pat 解题 Pat's Decryption

很多同学在出国前，都爱幻想（fantasize）国外是不是比中国好玩。

这个……那得看你喜欢什么了。

如果你喜欢 sports，那绝对应该出国。连 golfing 这样国内的贵族运动（high-class sports），在美国也不过只是大众运动（popular sports），因为价格并不贵（not so pricey）。

但 Pat 这里要澄清（clarify）两件事，一是 Pat 在国内时发现有些考生甚至老师谈运动时说自己经常去 scuba diving。这个可能性其实比较小，因为在国外这个活动一般要经过专业训练的，偶尔玩玩还可以，经常去就比较有风险（hazardous）了。

还有一个常见误区是 bowling，这个一般在西方还是蓝领（blue-collar workers）玩得比较多，如果要强调自己很有品味（have exquisite taste），一般人就不大会去 bowling。比如最近美国总统 Barack Obama went bowling for the first time in 30 years, which was part of his effort to get closer to working-class people. 这可就是典型的美国式作秀了（That was just for show.）。

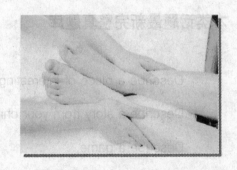

很多国内的朋友觉得 American football（橄榄球）很"暴力"，但其实美国的 football stars 却是美国智商最高的运动员群体（平均智商达到了 120 多）。您可能没看过 ice hockey（冰球）比赛，那才叫最暴力的运动，一半以上的观众基本就是抱着看打群架的心态去看冰球比赛的。

如果您既不喜欢 sports，也不喜欢 partying，甚至都不喜欢 going to the movies，那么真有可能你会觉得国外的生活挺单调的。西方人最喜欢的休闲活动除了 sports，基本上就是 fishing, hunting, camping, road trips, going to the movies, partying, clubbing, bar-hopping… 甚至连"看鸟"（bird-watching）也

成为了一种常见休闲活动。至于"洗脚城"（foot massage parlors）则少之又少，而卡拉OK（karaoke）也远没有国内这么"火"（in）。所以由于练习的机会不多，像 Susan Boyle 大娘那样自学成才的歌手还真得有点天赋（gift）才行。

不过国外的购物狂（shopholic）也很多，而且他们/她们还有一句座右铭（motto）叫 Shop till I drop.（生命不息，购物不止）。

到底哪种娱乐最好玩儿？那只能说是"萝卜白菜，各有所爱"了（Different strokes for different folks.）。

"娱乐"一词在地道英文里其实还有很多常见说法，只是国内的孩子们普遍过于依赖 entertainment，比如 diversions，pastime，amusement 等等不一而足，但却都很"娱乐"。

展开本类话题思路的线索　Brainstorming Techniques
（熟悉下面的表格可以确保你在拿到任何本类卡片题时都能有话说）

Leisure activities
What
Who
When
Why
How
My own feeling/Other "rounding off" remarks

本类话题最新完整真题库　The Complete Question Pool on This Topic

❉ Describe a piece of interesting news.

❉ Describe a story from your childhood.

❉ Describe a game.

❉ Describe an outdoor activity.

❉ Describe your favourite foreign culture.

❋ Describe a foreign country you wish to travel to.

❋ Describe a TV program that you like/dislike.

❋ Describe an advertisement that helped you buy something.

❋ Describe a film.

❋ Describe a book.

❋ Describe a song or a piece of music you heard in your childhood.

❋ Describe a website.

❋ Describe your favourite sport.

❋ Describe an extreme sport.

分级演示　A Spectrum of Sample Answers

1. 游戏 / 户外活动

> Describe a game you liked to play when you were a child.
>
> You should say:
>   where you played this game
>   how it was played
>   how it influenced you
> and explain why you liked it.

☆ 游戏之　捉迷藏

难度指数：★★★★☆

Pat 的答案

I played hide-and-seek lots of times when I was a kid. Normally we played this game in a park or in a building with lots of rooms.

The whole process was like... one of us, called the seeker, searched around for the

hiders.

The game started with the seeker covering his or her eyes and counting to 100 while everyone else ran off and found a place to hide.

When the counting was finished, the seeker began a painstaking search for the hiding kids. And that was my favourite part of the game, the highlight … you know, the climax, coz the suspense was just so intense. The hiders could really hold their breath, being afraid of getting caught. But then, there was always someone who got caught and this person would become the next seeker…

Hide-and-seek was fun because it was simple. These days we play PSP games and get fun from our iPods. But sometimes I really miss those simple pleasures in life…

轮到你了   It's Your Turn.

▶ Word Bank on This Topic

通常	normally / usually	过程	process
寻找	seek (v.)	躲藏	hide (v.)
悬念	suspense	亮点	highlight / climax

[剑桥例句] The election campaign will reach its climax next week.

宽敞的	spacious	简单的乐趣	the simple pleasures
伙伴	companions	团队精神	team spirit

[剑桥例句] The dog has been Julia's constant companion these past ten years.

拔河	tug-of-war / rope-pulling	跳绳	jumping rope / skipping rope

荡秋千   play on the swings （这个可不是中式英语，而是一个很地道的说法）

玩弹子球   play marbles

玩得很开心   have a blast = have a great time

非常仔细地寻找   a painstaking search

请参考Pat的思路，并适当借鉴这个词汇表里的单词，思考如果是您会怎么说

Pat 的海外生活英语实录

小朋友玩户外游戏除了"好玩儿"（fun 在口语里经常用作形容词）之外，另一个很重要的作用是可以锻炼孩子们的身体协调能力 **coordination**。

【剑桥例句】

（1）There are lots of fun things to do in this class.

（2）Gymnastics（体操）is a sport that requires a considerable level of coordination.

☆ *游戏之 "I spy with my little eye."*

Pat 指南

注意这里 "eye" 不用复数，这个游戏一直是 Pat 在游戏中的最爱，中文名字却真的不知道该怎么说，不过它在国外小孩子当中极度有名，长途旅行的时候一家人在车里经常可以玩。前两年还有一部 Eddie Murphy 拍的搞笑电影就叫 "*I spy*"。这里给大家简单介绍一下：

It's like one person, often an adult, picks an object that he or she can see, and then asks the kids " What is… (round / square / red / black / smooth…)?" The kids try to identify this thing. Simple as that.

What makes this game really fun is there can be multiple answers. So when the kids choose the wrong thing, the adult should tell them "No. " until they finally find the exact answer.

I remember once I asked a boy with black frames, "What is black?" Obviously, it was almost impossible for him to find the right answer…

▶ Word Bank on This Topic

确定　identify　　　　　　　　　　眼镜框　frame(s)

[剑桥例句] The research will be used to identify training needs.

Some other games I can think of now:

math games, spelling bees (拼字比赛), guessing games, Bingo, Blackjack (这个在 Las Vegas 的赌场里挺常见的), hopscotch (跳格子), Pin the Tail on the Donkey (补上驴尾巴, 是很常玩的 party 游戏之一)

> 请参考Pat的思路, 并适当借鉴这个词汇表里的单词, 思考如果是您会怎么说

Pat 的海外生活英语实录

　　凡是涉及到"猜"的游戏, 比如 riddle (谜语) 和 puzzle (拼图游戏), 一定都会给小朋友很多的悬念。"悬念"在地道英文中叫做 suspense, 而让人保持悬念的英文则是 keep sb. in suspense。

　　【剑桥例句】Ruby kept William in suspense for several days before she said she would marry him.

---

2. 有趣的新闻

☆ 一条有趣的新闻之　银行劫匪

Describe a piece of interesting news.

You should say:

　　when you heard the news

　　who was/were involved in the news

　　why it was interesting

and explain how you felt after you heard the news.

难度指数: ★★☆☆☆

Pat 的答案

Let me share with you a piece of interesting news I heard last weekend.

Last Friday a guy went to a bank in New York and tried to rob it. Actually I thought he was kind of a nice guy. Just that... you know, he lost everything in the financial crisis: he got fired, he lost his house and his wife. The only thing he had was debt. So he decided to rob the bank and get some money... or maybe to get his revenge on society.

"Fill the bag up?.. With what?!"

But the problem was he didn't have a gun. So this guy just took a banana and put it in his pocket. He thought that could fool the bank tellers.

Then, he entered the bank, approached a teller, told her he had a gun and asked her to give him cash. Of course the police came. This guy got so scared and he pulled out his "gun", I mean, his banana...

The news was interesting. But actually, it was a sad story. Obviously many people have lost their jobs in this crisis. I feel sorry for them.

轮到你了   It's Your Turn.

▶ **Word Bank on This Topic**

金融危机	financial crisis	债务	debt
复仇	revenge	愚弄	fool (v.)
银行柜员	bank teller	走近	approach
现金	cash	害怕的	scared
记者	journalist	报道	report / cover (v.)
丑闻	scandal	夸张	exaggeration (n.)

[剑桥例句] Paul said over sixty people were there but I think that's a slight exaggeration.

及时的	up-to-the-minute	轰动的	sensational
引人深思的	thought-provoking	面具	mask

[剑桥例句] This is a truly thought-provoking flim.

荒唐的 absurd / ridiculous

请参考Pat的思路，并适当借鉴这个词汇表里的单词，思考如果是您会怎么说

249

Pat 的海外生活英语实录

　　再好笑的笑话听的次数多了也就没意思了，说话也是一样。要说一件事情"搞笑的"，人人都用 funny，出国之后这么说话倒没问题，但考口语一个半天近四个小时里考官连着听将近二十名考生不停地说 funny，实在是一件非常不 funny 的事情。其实 amusing 在国外生活里用得也一样多，口试时何必总拽着人家 funny 不放呢？

【剑桥例句】One amusing story after another kept the audience laughing.

Time to Branch Out.
推而广之

Describe something that made you laugh.

补充弹药

laugh one's head off	这是个非常地道的成语，指某人笑个不停
crack sb. up	让某人大笑（我自己最喜欢的一部 comedy 叫 *The Nutty Professor*. Check it out！）
amusing　搞笑的	hilarious　超级搞笑的
punch line	一个笑话最后的那一句话

3. 电视节目

> Describe your favourite TV program.
>
> You should say:
>
> 　　what kind of program it is
>
> 　　what it is about
>
> 　　why you like it
>
> and explain whether it is popular in your country.

☆ 电视节目之　家庭滑稽录像

难度指数：★★★☆☆

Pat 的答案

I'm really into the TV show *America's Funniest Home Videos*. It's a famous comedy series, not just popular in America, but in China as well.

You know, it's like ... people send in some funny moments recorded by their video cameras.

The host gives his amusing comments about these videos, which often show wedding or party-planning mistakes. Sometimes the videos are organized around themes such as Christmas, Easter (Easter "复活节" 其实是英美极为重要的节日之一，但国内考生普遍都只是似曾相识。Easter 通常是在三到四月的某一个周末，而且总会有大型的 parade 花车游行）or Thanksgiving.

And the coolest thing about it is the top videos of the week are selected for prizes. The host has a great sense of humor and often says to the audience, "Remember, if you get it on tape, you could get it in cash."

I like this 'cause it's about family life, which is really a subject that all of us can relate to.

轮到你了　　　　　　　　　　　　　　　　　　　　It's Your Turn.

▶ **Word Bank on This Topic**

喜剧	comedy	系列	series	摄像机	video camera
主持人	presenter/host	评语	comment	组织	organize (*v.*)
主题	theme	观众	audience	录像带	tape

[剑桥例句] The theme of sadness runs through most of her novels.

现金 cash　有认同感 can relate to...　优雅 elegance(*n.*) / elegant (*adj.*)

真人秀 reality show　竞赛节目 game show　综艺节目 variety show

问答节目 quiz show　纪录片 documentary

搞笑的　amusing（如果搞笑到让观众"爆笑不止"，则要用 hilarious）

请参考Pat的思路，并适当借鉴这个词汇表里的单词，思考如果是您会怎么说

Pat 的海外生活英语实录

想说电视节目 "引人入胜的",国内同学一般会想到 interesting / attractive 等词汇,但其实最准确的应该是 engaging 这个词。

【剑桥例句】A good radio show script is always able to engage the listener.

此外,时常露一小脸儿的话题 Describe a quiz show. (有奖问答节目)也可以通过 www. dooyoo. co. uk/discussion/top-ten-quiz-shows/385040/和 www. dooyoo. co. uk/ discussion/top-ten-quiz-shows/上大量真实的英国观众逐一点评他们/她们心目中的十大 quiz show 轻松搞定。

Time to Branch Out.
推而广之

Describe a radio program.

补充弹药

talk show	聊天节目	a panel of guests	嘉宾团队
call-in show	电话参与的节目	live phone calls	现场打进的电话
broadcast	播放	regularly	定期的
talented	有才华的	well-received	受欢迎的
discussion	讨论		

Extra Ammo

☆ 电视系列剧之 欲望都市

Pat 指南

试了几次想写一段描述 Prison Break 或者或者 Heroes 的,但是每次发现内容都写得太复杂,实在不适合当作卡片题的答案(coz they were so full of twists and turns)。只好改为描述比较容易说的 *Sex and the City* 和 *The Big Bang Theory* 了。

难度指数:★★★★☆

Pat 的答案

Well, let me talk about Sex and the City. You probably watched it too.

It was a sitcom about four charismatic girls who lived in New York. They were close friends. Carrie was a columnist who enjoyed talking about views on sex. Miranda was an aspiring lawyer. Charlotte was a lady who had conservative ideas while Samantha was a PR agent who believed women should have sex just like men.

The conversations in this sitcom were pretty funny coz the four ladies were totally different in personality. The soundtrack was good too.

It won many awards coz it was about an interesting subject: the influence of men on women and women on men.

But for ladies, what were most attractive about the series were probably not the girls, but the trendy clothing and the high heels…

轮到你了　　　　　　　　　　　　　　　　　　　　　　　　　　　It's Your Turn.

▶ **Word Bank on This Topic**

情景喜剧　sitcom

有魅力的　charismatic（就应试而言这个词远比被用滥的 charming 值得推荐）

[剑桥例句] Few were able to resist this charismatic leader.

专栏作家	columnist	志向远大的	aspiring
保守的	conservative	公关经理	PR agent
谈话	conversation	性格	personality
原声音乐	soundtrack	奖项	award

[剑桥例句] The best thing about the film is its soundtrack.

有吸引力的	attractive	时尚的	trendy / fashionable / stylish
高跟鞋	high heels	一季	season
一集	episode	娱乐性的	entertaining
教育性的	educational		

请参考Pat的思路，并适当借鉴这个词汇表里的单词，思考如果是您会怎么说

Pat 的海外生活英语实录

电影版的 *Sex and the City* 更是把纽约的时尚生活展现到了极致。而"时尚的"这个词，其实并不只有 fashionable 一种表达。*trendy*，*stylish* 和 *chic*（请特别注意它的准确发音是／ʃiːk／）都是在国外生活里描述某东东很时尚的地道常用词。

【剑桥例句】

（1）Jake writes for some trendy magazines for the under-thirties.

（2）The ladies in the film were stylishly dressed.

（3）I like your haircut — it's very chic.

☆ 电视系列剧之　生活大爆炸

难度指数 ★★★☆☆

Pat 的答案

Let me talk about my favourite sitcom *The Big Bang Theory*. The central characters in this show are Leonard and Sheldon. Both of them are Caltech physicists and they

share an apartment. Leonard has an IQ of 173 but basically has no problem communicating with the "average" people. Sheldon is even smarter with an IQ of 187, but always sticks to routines and totally has a hard time interacting with the "ordinary" people. Penny, their next-door neighbor, is a waitress who dreams of being an actress. Leonard has a crush on her but they just seem to be completely different people. So Penny starts to show the two geniuses what "real life" is all about.

The show is funny... hilarious, you know. And most of the conversations are not just amusing, but witty as well. I totally recommend it!

轮到你了

It's Your Turn.

▶ Word Bank on This Topic

情景喜剧 sitcom   电视系列剧 TV series

中央的，核心的 central / core

[剑桥例句] People have to pay more for flats（公寓）with a central location.

影视剧中的人物 character（全体演员阵容的地道说法则是 cast）

加州理工 Caltech（顶级牛校，去年该校物理专业的排名全美第一）

物理学家 physicist

基本上 basically（它可是地道英文中灰肠常用的一个并没有实质意思的插入语）

[剑桥例句] "So what's the difference between these two TV sets?" "Well, they're basically the same, but the more expensive one comes with a remote control.

坚持，执着于 stick to   交流 interact with

[剑桥例句] Olivia's teacher says that she interacts well with the other children.

梦想做某事 dream of doing sth.

暗恋某人 have a crush on someone（不明白这个词组的意思在 Facebook 上就是绝
　　　　　对的"土人"）

[剑桥例句] It wasn't really love, just a schoolboy crush.

天才 genius   书呆子 nerd / geek

很逗的 amusing（在地道口语里它比 humorous 更常用）

机智的 witty   推荐 recommend

[剑桥例句] Holly tried to think of something witty to say.

绝望主妇 *Desperate Housewives*   英雄 *Heroes*

绯闻女孩 *Gossip Girl*   迷失 *Lost*

吸血鬼日记 *The Vampire Diaries*   尼基塔 *Nikita*

办公室 *The Office*   皮囊 *Skins*

梅林传奇 *Merlin*   娱乐性强的 entertaining

一季 a season

请参考Pat的思路，并适当借鉴这个词汇表里的单词，思考如果是您会怎么说

Pat 的海外生活英语实录

《生活大爆炸》里的 Sheldon 给人的感觉是个"愤世嫉俗者"，用当代英语里很常用的一个词 **cynic** 来描述他真是量身定做，而这个词的形容词形式 **cynical** 也是当代英美生活里的高频词之一。

【剑桥例句】

(1) I'm too much of a cynic to believe that he'll keep his promise.

(2) Adam is always deeply cynical about politicians.

4. 电影

> Describe a film that you enjoyed watching.
>
> You should say:
>   what type of film it was
>   what it was about
>   why you enjoyed it
> and explain whether this film was popular in your country.

☆ 卡通电影之 怪物史瑞克

难度指数：★★★☆☆

Pat 的答案

No doubt about it, my favourite animated movie is *Shrek*!

Actually, when I first saw it, I didn't expect much from it coz I was not very much into animations back then. But this one turned out to be a really good one.

The plot was like this: Lord Farquaad wished to marry Princess Fiona. But the princess was held in a castle by a dragon. So Lord Farquaad talked Shrek, an ugly ogre, into saving the princess. Shrek fulfilled this task but he fell in love with the Princess too. At first, the princess was not impressed. But eventually, Shrek won Fiona's heart.

The movie was full of famous fairytale characters like Snow White, Cinderella and the Three Little Pigs.

The soundtrack was good too...

轮到你了

It's Your Turn.

▶ Word Bank on This Topic

期望 expect (v.)	卡通片 animation / cartoon / animated movie
剧情 plot / storyline	城堡 castle
Shrek 那一类的怪物 ogre	最终 eventually

[剑桥例句] It might take him ages（ages 是口语里表示"很长时间"的常用说法）but he'll do it eventually.

童话 fairytale	灰姑娘 Cinderella
原声音乐 soundtrack	
不能以貌取人 Don't judge a book by its cover.	
票房很成功 a box office hit	完成任务 fulfill the task

请参考Pat的思路，并适当借鉴这个词汇表里的单词，思考如果是您会怎么说

☆ 童年时看过的电影之 狮子王

难度指数：★★☆☆☆

Pat 的答案

I saw *The Lion King* quite a few years ago but I still remember the plot clearly. It was about a lion prince named Simba. When Simba was a cub, his uncle murdered his father and made himself the ruler. But Simba was held responsible for the death. So Simba ran out of guilt

After many years, Simba was told that the kingdom was in serious trouble. So he faced up to his responsibilities, returned, defeated his uncle and saved the kingdom…

The animation was terrific and the soundtrack was amazing. I particularly liked the song " *Can You Feel the Love Tonight.* " by Elton John.

And I learned lessons from this movie. It was about living up to our responsibilities, no matter how hard it is…

轮到你了   It's Your Turn.

▶ **Word Bank on This Topic**

很久以前	quite a while back	卡通片	animation / cartoon / animated movie
剧情	plot / storyline	王子	prince
统治者	ruler	让某人负责任	hold sb. responsible

[剑桥例句] She held Larry responsible whenever anything went wrong in the project.

请参考Pat的思路，并适当借鉴这个词汇表里的单词，思考如果是您会怎么说

小狮子	cub	打败	defeat
内疚	guilt	票房很成功	a box office hit / a box office smash
原声音乐	soundtrack	特好的	terrific / marvelous

Pat 的海外生活英语实录

美版的卡通片（animation）与日版的卡通片（anime）不同，美版不论故事情节多么紧张都一定会有一两个很可爱的卡通形象出现在电影里，但日系的则不一定。"可爱的"大家都用哪个词咱就不啰嗦了，但 adorable 在考试时其实更值得推荐。

【剑桥例句】

（1）Erin has the most adorable two-year-old girl.

（2）Theo is an absolutely adorable child.

☆ 搞笑的电影之 美国派

难度指数：★★★☆☆

Pat 的答案

My favourite movie is *American Pie*. And Lots of friends of mine like this movie, too.

It was totally funny, hilarious, you know. The plot was like four high school students were trying to get sexual experience. The problem was, only one of them had a girlfriend. So they started courting girls, and eventually, all of them got the experience, although some of them felt so disappointed with the experience...

Well, I guess I'm not supposed to talk about the details here, coz this movie dealt with sex. But it was good. These days too many high-school movies are about violence but this one just made people laugh. And the film had a feeling of reality.

The soundtrack was amazing, very delightful and catchy. It had all the ingredients of a good movie!

轮到你了   It's Your Turn.

▶ Word Bank on This Topic

超级搞笑的 hilarious	追求（其人） court（*sb.*）
是关于……话题的 deal with / be concerned with	
暴力 violence	现实 reality（*n.*）
让人开心的 delightful / enjoyable	（音乐）好记的 catchy

[剑桥例句] This is a song with catchy lyrics（歌词）.

成分，原料 ingredients	喜剧 comedy
夸张的 exaggerated	观众 audience
受欢迎的 well-liked / well-received　受到好评的 receive rave reviews	

[剑桥例句] The show has received rave reviews in all the papers.
（英美生活中说 papers 时很多时候并不是指论文，而是指 newspapers）

请参考 Pat 的思路，并适当借鉴这个词汇表里的单词，思考如果是您会怎么说

☆ 电影之 黑天鹅

Pat 指南

最近在北美最火的电影之一《黑天鹅》剧情可真是够"跌宕起伏"的（The plot has many twists and turns.），可 Pat 还就偏偏想挑战一下自己，看看能不能用简单易懂的英文把这个电影跟考官介绍清楚。Here we go:

难度指数 ★★★☆☆

Pat 的答案

Hmm, the Oscar winner *Black Swan* is pretty impressive so I'd like to say something about it. The movie is what they call a "psychological thriller", you know, full of fear and darkness. But it's also a beautifully-shot movie, not to mention the beauty of ballet and of course the gorgeous actress Natalie Portman. All these make this thriller a really unique one.

In the movie, Natalie Portman played Nina, a young ballet dancer who was chosen to replace the former ballet star in a famous company. Nina's role in the company's new production of *Swan Lake* would be a dual one: She would play both the nice and sweet White Swan and the evil Black Swan. Nina was best suited for the first role but was not ready for the second one. And her drive for perfection dragged her into a horrible situation...

It's a cool movie from beginning to end. And Natalie Portman totally deserves the Best Actress Award she received!

轮到你了　　　　　　　　　　　　　　　　　　　　　　　It's Your Turn.

▶ **Word Bank on This Topic**

心理惊悚片	psychological thriller	爱情片	romantic movie
动作片	action movie	搞笑片	comedy / funny movie
贺岁片	new-year celebration movie	悬念片	suspense movie
恐怖片	horror movie	拍摄得很美的	beautifully-shot

更不用说　not to mention（固定习语）

[剑桥例句] Joe's one of the kindest and most intelligent, not to mention good-looking, men I know.

扮演　play

双重角色　dual role / double role

非常适合　be best suited for

驱动力　drive / motivation

[剑桥例句] With her experience, Mia would seem to be best suited for the job.

令人恐怖的　horrible

值得拥有　deserve

剧情　plot / story line

跌宕起伏的　full of twists and turns

很有悬念的结尾　the cliffhanger ending

紧张感　tension

[剑桥例句] We could feel the tension in the room as we waited for our test results.

> 请参考Pat的思路，并适当借鉴这个词汇表里的单词，思考如果是您会怎么说

Pat 的海外生活英语实录

　　Black Swan 之所以好看只靠 Natalie Portman 是不够的，事实上该电影的演员阵容相当强大，即使扮演配角（supporting role）的 Wynona Ryder 其实也是一巨星。那么怎样用地道英文来表达"演员阵容强大"呢？It has a strong cast. 就是它了。

【剑桥例句】

(1) After the final performance, the director threw a party for the cast.

(2) Part of the film's success lies in the strength of the cast.

☆ 电影之　国王的演讲

Pat 指南

　　The King's Speech 在 2011 年的奥斯卡之夜（Oscar Night）可谓大出风头（was in the spotlight）。这部电影不谈早已被 moviemakers 们拍摄过无数次、"不爱江山爱美人"的 King Edward VIII（爱德华八世），却讲了他的继任者 King George VI 如何克服口吃缺

陷（stammer），并最终在第二次世界大战中能用演说激励英国人民的历史故事。

对于说有关国王的电影 Pat 表示"鸭梨"很大，但我仍然坚信使用简单、清晰的英文说句子才是说好 Part 2 的秘诀。同时请您仔细听光盘里是如何对 VI 这样的罗马数字发音的，其实很简单。真正的英语从来就不是一种以难著称的语言……

难度指数 ★★★★☆

Pat 的答案

I watched the movie *The King's Speech* recently and was totally impressed. The acting was so good I couldn't possibly take my eyes off the big screen.

The movie told us the story of how an Australian speech therapist helped King George VI overcome his stammer. His stammer was so serious his speeches often made listeners very upset. He was even considered unfit to be a king because of this, which made him totally frustrated. But the speech therapist tried really hard to cure him and never gave up. When he noticed the only time his patient didn't stammer was when he cursed, he even encouraged his patient to use this as a practice tool. Eventually, King George VI overcame his stammer and delivered many successful speeches during World War II... A really fun movie. If you haven't watched it yet, you definitely should!

轮到你了   It's Your Turn.

▶ **Word Bank on This Topic**

表演 acting   实在无法（做某事）can't possibly

[剑桥例句] The team just couldn't possibly win the match.

语言矫正师 speech therapist   战胜，克服 overcome

[剑桥例句] Eventually she managed to overcome her shyness in class.

口吃 stammer   很烦的 upset

不适宜的 unfit   沮丧的 frustrated

治愈 cure   放弃 give up

骂街　curse

最终　eventually（这个词在描述一个较长的过程时在地道英语里超级常用）

发表演讲　deliver a speech

有趣的，有意思的　fun（请注意这个形容词与 funny "搞笑的" 之间的细微区别）

[剑桥例句] There are lots of fun things to do in Lesley's class.

历史片　historical drama　　　　感人的　moving/touching

特逗的　amusing（这个词在地道英文里用得挺多，可国内孩子们却坚
　　　　持只用 funny 那一个词）

首映 première（BrE /ˈpremiɛə/；AmE /priˈmir/）

[剑桥例句] The world première of the opera will be at the Metropolitan
Opera House.

请参考 Pat 的思路，并适当借鉴这个词汇表里的单词，思考如果是您会怎么说

Pat 的海外生活英语实录

　　虽然有些影评家（film critics，请注意 critics 在这个短语里不是 "批评者" 而是 "评论家" 的意思）认为 *The King's Speech* 的某些细节与历史真相不符，但本片仍然属于相当典型的传记电影。那么传记电影在真实的英文口语里怎样表达呢？biography films? film biography? 都不是，最常用的口语说法其实是 biopic，而最常看到的书面说法则是 biographical film。

　　【剑桥例句】A biopic is about the life of a real person.

5. 歌曲之　加州明信片

> Describe a song or piece of music.
>
> You should say:
>
> 　　what the song or piece of music is
>
> 　　when you first heard it
>
> and explain why you like it.

难度指数：★★★☆☆

Pat 的答案

I'd like to describe my favourite song, *picture postcards from LA.*

Of course, LA stands for Los Angeles, a city best known for its entertainment industry on the West coast of America. This song is about an average-looking waitress who always dreams about becoming a superstar in Hollywood. But whenever she shares her dream with the singer of this song (Joshua Kadison), he's like, " So send me picture post cards from LA. And if you find me one, I'd love a picture of the California sun" The melody of this song really calms me down, very very peaceful. And the lyrics are totally touching.

It's all about the average people's lives, our joys and sorrows. Maybe all of us, at least at some points of our lives, have dreamed about making it big. But very few of us manage to make our dreams come true. Few of us have the good fortune to become a super star. The singer has a deep and rich voice. I simply adore him and I love this song sooooooo much. It's just so moving coz it's about us, the average people who wish to make it big someday.

轮到你了　　　　　　　　　　　　　　　　　　It's Your Turn.

▶ **Word Bank on This Topic**

是……的缩写	stand for	洛杉矶	Los Angeles
外表普通的	average-looking	女服务生	waitress
一首歌的词	lyrics/words	一首歌的曲	melody / music
成功	make it big	喜怒哀乐	joys and sorrows

[剑桥例句] The sorrows of her earlier years gave way to joys in later life.

舒缓的，让人放松的	soothing	感人的	moving / touching

[剑桥例句] I put on some nice, soothing music.

国歌	national anthem	让人振奋的	uplifting
节奏	rhythm	热情的	passionate

[剑桥例句] The Italians are said to be the most passionate people in Europe.

拍子　beat

……说，… he's /she's like, "…" （这个表达在国外日常交流中转述别人说的某句话时比 he/she said 更常用，真可惜 Pat 居然就没听一个国内考生用过）

> 请参考Pat的思路，并适当借鉴这个词汇表里的单词，思考如果是您会怎么说

Pat 的海外生活英语实录

　　Pat 有时会在线收听来自国内的音乐节目。最近很流行说一首歌"给力"，对应的英文就可以这么说，"It's an uplifting/ inspiring/ inspirational song." 而如果您想说一个故事（story / tale）或一次谈话（conversation）"给力"，则不妨说，"It was a motivating / stimulating / engaging story / conversation." 介绍一种最新的科技"给力"，地道的英文可以用 It's highly empowering. 而一部电影或一次表演（performance）"给力"则要说：It was phenomenal. （phenomenal 这个词貌似很书面，但其实在当代英美日常口语中的使用已经相当普及）。如果觉得一篇剑8范文的逻辑论证"给力"，您则可以说 It's a compelling / convincing / cogent / forceful essay.

　　如果实在懒得去判断自己所要描述的对象到底属于哪种"给力"，那就用 desirable 吧。它未必最准，但却是最万能的"给力"。

　　较真儿的话，在当代英文口语里与中文"给力"最为酷似的一个表达其实是 It's a knockout. 意即 overwhelmingly attractive。但这个表达已涉及到较"痞"的领域，容易导致烤鸭朋友们在考场里误用，所以不记也罢。此外尚有 two thumbs up 等地道表达，都是英文里的"给力"之选。

【剑桥例句】

(1) Reducing class sizes in schools is a desirable aim.

(2) It's regarded as a highly desirable job.

(3) His first novel was phenomenally successful.

IELTS SPEAKING TEST

6. 广告

> Describe your favourite advertisement.
>
> You should say:
>> what it advertised
>>
>> where you saw it
>>
>> what it was like
>
> and explain why you still remember it.

难度指数：★★★★☆

Pat 的答案

My favourite TV commercial is a shoe commercial.

A businessman rushed to the airport in a taxi and hopped onto an airplane and flew a city far away from his.

Having arrived at an office building, he got into the lift and rode up to the 20th floor, looking totally nervous. He looked down at his shoes, only to notice that they didn't match at all. He completed the interview.

The businessman seemed very disappointed. He looked sadly at his mismatched shoes. All of a sudden, his mobile phone rang — he got the job. He was so excited and jumped into the air. The narrator said calmly. "Converse can always take you there."

轮到你了   It's Your Turn.

▶ **Word Bank on This Topic**

电视广告	commercial	跳	hop / skip / jump
不相配的	mismatched	失望的	disappointed / frustrated

[剑桥例句] Is Sophie feeling frustrated in her present job?

旁白	narrator	匡威	Converse
广告牌	billboard	广告传单	flyer
可信的	dependable	顾客群	customer base
乘电梯上楼	ride up in the lift (BrE) / elevator (AmE)		

请参考Pat的思路，并适当借鉴这个词汇表里的单词，思考如果是您会怎么说

*D*o you know what amazes me more than anything else?
The impotence of force to organize anything.

—Napoleon Bonaqarte

Pat 的海外生活英语实录

"有创意的"大家都知道是 creative，部分同学也知道 innovative 那个不错的词。但在英文口语里还有个固定短语叫作 think out of the box，也是用来形容人在思考或设计时充分发挥自己创造力的常用表达。例如：

【剑桥例句】People who can think out of the box usually run their own companies rather than manage others' companies.

☞ The 10 Best Ad Slogans （广告语）in History

① Just do it. （Nike vs. the Adidas slogan "Impossible is nothing."）

② Melts in your mouth, not in your hands. （M&Ms）

③ It's the real thing. （Coca Cola）

④ Come to where the favor is. Marlboro Country. （Marlboro）

⑤ Think small. （Volkswagen）

⑥ Think different. （Apple）

⑦ The taste is great. （Nestle）

⑧ Let's make things better. （Phillips）

⑨ Connecting People. （Nokia）

⑩ Start ahead. （Rejoice）

7. 故事

☆ 童年听过的故事之　三只小猪

> Describe a story from your childhood.
>
> You should say:
>
> 　what the story was about

> how you first heard this story
> why you remember this story
> and explain whether it is still popular today.

难度指数：★ ★ ★ ☆ ☆

Pat 的答案

Let me share with you the Three Little Pigs.

Once upon a time there were three little pigs. They moved to a new village and built their homes.

The first little pig built a straw house simply because that was easy. But the house was not sturdy at all.

The second little pig built a stick house for himself. He didn't spend much time building it either.

The third little pig was pretty hard-working. He built a brick house, which was very sturdy.

Then of course, the wolf came along, blew the first house down and ate the first little pig.

And then in the same way, the wolf ate the second piggy.

The only house the wolf couldn't blow down was the house built by the third pig coz he built the house as well as he possibly could. The wolf gave up. And the third piggy just lived happily ever after.

My grandma told me this story when I was just 5 or maybe 6. But I still remember it coz it taught me as an important lesson: Hope for the best, but prepare for the worst.

轮到你了   It's Your Turn.

▶ **Word Bank on This Topic**

很久很久以前 once upon a time   从此之后幸福地生活着 lived happily ever after
(这两句基本是英文童话的固定开始和结尾，小孩子们都会背的)

坚固的　sturdy　　　白雪公主和七个小矮人　Snow White and the Seven Dwarfs

[剑桥例句] They put up a sturdy defence of their proposal.

灰姑娘　Cinderella　　　　皇帝的新装　The Emperor's New Clothes

美人鱼　The Little Mermaid　　安徒生　Hans Christian Andersen

丑小鸭　The Ugly Duckling　　孙悟空　The Monkey King

童话　fairytale

> 请参考Pat的思路，并适当借鉴这个词汇表里的单词，思考如果是您会怎么说

Pat 的海外生活英语实录

童话故事的"寓意"英文怎么将？只说 meaning 可不够准确，**moral** 才是 the right word for it，请注意当用作这个意思时 moral 是名词。

【剑桥例句】The moral of/to the story is that honesty is always the best policy.

Pat 指南

从今年年初开始，雅思口试还时常偷着考这个卡片题 **Describe your favourite childhood song**.

下面这个很轻松的网站提供了大量的儿歌，www. mamalisa. com。您登录后点击地图里的 Asia，再点击 China 就看到中国的儿歌了，从"小燕子"到"两只老虎"都有。

8. 自己喜欢的网站

☆ **网站之　雅虎**

> Describe your favourite website.
>
> You should say:
> which website it is
> when you first visited this website
> how often you visited this website
> and explain why you like it.

难度指数：★★★☆☆

[Pat 的答案]

My favourite website is Yahoo!. I'm sure you've heard a lot about this website coz it's definitely one of the most popular websites in the world.

I like this website so much primarily because it's very informative and entertaining. It offers loads of information like the latest world news, changes in the financial market and reports about sporting events. Also, it gives us the newest stories about the showbiz, you know, the movie stars, famous singers and TV programs. And the layout of the web pages is very organized and user-friendly.

Another reason I really adore Yahoo! is its founders are like heroes to young folks. Jerry Yang and David Filo started Yahoo! back in 1994, when they were both just 24. So you see, Yahoo! is more than a leading website. It's also an inspiring success story to us...

轮到你了

It's Your Turn.

▶ **Word Bank on This Topic**

首先是因为	primarily because	信息量大的	informative
娱乐性强的	entertaining	金融市场	financial market
娱乐圈	showbiz	排版	layout

[剑桥例句] Application forms vary greatly in layout and length.

有秩序的	organized	超级喜欢	adore
创建者	founder	激励人的	inspiring

[剑桥例句] She is the founder and managing director of the company.

点击率	hits	方便使用的	user-friendly

请参考Pat的思路，并适当借鉴这个词汇表里的单词，思考如果是您会怎么说

Pat 的海外生活英语实录

二十一世纪谁都知道网站叫 website，可网络公司的英文是……? 出乎您的意料，答案居然就是多数网站域名的最后部分：dotcom。惊奇，但是事实。dotcom 的确就是英文口语里对网络公司的最地道称呼。

【剑桥例句】

(1) A survey found that 20 of the top 150 European dotcoms could run out of cash within a year.

(2) Connor is a dotcom millionaire.

☆ 关于网站的双语感悟

Random Bilingual Reflections on Websites

The Internet is such a miracle!

互联网真是神奇！说到 the Internet，就想起上大学的时候我教班里的同学说"互联网"这几个中文字，结果说成哪国文字的都有，就是没有说得像中文的。所以大家永远不要说"My English is very poor." 很多老外说外语可比你的英语说得差多了！首先，要知道点击率英文叫 hits。This site gets tons of hits daily. 就是说这个网站点击率很高。网页的布局叫 layout。The layout of this website is pretty neat. 就是说网站布局很清晰。Users just follow the links. 就是说用户只要逐个点击就可以到达目的地了。This website is very user-friendly. 就是说这个网站用户使用起来很方便。This site is very entertaining. 是说网站娱乐性很强。It is incredibly informative. 就是说信息量超大呀！I can pull an awful lot of cool stuff from it. 是说我可以从上面下载很多酷毙了的东东（当然下载也可以说 download），如果是一个专门关于流行音乐的网站，就说 It specializes in popular music.，如果要说是关于新闻时事的 www. cnn. com 或 www. foxnews. com 这类的网站，就说 It is dedicated exclusively to current world affairs.，要是如果说新闻都很及时而且有价值，就说 It presents up-to-the-minute coverage of newsworthy events.，如果要说它极大地充实了你的生活，就说 It really brightens up my life.，如果说它独一无二，就是 It is one of a kind.，或者 It is unique.，如果说你对它很着迷，就说 I am really hooked on it!

9. 最喜欢的外国文化

☆ *最喜欢的外国文化之　英国文化*

> Describe a foreign culture you're interested in.
>
> You should say:
>   which culture it is
>   why you like it
>   how you get information about this culture
> and explain how you'll try to learn more about it.

Pat 指南

其实完全可以说是因为你会去那里学习，因此特别关注那里的文化，即使你其实正在玩儿命地申另一个国家的学校。不过英国文化即使在已经略显没落（declined）的今天也确实还是有它的优秀之处，否则老美们也不会对威廉王子的婚礼那么兴师动众地报道（It dominated the headlines.），而且一听说哪个朋友打算去英国旅游就妒忌得不行（get green with envy）。

Pat 给这个答案标了五星级，因为毕竟 culture 还是一个相对抽象的概念。但在这个答案里我还是尽可能多地用了一些简洁的表达来让它变得更清晰易懂。请您重点体会描述清楚一种文化的思路（train of thought）以及"小词们"的使用。

难度指数：★★★★★

[Pat 的答案]

Well I'm planning on studying in London. So let me share with you some thoughts about the British culture.

I've heard and read a lot about the Houses of Parliament, the Tower of London and Buckingham Palace ... So for sightseeing trips, I guess Britain would be a perfect place because of the gorgeous architecture.

And ... Britain is the birthplace of sooooo many great minds, you know, like Shakespeare, Newton and of course, J. K. Rowling, the author of the *Harry Potter* series. She's my idol!

And what else? ... Practically all of my favourite bands have been British bands, like the Beatles, Pink Floyd, And what else? the Rolling Stones, Coldplay, Radiohead and the Stone Roses... So many musically-talented people there!

Another thing I should emphasize here is there're a multitude of world-class universities in the UK, like Oxford, Cambridge and LSE. That's exactly why I'm planning on studying in this country...

In terms of personality, the British people are probably kind of reserved. But it also depends on which part of the UK they live in I guess.

I don't really know much about the British food. I heard fish-and-chips was very popular there. But how it tastes... I have no idea.

I used to think the cities there were pretty foggy all year round but some British friends of mine told me that was not the case anymore.

So far, most of the information I have about the British culture has been from magazines or TV programs. I really hope I'll get into one of the fine universities there. That way, I will learn a whole lot more about this brilliant culture...

轮到你了   It's Your Turn.

▶ Word Bank on This Topic

计划做某事　　plan on（plan on doing sth. 在日常口语里面其实比 plan to do sth. 更加常用）

议会大楼　　the houses of parliament（这里的 house 用复数）

观光　sightseeing　　是……的出生地　is the birthplace of（这里不需要过去时）

作者　author　　几乎　practically（用来代替 almost 不错）

[剑桥例句] He blamed Daniel for practically every mistake in the report.

有音乐天赋的　musically-talented　　　强调　emphasize

大量的　a multitude of / a host of（这两个比 tons of/loads of 听着正式一点）

世界级的　world-class

[剑桥例句] He's regarded as a world-class athlete.

内向的　reserved（注意 introverted 是个口语中基本不用的词）

炸鱼土豆条　fish and chips

（在英国超级常见的快餐食品，在 Vancouver 偶尔有人也吃，不过在 California 就比较少有人吃这个，所以总的来说是一种很英式的东东）

有雾的　foggy　　　　不是那样了　that's not the case

录取　get into / get admitted to

（在口语里面第一个说法占据绝对优势 has the absolute upper hand）

好的　fine

（口语里面这个经常用来代替 good，可惜国内考生用这个词只限于 I'm fine, thanks.）

那样的话　That way, ...

了解　learn（在口语里很多时候这个词并不是"学习"而是"了解到"）

[剑桥例句] I just learned you would come over soon.

"伦敦眼"　the London Eye（伦敦很有名的一个摩天轮 Ferris wheel）

伦敦著名的一家高端百货商店　Harrods（不过这家店由于坚持卖"皮草" real animal fur 而时常遭到 animal rights activists 的批评）

请参考Pat的思路，并适当借鉴这个词汇表里的单词，思考如果是您会怎么说

Pat 的海外生活英语实录

　　说起英国人，同学们往往容易想到"温文尔雅的"这些词，尽管这个词并不适合所有的英国人，但总体而言还是比较准确的。Pat 在北京时问过学生们"温文尔雅的"英文该怎么说，大家全都异口同声地回答 gentleman（晕，连词性都不对）。其实如果在口试时要说一个人的言谈举止有风度，除了 polite / well-mannered 这些词之外，refined 也是个好选择。而形容男士"温文尔雅的"在地道英文里最精准的词其实应该是 urbane（/ɜːˈbeɪn/，注意不是 urban），不过 urbane 对于多数 IELTS 考生来说就有点难了，出国前不记也罢。

【剑桥例句】

（1）The hotel lobby reflects the refined taste of the owner.

（2）Refined people tend to be very polite and show knowledge of social rules.

Time to Branch Out.
推而广之

> Describe a foreign country you wish to travel to.

补充弹药

by air 乘飞机	travel half way around the globe 绕地球转半圈
exotic 异国风情的	check out... 体验……
explore 探索	tourist attractions 旅游景点
cost sb. an arm and a leg 花某人一大笔钱	

10. 最喜欢的运动

☆ **最喜欢的运动之 游泳**

> Describe your favourite sport.
>
> You should say:
>> what the sport it
>> when you took up this sport
>> what benefits it brings
>
> and explain whether this sport is popular in your country.

(男生女生都可以说的最常见运动的应该就是 swimming 了)

难度指数：★★★★☆

Pat 的答案

My favourite sport is swimming. Actually it's my favourite hobby.

It's a good work-out coz it exercises every muscle in my body. Also I guess swimming skills are important coz sometimes it can really save lives.

The fun it gives me is yet another reason I'm into swimming. Actually, when I was a kid, I didn't know how to swim. Some friends of mine even laughed at me for that. My parents were afraid I would get hurt emotionally so they sent me to swimming lessons.

The instructor was very nice. At first, I just swam like a brick. My wonderful instructor showed me patiently how to kick my legs and put my face in the water, a pretty good way to "get my feet wet." Then he taught me how to control my breathing. Little by little, I got the hang of it and felt comfortable with the water. Eventually, I could control my breathing perfectly and do the swimming strokes pretty well.

Now I can swim like a fish. I can swim twenty laps and still feel great. I'm thankful for my instructor. He was awesome. He gave me so much confidence in myself…

Swimming is very popular in China coz it's the best all-around exercise. It keeps us fit and keeps our body in shape…

轮到你了　／／／　　　　　　　　　　　　　　　　　It's Your Turn.

▶ **Word Bank on This Topic**

锻炼　work-out (*n.*) /work out (*v.*)	肌肉　muscle
受伤害　get hurt	情感上　emotionally
[剑桥例句] Fiona spoke emotionally about her experience.	
教练　instructor（这里不要叫 coach）	不会游泳　swim like a brick
超级会游泳　swim like a fish	逐渐掌握　get the hang of it
[剑桥例句] "I've never used a word processor before." "Don't worry — you'll soon get the hang of it."	
最终　finally / eventually	信心　confidence
（泳道的）一趟　a lap	全面的　all-around
热身运动　warm-up exercises	蛙泳　breast-stroke
仰泳　back-stroke	蝶泳　butterfly-stroke
自由式　freestyle	狗刨　doggy-paddle
潜水　dive	浮板　kickboard
菲尔普斯　Michael Phelps	

请参考Pat的思路，并适当借鉴这个词汇表里的单词，思考如果是您会怎么说

Pat 的海外生活英语实录

在 IELTS 口试里，谈到体育运动时往往会说到一项运动很"耗费体力的"，多数同学都是用 tiring 或者 exhausting。但在地道口语里还有个常用词叫 strenuous，口试时是个拿分效果挺明显的表达：

【剑桥例句】

(1) Lucas rarely does anything more strenuous than changing the channels on the television.

(2) Hannah's doctor advised her not to take any strenuous exercise.

Time to Branch Out.
推而广之

Describe a skill.

Describe something that you are good at.

Describe a difficult thing that you can do well.

Describe something you hope to learn.

补充弹药

tough	困难的	challenging	有挑战性的
overcome the difficulties	战胜困难	boost my confidence	提升我的自信
self-esteem	自尊	get used to	适应

Extra Ammo

11. 绘画（双语感悟）Random Bilingual Reflections on Painting

我自己小时候画过五年油画（oil painting）。国外的 paintings 主要分成三种：景物画（landscape painting）、静物画（still life painting）和人像（portrait），自画像叫做 self-portrait，中国的水墨画我会把它叫做 Chinese ink painting。画的构图叫 composition，光线叫 lighting，画布叫 canvas，画框叫 frame，画室是 studio，而画廊当然就是 gallery 了。

277

一幅"杰作"叫 a masterpiece，而仿制品只能叫 a fake/ a knockoff / a reproduction。说一幅画有创意除了 creative，还可以用 original 这个形容词。具象画叫 representational paintings，抽象画是 abstract paintings，美术欣赏课英文叫 art appreciation classes。

如果画的颜色很浓，说 It has intense colours.，画的颜色很鲜艳，叫 It has vivid colours.

全世界最有名的一幅画肯定是 *Mona Lisa*，它是一幅半身像（a half-length painting），是文艺复兴时期的作品（It dates back to the Italian Renaissance.）。Now it hangs in the Louvre（挂在卢浮宫里）and attracts a host of admirers（大量的崇拜者）each day.

它的作者是 Leonardo Da Vinci（这个不用解释了吧?），What 's really special about it 就是 Mona Lisa 神秘的微笑（her enigmatic / mysterious smile）。

有的人觉得这幅画很真实（realistic / true-to-life），但是也有人认为它太虚幻了（so ethereal）。但是不管怎样，它一定会在你的心里产生强烈的震撼（It evokes strong feelings.）。

《达芬奇密码》（*The Da Vinci Code*）那本 detective novel 几年前曾经极度火爆（It was a smash.），而关于这幅画也有太多的猜测（Speculations abound about this masterpiece.）。有人说 Mona Lisa 是 the wife of a wealthy merchant（富有商人的妻子），有人甚至认为它是作者的自画像 a self — portrait of Leonardo Da Vinci himself（or herself?!），这也太不靠谱了吧（That was way off base.）。

更多本类相关句型　Bonus Sentences（高分内容）

There are certain fads that come and go.

Advertisers are experts at persuading people to spend their money.

Advertisers like to catch people young coz they know the significance of loyalty.

This newspaper is aimed at teenagers.

This newspaper has a middle-class readership.

I always read the headlines on the front page first.

I scan the classified ads too.

I love the comics. （请注意在地道口语里 comics 不是 comedy "喜剧"，cmoics 是指漫画书）

I prefer to read leisure magazines.

I'm into the travel section.

I pick it up at the newsstand.

I have a one-year subscription to it.

The text is very amusing.

It has incredible photographs of the natural beauty of the places authors have visited.

It comes out once a week.

It's published weekly.

The layout is very organized.

It gives me a lot of new tips about learning English.

It's inexpensive.

I read a variety of magazines, like outdoors, scholastic, fashion and political magazines.

Its circulation has risen dramatically in recent years.

It's the best way to build your strength, balance and coordination.

It builds up team spirit.

It helps you release all your stress.

It keeps you fit.

Many people enjoy noncompetitive activities like hiking, biking, horseback riding, camping or hunting.

They try to work off all those calories they ate.

临时抱佛脚

近期亚太考区的一道考题吓倒了无数英雄：

Describe an extreme sport.

不要说描述，估计至少有一半的 IELTS 考生长这么大都还没参加过极限运动，所以很多孩子感觉描述这道题本身就是他们/她们人生里参加的第一项极限运动。不过这道题加上点外貌描述就可以立刻帮我们同时准备好另一个难题 Describe an adventurous person. 所以还是值得一试的。

这种题想说得"完美"当然不容易（如果真有所谓"完美"的话），但介绍一下某种极限运动的基本情况其实还不算太痛苦，甚至可以变得有趣。先熟记 3 个关键词：risky / hazardous（任选一个：有风险的），adventurous（勇于冒险的）和 excitement / exhilaration /thrill（程度依次递增，但用一个就够，名词：兴奋）。然后再记住两个短句：It's an ultimate challenge（它是终极挑战）. 和 Overcoming such a challenge gives people an overwhelming sense of satisfaction（成功应对这样的挑战给人极大的心理满足感）. 有空还可以看看 BBC 怎么介绍常见的极限运动的 news. bbc. co. uk/cbbcnews/hi/find_out/guides/sport/extreme_sports，彩色图片还可以进一步减少挑战这个话题给你带来的"极限感"。

更棒的是，近期的常见考题 **Describe an adventurous person.** 同时也就有的可聊了。

另类话题 Off-the-Wall Topics

如果在国外生活中听到有人问你 What's your sign? 那是什么意思呢？是在问你的星座是什么。如果说两个人的 signs are compatible，就是说两个人的星座配合度（compatibility）很高。

我小时候除了爱画画，还特喜欢研究星座（horoscope）。下面的星座描述，一定会让你更了解自己（get a fair and accurate self-image），满眼都是描述人的卡片能用得上的又简单又实用的英文。更棒的是，通过熟悉以下各种性格的英文描述还可以帮您准备好 **Describe your personality.** 这个题，而且其实多数人的性格都是以下各类性格特征（地道英文里叫做 personality traits）的"混合物"（Most people are actually a rich blend of different personality traits.）。

Aquarius（Jan 23-Feb 22）水瓶座

You are very creative, inventive and you take a unique approach（途径）to living your life. Many of your friends call you a true original（地道习语：确实有创意的人）. But you also tend to question your decisions and can lack self-confidence when suggesting something new.

Pisces（Feb 23-Mar 22）双鱼座

You love music and art and can get lost in a movie. You tend to be shy and quiet, but you have a great memory. However, you tend to blame yourself for everything that goes wrong and often have way too much self-pity.

Aeries（Mar 23-Apr 22）白羊座

You are a practical Earth sign who is realistic and hard-working. You are filled with determination（决心）when you set your sights on something.

Taurus (Apr 23-May 22) 金牛座

You are very loving and <u>dependable</u> and your calm personality always <u>puts</u> everyone <u>at ease</u>. You love nice things, but remember: you have to work hard to get them!

Gemini (May 23-Jun 22) 双子座

You are <u>an excellent communicator</u> and you love to talk! Your wit (机灵) often help you <u>persuade</u> (说服) people to see things your way. You pay close attention to details and are very curious (好奇的). But you can be known to have a dual (double) personality.

Cancer (Jun 23-Jul 22) 巨蟹座

You truly care when friends tell you their problems. If you have a younger <u>sibling</u> (brother or sister), you are <u>very protective of</u> them because you love your family so much! (The bad things are left out coz this is my sign ho ho...)

Leo (Jul 23-Aug 22) 狮子座

You are fun and <u>playful</u> and enjoy being around people who are exciting. You always <u>liven up</u> a party and you make a great cheerleader for your friends. You give a lot of praise to others, and you expect it back in return.

Virgo (Aug 23-Sep 22) 处女座

Cleanliness and <u>a healthy lifestyle</u> are very important to you, which can sometimes make you nervous and worried.

Libra (Sep 23-Oct 22) 天秤座

You are an honest friend and people trust you with their deepest secrets. You are also very artistic and love drawing, painting, singing or anything else creative. Sometimes you are afraid of making the wrong choice, so you <u>mope around</u> (踱来踱 去) and worry about it much longer than you should.

Scorpio (Oct 23-Nov 22) 天蝎座

You love magic and <u>mystery</u> and <u>people are naturally drawn to you</u>. A Scorpio will always forgive — but will never forget. Once you break the trust of a Scorpio, things are never the same again.

Sagittarius (Nov 23-Dec 22) 射手座

You are kind and <u>caring</u> to those who need your help. You also love coming up with different ideas on how to solve a problem. But you also can be very <u>sensitive</u> and get your feelings hurt when friends don't view the world as you do.

Capricorn（Dec 23-Jan 22）摩羯座

You are very <u>generous</u> and make an extremely <u>loyal</u> friend. Once you love somebody, you love them forever. But you sometimes test your friends to see if you can really trust them.

It's really about horoscope. It all comes down to how effective simple English can be. Guys, have a good one.

对本类话题有价值的网址

下面的网址对骨灰级 DIYer 准备关于 leisure activities 的答案会非常有用：
游戏：

http://www.tradgames.org.uk/（It provides loads of info on traditional games from around the world.）

电影：

http://www.imdb.com/（This is by far the most comprehensive movie database online.）

图书：

http://www.amazon.com（Well, obviously all of you have heard a great deal about this site. Or maybe some of you have had shopping experiences with it already. Jeff Bezos, its founder, is an extremely talented guy.）

音乐：

http://www.unsignedbandweb.com/forum13.html（an online forum where you can get lots of info and thoughts about music）

运动：

http://www.justlanded.com/english/UK/Tools/Articles/Travel-Leisure/British-Sports（Actually, it's far more than that. You can find practically everything about the British culture there.）

E 物质诱惑

Pat 解题　Pat's Decryption

本节我们会学到很多描述物品的地道词汇和表达。

比如一般同学说衣服这个词都喜欢用 clothes，其实您身上穿的一套衣服国外生活中的很多时候也可以叫 outfit，而人身上戴的首饰则叫 accessories，比如 earrings，nose ring，belly-button ring（脐环）等，在国外总称为 body piercing。在北京的时候一次看报纸时发现有个作者居然误以为在国外戴耳环的男人都是 gay，这可就不靠谱儿了（way off base）。在英美戴耳环的男性很多，甚至连大学男教授也有戴的，但大部分人都只是把它当成装饰（stuff that enhances your appearance）。

本节我们还会学到很多 electronic devices，比如 digital cameras。不过最近 Pat 最感兴趣的电子东东是 ipad 2。英文里有一个特棒的词来形容这些电子小东西，叫 gadget，考试的时候可以用 1~2 次。

当然我们还会学习更大型的 objects，比如 automobiles。我的学生和读者当中车迷（car buffs）从来都不少。另外，我们还可以看看两种这辈子还能买得起的车型。

handicraft（手工制作的物品）一直是个难点，本节我们也得突破。

一口气谈了这么多 objects，希望咱们不会变得 太 materialistic（物质化）！

展开本类话题思路的线索　Brainstorming Techniques
（熟悉下面的表格可以确保你在拿到任何本类卡片题时都能有话说）

Objects
How I got it
Exterior
Function
Price
Role in my life
Role in others' lives
My own feeling/Other "rounding off" remarks

本类话题最新完整真题库　The Complete Question Pool on This Topic

❋ Describe a vehicle (such as a car or a bicycle) that you'd like to own.

❋ Describe a photo.

❋ Describe something electronic that you use often/that you do not use often.

❋ Describe a piece of equipment you use every day.

❋ Describe an old piece of furniture/an antique (本话题请看 Day 10) .

❋ Describe an object you use every day.

❋ Describe an item of clothing/a piece of jewellery that you like.

❋ Describe a handicraft/something that was made by yourself.

❋ Describe a national product.

❋ Describe something expensive you'd like to buy.

❋ Describe a gift or a present you have received.

❋ Describe something you made yourself.

❋ Describe an important conversation. (请见 Day 10)

分级演示　A Spectrum of Sample Answers

1. 交通工具

☆ **交通工具之　*Mini-Cooper***

> Describe a vehicle you'd like to own.
>
> You should say:
>> what the vehicle is
>>
>> why you would like to own it
>>
>> whether it would be expensive to buy
>
> and explain whether you think you'll buy it in the future.

这个题目 Pat 上课让孩子们练习时候大家总是会想到一大堆超级大词，真想试试用简单词能不能搞定它（sort it out）。

难度指数：★★★☆☆

Pat 的答案

A friend of mine bought a Mini Cooper last month. It cost her like 250,000 renminbi. But it looks like a 500,000 renminbi car, I have to say.（真实的英文谈话里像 I would say... / ... I should say 这类小短语特别多，其实也不是真的就"非说不可"了，但说了却更像是人类之间的交流，而不是两台机器间的互殴）

Back then, that friend of mine was looking for a small car with good performance and she got totally impressed by Mini. The exterior was sooooooo cute, like a chubby baby coz it looked pretty compact. The car is sleek too. You know, shiny.

Unlike Beetles, Mini had a powerful engine, which makes it similar to other BMW cars. It can even handle the bumpy roads in the suburbs. It has good gas mileage as well. That's definitely good news when the petrol price（＝gas price）is still sky-high here in China.

It looked small, but the interior turned out to be very spacious. The backseats were probably only good for kids, though. You can park it anywhere because of its small size, which is really nice in a city where there are not enough parking spaces.

I'm starting to envy my friend. I'm sure I'll buy a Mini too coz it's just so fun. It's almost like if you test-drive a Mini, you'll buy it...

轮到你了　　　　　　　　　　　　　　　　　　　It's Your Turn.

▶ **Word Bank on This Topic**

性能　performance

性价比　performance / price ratio（生活里也经常会简单地说 It offers good value for money.）

外观　exterior　　　　　　　内部　interior

[剑桥例句] The car's interior is very impressive — leather（皮革）seats and a wooden dashboard（dashboard 就是方向盘前方安装有很多仪表和空调开关等的那个控制板）。

轮到你了

It's Your Turn.

胖乎乎的	chubby	紧凑的	compact
光亮的	sleek（大众的）	甲壳虫	Beetles
发动机	engine	类似的	similar
耐用的	durable	坑坑洼洼的	bumpy
可以承受	can handle...	油耗低	good gas mileage / good fuel economy
郊区	suburbs	宽敞的	spacious
汽油	petrol（BrE）/ gas（AmE）	很快	shortly / soon
羡慕	envy	方向盘	steering wheel
气囊	airbags	没有任何多余装饰的实用型东西	no-frills

[剑桥例句] It's a no-frills shop supplying only basic goods at affordable prices.

装备齐全	It's loaded..	手动挡	stick shift / manual
自动挡	automatic（transmission）	敞篷车	convertible
跑车	sports car	流线型的	streamlined

[剑桥例句] Streamlining cars can increase their fuel efficiency.

底盘 chassis（真正爱车的人都知道，engine 和 chassis 才是最重要的，exterior 其实真的不值多少钱）

商务用车（一般车正面是倾斜的那种长面包车）minivan / MPV

国内同学时常发错音的汽车品牌（请您注意听光盘里的发音）

Mercedes Benz（其实在地道英文中说"奔驰"时经常会只说前面的第一个单词）

Land Rover	陆虎	Rolls Royce	劳斯莱斯
Volkswagen	大众	Hyundai	现代
Lexus	雷克萨斯	Lamborghini	蓝博基尼
Cadillac	卡迪拉克	Volvo	沃尔沃
Bentley	宾利	Renault	雷诺
Citroen	雪铁龙	Porsche	保时捷

Do you know what amazes me more than anything else?
The impotence of force to organize anything.
—Napoleon Bonaqarte

Mazda	马自达	Nissan	日产
Saab	萨博	Toyota	丰田
Audi	奥迪		
Chevrolet	（生活里谈话时也经常简称为 Chevy） 雪佛兰		

请参考Pat的思路，并适当借鉴这个词汇表里的单词，思考如果是您会怎么说

Pat 的海外生活英语实录

最近利比亚（Libya）局势不稳导致油价飞涨，大家在加油时免不了都得骂上几句。怎样用地道的英文来说一辆车"省油"或者"费油"。是不是您的脑子里已经飘出了 save oil 和 waste oil？太堕落了哈。下次跟老外聊车的时候请您一定要记得用 **It gets good mileage**（发音/'mailidʒ/）. 或者 **It' pretty fuel-efficient.** 来形容一辆车很省油，而用 **It's a gas-guzzler**（发音/gæs'gʌzlə/）. 来表达对"油老虎"的无奈。

【剑桥例句】

(1) Smaller cars get better mileage and so cost less to run.
(2) Gas-guzzlers are expensive to drive because they use more fuel.

☆ 交通工具之 森林人

Pat指南

Mini-Cooper 和 Beetle 都是 MM 们的最爱。而 Pat 发现国内的男同学们一提起适合男性开的车就会立刻想到"悍马"（Hummer），可在油价飞涨而且全球都"Go green."的年代里，像 Hummer 这样的"油老虎"（gas-guzzler）即使能买得起也不是谁都能养得起的。2011 年在美国和加拿大进行的一项最新调查显示，Subaru Forester（森林人）拥有很多受过良好教育的男性车主，而且性能不俗。Forester 左右对称的全时四轮驱动（symmetrical all wheel drive）正在悄悄地改变着英美传统观念中的"猛男"形象。

难度指数 ★★★★☆

Pat 的答案

The vehicle I will probably buy is a Subaru Forester 2011. I test-drove one last month and was quite impressed with it.

It has a sleek exterior and the build quality feels good. The interior is roomy, but not luxurious. The leg room and head room are just perfect for me and there's plenty of cargo room as well.

As for the performance, the handling is good and the acceleration is quiet and smooth. The engine is kind of noisy but... tolerable.

There isn't much snow in my area. But during the summer it can rain really hard so I guess the AWD feature of Forester would mean more safety on the road.

Frankly, Forester is not for people who look for an upscale interior. Some interior materials are even on the cheap side. It's simply not a luxury car, you know. But it offers the best value in its class and provides comfortable rides. I'm a person who favors function over form so it's a great choice for me anyway.

DIYer工具箱

▶ Word Bank on This Topic

试驾 test-drive   （外型）柔顺的 sleek

[剑桥例句] Who owns that sleek car parked outside your house?

物品的外观 exterior   汽车或建筑等的内部空间 interior

车身工艺 build quality   宽敞的 roomy / spacious

奢侈的 luxurious   腿部空间 leg room

头顶空间 head room   储货空间 cargo room

性能 performance   操控性能 handling

[剑桥例句] High-performance cars tend to be expensive.

加速 acceleration   转向性能 steering

可以忍受的 tolerable

[剑桥例句] The heat in the room was hardly tolerable.

全驱　all wheel drive/ the AWD feature（在冰天雪地或者路面湿滑的地方这种配置很有用）

四驱　four wheel drive（这个也尚可）

前驱　front wheel drive（下雪天应对路面就会难一些）

坦白说　frankly　　　　　　　奢华的　upscale

豪华车　luxury car　　　　看重功能而不看重外型　favor function over form

转向性能　steering　　　　反映灵敏的　responsive

紧凑型 SUV　compact SUV

二手车的售出价格　resale value（有些人把"老外"全想象成富翁，其实在英美开二手车甚至五、六手车的车主比例要比国内高多了，所以二手车的卖出价格也是判断新车保值率的重要依据）

> 请参考Pat的思路，并适当借鉴这个词汇表里的单词，思考如果是您会怎么说

Pat 的海外生活英语实录

形容车的外观漂亮，有些孩子肯定会想到 gorgeous，这个词在国外生活里确实属于绝对的高频词，但是它的语气很强，有点像中文"超靓的"，并不适合像 CR-V，RAV 4，Tiguan 这类"一般好看"的车。那么请试试 **neat** 吧，它在实际生活中不仅可以用来指"干净的"，而且也常常被用来表示"挺好看的"的意思。

【剑桥例句】

（1）It's a neat little cottage.

（2）You've got such neat handwriting.

2. 物品之电子用品

> Describe something electronic that you use often.
>
> You should say:
>
> 　　what it is

> where / when you bought it
>
> what you use it for
>
> and explain why you like it.

☆ *电子物品之* iPhone 4

Pat 指南

在这个答案里我汇集了在国外喜欢数码东东的弟兄们常说的几乎全部高频词汇，但如果你觉得不好记，那就看下面的数码相机那一段吧。

难度指数: ★ ★ ★ ☆ ☆

Pat 的答案

Of course I'll describe my iPhone 4. I waited in line for hours to get it. And I should say it was well worth all the waiting!

You know, I've used many smart phones but iPhone 4 is definitely the best, hands down. It's thinner, faster and prettier. The touch screen is gorgeous and helps me type much faster than on other screens. And the ring tones are pleasant as well.

The operating system of iPhone 4 is super user-friendly I felt comfortable with it right away. And I love the Google maps. So vivid and detailed. Now I can even use my iPhone 4 to watch YouTube videos!

It comes with so many features but it's not cumbersome at all. I can easily slip it into my pocket. Oh, by the way, as a phone, its call and reception quality is perfect. And I can even make video calls with Facetime.

The only thing that bothers me a bit about this gadget is it only offers 32 GB of storage. But anyway that's not much of a problem.

Some folks complained about the battery life. I feel fine about this, though It's like a full day or something…

轮到你了   It's Your Turn.

▶ **Word Bank on This Topic**

电子用品　electronic device / electronic gadget（后面这个数码迷们用得超多）

排队　wait in line（这个短语在国外生活里也非常常用，而且队伍很长时还经常会有人
　　　向你确认 Are you in line?）

值得这么等　well worth all the waiting　　智能手机　smart phone

轻松胜出　is the best…, hands down　　触摸屏　touch screen

铃声　ring tone　　　　　　　　　　　操作系统　operating system

方便使用的　user-friendly　　　　　　　鲜明的　vivid

具体的　detailed　　　　　　　　　　　笨重的　cumbersome

[剑桥例句] Modern hand-held cameras are far less cumbersome.

特色功能　features　　　　　　　　　　让人心烦　bother sb.

[剑桥例句] Our latest model of mobile phone has several new features.

接收　reception　　　　　　　　　　　存储　storage

抱怨　complain 电池一次充电后的使用时间（容易只看字面而误解为电池的终生寿命）
　　　battery life

……兆内存　…GB（考试时对它的发音请说 gigabytes /ˈgigəˌbaits/）

其他的手机常见功能：

内置相机　built-in camera　　　　　　折叠键盘　folding keyboard

发短信　texting / text-messaging（我在国外几乎从没听人说过 send short
　　　messa-ges，而且生活里 text 也还经常当动词用：I'll text you.）

限量版·　limited edition / special edition（这两个很地道的英文表达最
　　　开始只是用在出版物的限量发行，但现在英美生活里已经被广
　　　泛地用于各种产品了）

请参考Pat的思路，并适当借鉴这个词汇表里的单词，思考如果是您会怎么说

Pat 的海外生活英语实录

　　在英美，数码爱好者们对于 gadget（它可以指任何小型的电子或者数码产品）
这个词真的是情有独钟，几乎已经达到了"逢码必用的程度"。而另一个经常会与它
伴随使用的词则是 handy（灵巧轻便的）：

【剑桥例句】

(1) Have you seen this handy little gadget?

(2) This handy gadget is great for storing important data.

☆ 电子物品之 数码相机

这个简单给大家描述一下。

难度指数：★ ★ ★ ☆ ☆

Pat 的答案

I'd like to talk about my digital camera. It's a Nikon. I bought it in Hong Kong. I think it's cool.

It's got a sleek black body, is light and pretty handy. The 2.5 inch LCD screen is large and clear. The touch-screen menu control is very convenient.

And... what else? Oh, I almost forgot. It's a 10X-zoom camera so the photos look great.

It uses an SD card so I can download everything onto the hard drive of my PC.

Most importantly, the 5 mega-pixel sensor gives me sharp pictures. You know, the colours are always accurate...

轮到你了

It's Your Turn.

▶ **Word Bank on This Topic**

光亮的 sleek

请注意听 CD 朗读下面品牌的英文名称：

| Nikon | Canon | Lenovo | Kodak | Fuji |
| Sony | Samsung | Ricoh | Olympus | |

小巧的 handy   触摸屏 touch-screen

变焦　zoom（光学变焦叫做 optical zoom，而数码变焦则是 digital zoom）

百万像素　mega-pixel　　　　感光器　sensor

精确的　accurate

[剑桥例句] We hope to become more accurate in predicting earthquakes.

> 请参考Pat的思路，并适当借鉴这个词汇表里的单词，思考如果是您会怎么说

Pat 的海外生活英语实录

　　英文里的相机叫做 camera，摄像机是 video camera，监控录像机叫 surveillance（它的读音是/səˈveiləns/）camera。但网络聊天时用的"摄像头"地道英文又叫什么呢？不能叫 computer camera ⊠，而要说 webcam 才够地道。另外还要提醒大家一下：出国后当您看到 CCTV 这个缩写，千万不要以为是央视驻英国记者站，其实它在英美生活里是指"闭路电视"。而"有线电视"在国外实际生活里就是被很简单地称为 cable（TV）才最地道。

　　【剑桥例句】Webcams allow moving pictures and sound to be broadcast on the Internet as they happen.

Time to Branch Out.
推而广之

Describe a gift you received.

Describe something that you lost.

补充弹药

It's the thought that counts.　（固定习语）重要的是心意。	
considerate　体贴的	thankful　感激的
precious　珍贵的	look high and low for...　到处找……
upset　心烦的	regret doing sth. / having done sth.　后悔做某事

☆ 电子物品之 iPad 2

Pat 指南

早在 Pat 还上大学的时候 Apple 就已经掳得了相当多北美大学生的倾心，每次做集体的 presentation 放眼望去尽是一只只闪亮的 Mac 大白苹果。而现在，Apple 则又通过 iPad 2 进一步加固了它在年轻人心目中的崇高地位（exalted status）。但 Pat 关心的并不是 iPad 2 怎样迎接 Motorola Xoom 的挑战，而是咱们怎样才能用最浅显的英文来介绍它。

难度指数 ★★★☆☆

Pat 的答案

Honestly, to get my iPad 2, I waited for five hours in line. So you can imagine how excited I was when I finally got my hands on it!

It's super slim, nothing like my bulky laptop, and light as well, which makes it perfectly portable. I can easily carry my iPad 2 with just one hand. The display is bright and sharp. And the A5 processor is so speedy it loads websites even faster than my laptop.

The only complaint I have with my iPad 2 is the front-facing camera. The picture quality is kind of disappointing, I have to say. But the back camera is pretty decent and records nice videos.

What else? Oh, the batter life... Well, I can spend a whole afternoon on it and still don't need to recharge the battery, so can't complain.

I should say iPad 2 is an amazing device. All Apple fans should be thankful to Steve Jobs for this, I guess.

轮到你了   It's Your Turn.

▶ **Word Bank on This Topic**

排队等候 wait in line

纤细的，苗条的 slim （这个词在现代英语里经常也会被用来形容轻薄的电子产品）

*D*o you know what amazes me more than anything else?
The impotence of force to organize anything.

—Napoleon Bonaqarte

笨重的　bulky

[剑桥例句] The book was too bulky to fit into her bag.

笔记本电脑　laptop/notebook （但在真实的国外生活里 laptop 这个词远比 notebook 更
　　　　　加常用）

便于携带的　portable　　　　　处理器　processor

[剑桥例句] Computers become lighter and more portable every year.

快速的，迅捷的　speedy

加载网页　load websites

抱怨，不满　complaint （请注意这是名词，动词则少一个 t 是 complain）

不错的　decent （这个词在日常口语里其实和"体面的"真没啥关系，反倒是很像
　　quite good）

[剑桥例句] Are there any decent restaurants around here?

充电　recharge　　　　　　　设备，仪器　device

[剑桥例句] Rescuers used a special device for finding people trapped in the building.

史蒂夫·乔布斯　Steve Jobs （大名鼎鼎的 Apple's CEO，截至本书完稿时 Steve Jobs
　　　　　先生仍在病重休养，在此衷心祝愿他能早日康复）

粉丝　an avid fan of... （当你发现仅仅用 fan 已经不能表达出对于某事的热衷程度的时
　　候，avid 将是你的最拿分选择）

同系列里在它之前的产品，前身　predecessors

[剑桥例句] The latest Ferrari is not only faster than its predecessors
but also more comfortable.

请参考Pat的思路，并适当借鉴这个词汇表里的单词，思考如果是您会怎么说

电子游戏机　game console / game device （在英美人们玩得比较多
的是 Wii /wiː/, PS3, Xbox 360 和 GameCube）

Pat 的海外生活英语实录

　　平心而论，Apple 的很多产品已经超出了生活必需品（necessities）的范围，而
成为奢侈品（luxuries）。它们的主要意义已不再是满足人们对功能（functionality）的
需求，而是给我们提供了更多的休闲选择。"休闲"，除了 relax，还有个相当常用的口
语词叫 unwind（发音/ʌnˈwaind/）。如果您觉得这个表达不好理解那么可以这样想——
英文里的 wind up 是把东西拧紧，而 unwind 则是让绷紧的弦彻底放松下来。

【剑桥例句】

(1) A glass of wine in the evening helps me to unwind after work.

(2) I'm just going to watch some TV and unwind.

☆ 电子物品之 优盘

难度指数：★★★☆☆

Pat 的答案

I just bought a USB disk yesterday. Actually it's just like any other USB disks. You know, tiny, light but sturdy. It has a storage capacity of 1 Gigabytes.

What I really like about this USB disk is it has a fast transfer rate, fast as lightning.

How do I use it? Well, I just connect it to my computer via a USB port and all set. It's compatible with both Microsoft and Mac systems…

It's a keeper.

轮到你了   It's Your Turn.

▶ **Word Bank on This Topic**

电子用品 electronic device / electronic gadget

坚固的 sturdy   储存容量 storage capacity

输送速度 transfer rate

像闪电一样快（这是一个很地道的英文成语） fast as lightning

通过……（传输） via (prep.)   接口 port

一切就绪。 All set.   兼容的 compatible with…

[剑桥例句] This new software may not be compatible with old operating systems.

苹果的操作系统 Mac / Macintosh   值得保留的东西 keeper

一张图片可以说明一千个文字才能说明的问题（常用成语）

A picture is worth a thousand words.

请参考Pat的思路，并适当借鉴这个词汇表里的单词，思考如果是您会怎么说

Pat 的海外生活英语实录

除了 USB disk 之外，优盘有时在生活里也有人会说 USB drive。这个似乎不好理解，但在实际生活里大家就这么说。那么电脑的"硬盘"又应该叫什么呢？严格来说应该是叫 hard disk，但是在实际日常生活里绝大多数人却都是用 hard drive 来指"硬盘"，也许不够严谨，但对于交流来说却已足够有效。英语在欧洲语言里没有法语优雅，没有德语严谨，也不像希腊语那样"富于哲理"，但它最终还是凭借其实用性成为了全世界最通用的语言。忽视英语在现实生活里的实际用法去闭门造车，只会导致更多的沟通不畅。

【剑桥例句】The hard drive is fixed inside your computer and stores a large amount of information.

3. 照片

☆ 照片之 合影

> Describe a photo that you like.
>
> You should say:
> what the photo is
> when it was taken
> why you like it
> and explain whether you still keep it.

Pat 指南

很多同学都觉得这道题即使用中文也很难讲到 1'30" 以上，而且即使说了一点也会很生硬（so artificial and mechanical）。我仔细想了一下，确实即使让考生用自己的母语描述一张 photo 也很难，因为照片是平面的（two-dimensional），放大过之后也只有那么大，只能从一个 corner 描述到另一个 corner。其实说 wedding photo 不错，可以顺便把明天我们要学到的 wedding 扯进来，不过如果你自己还没结婚却总惦记着人家的 wedding photo 可能会有点怪（weird）……

所以 Pat 坚定地认为这个话题至少应该说人的照片，这样内容马上就灵活了。否则内容肯定有限。比如说你和一个朋友怎样拍的合影（合影的地道英文就是 a photo of... and

297

me）就不会很难或者说无意中（by chance）拍到一个名人（celebrity）的照片也不错，至少可以合理合法地把这个名人描述 2 ~3 句吧（不要太多！Less is more.）。

难度指数：★★★★☆

[Pat 的答案]

My favourite photo is a photo of... (Put the celebrity's name here.) and me. It was taken a couple of months ago while I was at the Hong Kong airport, waiting for my flight.

It was like... I was chatting with a bunch of friends. All of sudden, I spotted a guy who looked exactly like... (the name again), which made me soooooo curious.

... is... （这里很自然地加入 2 ~3 句介绍这个 celebrity 的句子，不要长，这部分可以用现在时态）

So I just approached him and asked if he was ... That gentleman smiled politely and nodded yes. I got so excited and asked if I could take a picture with him 'cause I was such a big fan of him.

You know what he said? He was like, " Of course!" And he even said " cheese" and made a V sign ... He really made my day!

After I returned home, I got the picture framed and hung it on my bedroom wall. Honestly, I didn't expect such a famous person to be so laid-back and so approachable...

轮到你了　　　　　　　　　　　　　　　　　　It's Your Turn.

▶ Word Bank on This Topic

航班 flight　　　　　　　　　　看见 see / spot

[剑桥例句] If you spot any mistakes in the article just mark them with a pencil.

好奇的　curious　　　　　走近　approach　　　　　点头　nod

"茄子"　cheese（请注意中文照相说茄子，而英文照相说 cheese "奶酪"）

放松的　laid-back　　　　放在镜框里　frame

值得回忆的　memorable　　容易接近的　approachable

[剑桥例句] Graham's very approachable — why don't you just talk the problem over with him?

捕捉　capture　　　　　珍贵的瞬间　precious moments

V sign　V 形的手势以前我在国外一直听说是代表 peace，回国之后才听
　　　　说可以代表胜利，好像更有道理（victory）

让我一天都很开心　... really made my day！（这个在地道英文里太常用了，要多用）

请参考Pat的思路，并适当借鉴这个词汇表里的单词，思考如果是您会怎么说

Pat 的海外生活英语实录

说人 "很上镜的"，不能说 good on a camera ☒，而要说 He/She's very photogenic.（它的发音是/ˌfəutəuˈdʒenik/）照片照得比真人好看要说 It's a flattering photo. 而照片把人的缺陷全都给拍出来了则要说 The photo looks quite candid. 说一个人 "不喜欢照相" 在地道英文里则要说成他/她 "面对镜头害羞" He's / She's camera shy.

【剑桥例句】Freya is very photogenic. She has the type of face that looks attractive in a photo.

Time to Branch Out.
推而广之

Describe an important letter you received / you wrote.

补充弹药

Extra Ammo

a nice surprise	惊喜	emotional	动情的
convey	(v.) 表达	moving	感人的
be moved to tears	被感动得流泪		

4. 手工制作

☆ **手工制作之 风筝**

> Describe something you made yourself.
>
> You should say:
>   what the thing was
>   how you made it
>   why you made it
> and explain whether you still have this thing today.

Pat 指南

北京给我印象最深的是什么？不是 the Forbidden City，也不是 the courtyard houses，更不是 Peking Roast Duck，而是晴天时北京天空上的风筝，那么自由，那么悠闲（carefree）。世界各地的城市我去了很多，但就是没有一个城市的人像北京人这么爱放风筝，这是简单的快乐（simple pleasures in life）。上课练习的时候，让很多孩子描述 making a kite，但是怎么听都像在背百科辞典（encyclopedia）。Let me give it a try. 我一点也不怕话题跟你重复，只要我用的英语比你的简单。

难度指数：★★★☆☆

Pat 的答案

I made a simple kite for my cousin last week. Since I'd never made a kite before, I'd thought it must be tricky. But it turned out that making a kite was actually just a breeze.

I decided on its shape first. You know, I just chose a flat one coz obviously it was the most basic form and could be easily carried around. Then I got a sheet of coloured paper and cut out the shape.

My cousin found some thin plastic strips for me. I tied them together with a string, which, apparently, would be the frame of the kite. After that, we made the "bridle", which connected the frame to the control line. Finally, I glued the paper to the frame.

All set. Ready for the "maiden flight".

It flew pretty well. Our hard work paid off.

I have no idea what happened to it later — maybe it got thrown away. My cousin is just an 8-year-old, anyway...

轮到你了   It's Your Turn.

▶ **Word Bank on This Topic**

表弟/表妹/表姐/表哥　cousin（一个词有这么多可能的选择，这样的"万能"词汇可以提高你在考试时的快速反应能力）

一张纸　a sheet of paper　　　　　不容易做的　tricky

简单易行的事情　It's a breeze（国内考生普遍熟知 It's a piece of cake，却对这个使用频率同样极高的习语缺乏了解）

[剑桥例句] You won't have any problems with the entrance exam — it's an absolute（绝对的）breeze.

一条　strip　　　　　　　　　　困在一起　tie... together

绳子　string（这里最好不要用 rope）　　明显地　apparently / obviously

框架　frame　　　　　　　　　　粘贴　glue / stick

细的　thin（这也是个万能词，还能表示瘦的，薄的，稀的，甚至夏天穿的衣服少也可以叫 thin summer clothes）

一切就绪了。All set.（这个句子在国外生活里实在太常用，不论在学校、餐馆，还是体育场，都经常能听到，可惜咱们孩子们从来不用）

有回报　pay off　　　　　　　　首航　maiden fight

螺丝刀　screwdriver　　　　　　剪刀　scissors

镊子	tweezers	钳子	pliers
把……拧弯	twist	把……弄弯	bend

[剑桥例句] Make sure you bend your knees when you're picking up heavy objects.

支架	bridle	折纸	paper folding
剪纸	paper cutting	刺绣	embroidery

缝制　knitting（其实有不少英美老奶奶也挺喜欢"打毛衣"的）

| 拼贴 | collage /ˈkɒlɑːʒ/ | 陶艺 | pottery |

请参考Pat的思路，并适当借鉴这个词汇表里的单词，思考如果是您会怎么说

Pat 的海外生活英语实录

　　handicrafts 如果只是业余玩玩儿可以像咱们这样自学成才，但如果要成为高手（pro）那可就要付出艰苦的努力了。艰苦的努力，考生多数会用 hard effort，strong 或者 painful effort 这样的表达，但其实 arduous effort 才是表达这个意思最为精确的一个固定短语。不少国内朋友看过 Donald Trump 的 *The Apprentice*（学徒）那档节目，就能深刻体会"学徒"得需要付出多少的 arduous effort 才能变成"师傅"了。在地道英文里还有个习语叫 It's a long and winding road. 同样也是用来形容实现目标的艰辛过程。

　　【剑乔例句】The journey was long and arduous.

Time to Branch Out.
推而广之

Describe a toy.

　　Are kites toys? Well, it depends on how toys are defined. According to *Longman* and *Oxford* dictionaries, toys are just objects for children to play with. So...

补充弹药

run around	到处跑	flip（*v.*）	翻滚
high up in the sky	在高空	laid-back	放松的
pastime	业余爱好	kite-flying（*n.*）	放风筝

5. 服装

☆ 服装之 旗袍/唐装

> Describe an item of clothing you like.
>
> You should say:
> 　　what the item is
> 　　where / When you bought it
> 　　what it looks like
> and explain when you wear it.

Pat 指南

雅思口语中还有一个题目是描述 your favourite traditional clothing。所以建议大家准备旗袍（Chi-pao）或者唐装话题，这样就把两个题一起准备了。唐装有很多种翻译方法，但是大多数的英文听着特别扭（They sound so awkward.）。我会叫它 Tang suit，至少这个听着还算自然。说旗袍和唐装除了历史不一样，其实多数内容还是一样的，不过 Pat 个人感觉唐装比较宽松（loose-fitting），所以它的效果主要是让男士看起来更富贵（well-heeled / well-off），而不是像紧身的（tight-fitting）旗袍那样让女士看起来更优雅（elegant/graceful）。

难度指数：★★★★☆

Pat 的答案

Let me talk about my Chi-pao. It was a birthday gift from my folks.

It's essentially a one-piece dress. But it looks unique because of the fabric, I mean, the silk, and the embroidery. Also, the bell-like sleeves and the slits on the sides all make it so different from regular dresses.

My Chi-pao is pretty easy to slip on and really comfortable to wear. And it accentuates my figure coz it's pretty tight-fitting. Actually, I guess that's exactly why it's so popular these days.

I wear it during the Spring Festive and other family occasions like family reunions, as the embroidery feels very festive.

Now let me share with you something about the history of Chi-pao. (*If you don't think you'll have time for this during the Part 2 test, just skip it and go straight to the next paragraph.*) It was popular among the Manchurian women in the Qing Dynasty. But now it represents the traditional Chinese clothing in general and is often considered a national treasure.

The only minor quibble I have about my Chi-pao is that many waitresses wear Chi-pao in restaurants too. So sometimes it can be really confusing or even embarrassing...

轮到你了	It's Your Turn.

▶ Word Bank on This Topic

父母 folks / parents	本质上 essentially
连衣裙 a dress（这时候它是可数的）	独特的 unique
面料 fabric	刺绣 embroidery
铃铛 bell	袖子 sleeves
窄缝 slit	普通的，常规的 regular

[剑桥例句] Her heartbeat was regular.

穿上 slip on / put on	强调，突显 accentuate

[剑桥例句] The short black dress accentuated her slimness.

身材 figure	紧身的 tight-fitting
场合 occasion	家庭团聚 family reunion

[剑桥例句] We're having a family reunion next week.

喜庆的	festive	代表	represent / symbolise
国宝	national treasure	让人困惑的	confusing
小的抱怨	minor quibble	优雅的	graceful / elegant
让人羞愧的	embarrassing	复杂的	complicated
规则的花纹	pattern	制服	uniform
鲜花（图案）的	floral	丝绸	silk
庆祝	celebrates	棉布	cotton
绒布	velvet	皇族	the royal family
满族的民族服装	Manchurian costumes	身份的象征	status symbol
民族服装	ethnic costumes		

请参考Pat的思路，并适当借鉴这个词汇表里的单词，思考如果是您会怎么说

Pat 的海外生活英语实录

适度注意着装是必要的，甚至也可能成为竞争时的一个优势（a competitive edge）。但如果一个人过度地追求时尚，那么就会变成 a fashion victim 了。

【剑桥例句】Ellie is a fashion victim. She always wears trendy clothes even if the clothes sometimes make her look silly.

雅思口试中偶尔还会咕咕冒出一张卡片：

Describe an item of clothing / a piece of jewellery（首饰）**you like.** 如果真赶上这个卡片，那真的要好好反思一下考前是否虐待过小动物或者坐公车没主动给老年人让座了。点点 www.jewelinfo4u.com 上面的一堆链接也许是个不错的选择，对各种首饰的解释都细致入微。但 ad 就可以跳过不必看，出国之后欣赏好首饰的机会是无穷无尽的，先赶紧把考试过了再"小资"不晚。

下面是最有名的一些时尚名牌，很多还没有标准的中文翻译，请大家仔细听光盘中的发音。它们中大多数都不是英语，发音都是很容易错的哦。

BURBERRY	FENDI	CHANEL
GUCCI	CHOLE	HERMES
BVLGARI	DOLCE&GABBANA	LOUIS VUITTON
VERSACE	SALVATORE FERRAGAMO	MARC JACOBS
ANNA SUI	SWAROVSKI	

6. 双语感悟之　自行车 Random Bilingual Reflections on Biking

Describe an invention（before the age of computers）.

计算机之前的发明，bicycle 也许绝对是最值得我们继续使用也最环保的一种了。

首先，It was invented in the late 19th century by some Frenchmen. 然后，It became popular immediately coz it was inexpensive and easy to ride. 立刻流行起来了，原因很明显啊。

Now millions of people ride their bike on a daily basis.（"每天"也可以这么说的）Some people are bike commuters.（骑自行车上下班的人，commute 是每天上下班的过程。）Others just ride a bike for pleasure / recreation.（另一些人就是为了那种乐趣）I like biking coz I love the feel of the breeze on my face.（微风吹着就更舒服了）

再了解一下 bike 的组成部分（parts / components）：

铃铛叫 bell，不过好像我在北京骑过的几辆车铃铛都不响（on the blink），车把叫 handlebars，车闸叫 brake，横梁是 crossbar，车座叫 saddle，脚踏板是 pedals（所以英文也经常说 pedal my bike），链条叫做 chain，轮子当然就是 tyre（BrE）/tire（AmE）了。

有些比较贵的自行车还有变速器，这个日常口语里管它叫 shifter，正式英文怎么说真的不知道。

如果车很新就说 brand-new，很旧就说 worn-out/beat-up，已经很久没骑过了就说 It's gathering dust now.

另外，在 Day 7 里面我们讲过 biking 的好处也都可以拿过来说说，或者稍变化一下，比如 It's cool especially when the gas price is soaring（急速上升）, coz bikes don't need any fuel（燃料）.

biking 其实也可以叫 cycling，比如您就可以说 Cycling is ecofriendly coz it's zero-emission.（零排放）

上次回 Vancouver 的时候听说最新研发出了一种叫 e-bikes（网络自行车）的东东，这个我真的想不明白了（I reaaaaaaaally can't figure that out. / It goes right over my head.）。

Time to Branch Out.
推而广之

Describe a car or a bicycle.

补充弹药

transform（*vt.*）=fundamentally change　彻底改变

profound influence　深刻的影响

altered the course of history　改变了历史的进程

user-friendly　方便使用的

更多本类话题句型　Bonus Sentences（高分内容）

It's my lucky charm（护身符）.

It's our family heirloom（传家宝）.

It's so precious（珍贵的）to me.

At first, I couldn't afford it.

Eventually, I saved up enough money for it.

I rushed to the store and bought it right away.

It drives off my loneliness.

It's a source of pleasure and fun for me.

It's always at the center of attention because of its fancy-looking exterior.

This car consists of many parts, such as the hood, the trunk, the engine, bumpers, side mirrors, rear-view mirrors, the dashboard, speedometer, odometer, plus airbags and the ABS system.

It's so exquisite.

Actually, I have mixed feelings about it.

It's not my cup of tea.

另类话题 Off-the-Wall Topics

如果说奔驰（Mercedes）是身份的象征（status symbol），那么悍马（Hummer）在北京就是属于最有钱的那个群体了（the upper crust）。我自己在加拿大开过一次 Hummer H3，除了感觉到了 " the wow factor"（让身边的人们惊叹的效果），就是感觉汽油在不停地烧，这种车真不是给我们这种需要考虑油价的人设计的。

下面这段是一普通人 买了 Hummer 之后就像拿了个烫手山芋（英文里叫"烫手土豆" hot potato）的无比纠结的心态，请仔细体会用词简单却清晰易懂的效果，这才是每天人们在用的真实英文：

I bought this Hummer for my wife. She just loved it. But I hated it from the start. It was not comfortable for me to drive. As a matter of fact, I refused to drive it. I would rather drive my Ford 'cause it has a better ride and gets better mileage. Most ladies I have talked to enjoy it because they feel safe and yes it is a safe car to a certain point. We have had it for least a year and my wife and son both have had backing accidents due to the bad blind spots. If I had to drive it everyday, it would have a new home. But luckily I don't so it'll stay put till my wife gets tried of it as well.

(*gas mileage: We've learned this in our Mini Cooper segment, right?*

backing: When you back up your car, it goes backward.

blind spot: The part of the road that you can't see when you drive a car.)

对本类话题有价值的网址

下面的网址对骨灰级 DIYer 准备关于物品类的常考题也会很有帮助：

家用电器：

http://www.dixons.co.uk/gbuk/index.html（It gives detailed descriptions of tons of home appliances）

手工艺品：

http://www.estudychinese.com/web/aboutchina/culture/handicrafts/index.htm（This is a useful bilingual site focusing on Chinese arts and crafts.）

传统服装：

http://www.costumes.org/ethnic/1pages/asiancostlinks.htm#China（It's a very informative website dedicated to Asian costumes.）

F 曾经沧海

Pat 解题 Pat's Decryption

这一节我们突破最后一大类卡片：经历。

描述经历的题中，有很多是关于 an event 的。要描述好 an event，我们首先要对什么是 event 做个定义：

"A social occasion or activity"，这是 Merriam Webster 对 event 的解释。

"something that happens, especially something important, interesting or unusual"，这是 *Longman* 对 event 的解释。

所以真的不需要担心得太多，只要是符合卡片要求的"事件"都可以介绍，一般来说卡片要求你描述的 event 本身已经带有一些特殊性了。

解决了关于 events 的顾虑，我还要再提醒大家，说到 an event 或者 an experience 的时候经常会用到下面的词组（不一定每个都会用到，但是经常会用到其中的某几个）：At first, ...; But then, ...; So, ...; After that, ...; Then, ...; Next, ...; Finally / Eventually, ... 因为它们可以帮我们把顺序（sequence）讲清楚。

今天我们还会谈到人生中一个重要的 event —— wedding。如果说东西方婚礼的差异，Pat 观察到的是西方的婚礼仪式（wedding ceremony）比较强调 spirituality（精神意义），仪式本身相对比较 simple（其实花钱也不少，但把钱主要都留给后面的 wedding reception 和更贵的 honeymoon 了），而中国的婚礼仪式则更务实（pragmatic）。比如"闹洞房"（The couple's friends mess around in their bedroom.）就有很好的喜庆效果，好玩儿。

展开本类话题思路的线索 Brainstorming Techniques
（熟悉下面的表格可以确保你在拿到任何本类卡片题时都能有话说）

Experience
What
Why
When
Where
Who
How
My own feeling/ Other "rounding off" remarks

Do you know what amazes me more than anything else?
The impotence of force to organize anything.

—Napoleon Bonaqarte

本类话题最新完整真题库　The Complete Question Pool on This Topic

✱ Describe a happy event.

✱ Describe an exciting message/a piece of good news you heard on the phone.

✱ Describe a sports event.

✱ Describe a special meal you had recently.

✱ Describe an activity in an English lesson.

✱ Describe a science lesson.（本话题请见 Day 10）

✱ Describe a piece of work that was done quickly.

✱ Describe a difficult thing that you did well.

✱ Describe something you would like to succeed in doing.

✱ Describe a skill.

✱ Describe a happy family event.

✱ Describe a festival that is popular in your country.

✱ Describe an occasion that you were late for.

✱ Describe an unhappy shopping experience.

✱ Describe a wedding you have attended.

✱ Describe a family photo.

✱ Describe a birthday party.

✱ Describe a party you prepared for others.（本话题请见 Day 10）

✱ Describe an important change in your life.

✱ Describe an important letter you wrote.

分级演示　A Spectrum of Sample Answers

1. 让人开心的事

Describe a happy event.

You should say:

    what it was

    where it was held

    who went to the event

and explain why it was a happy event.

Pat 指南

    让人开心的事件选择挺多的，最重大的比如 wedding（今天咱们也将研究，谁让 Part 2 题库里有这个话题呢，但多数去留学的烤鸭应该至今还没作为主角出席过 wedding，所以对 happy 的程度感受可能还不够深）；意义比较小的比如被特许参加了某个新游戏的"封测"（internal testing／alpha testing）。

    不大不小又而最容易说清楚的，那就是毕业典礼了。不过在英美即使中学毕业典礼都是非常被家长们重视的（孩子自己倒不一定），也要"带博士帽穿袍子"（cap／mortarboard and gown）。而在北美的很多大学里毕业典礼还有个寓义深刻的说法叫 commencement（开始）。仔细想想挺对的，毕业典礼其实并不仅是上一个阶段的"毕业"，更标志着人生一个新阶段的"开始"不是么？

    难度指数：★★★☆☆

Pat 的答案

Let me talk about my graduation ceremony. Actually the ceremony was very short and kind of too formal but still, it was a happy event.

On that day, my classmates and I were all dressed in caps and gowns and arrived early. Our parents and friends also came, with bouquets or gifts in their hands. After the guests were seated, we lined up in order and walked in. Then the principal and some guest speakers delivered speeches and some awards were presented.

The most important part of the ceremony was, obviously, the awarding of diplomas, you know, when the students got called up to the podium, one by one, shook hands with the principal and received our diploma. Unfortunately, a couple of my classmates failed to get enough credits so they didn't get a diploma.

Then after the ceremony, I took lots and lots of pictures with my classmates, coz I knew graduation would be the end of the years with these wonderful friends of mine.

The graduation ceremony was not just a happy ending to a past academic experience, it also marked the beginning of a whole new stage, probably an even more challenging one, in my life…

轮到你了   It's Your Turn.

▶ Word Bank on This Topic

有点   kind of   正式的   formal

毕业典礼用的"博士帽"和"袍子"   cap and gown （这是口语里最常听到的说法，正式一点则可以说 mortarboard and gown）

花束（请注意听光盘里它的发音） bouquet   就座   be seated

[剑桥例句] Chris sent Evelvn a bouquet when she was ill.

排成队   line up in order

中学校长   principal （大学校长则多数叫 president）   做演讲   deliver a speech

发毕业证书   the awarding of diplomas

领奖台（对于毕业典礼来说则是"领证台"） podium

两三个   a couple of   学分   credit

一个好的结局   a happy ending   学术的   academic

标志着   mark / represent / symbolise   阶段   stage

高兴的   delighted / elated （后面这个词较为正式而且语气很强，但偶尔在生活里也能听到）

[剑桥例句] I was delighted by your news.

场合   occasion

[剑桥例句] We met on several occasions to discuss the issue.

请参考Pat的思路，并适当借鉴这个词汇表里的单词，思考如果是您会怎么说

Pat 的海外生活英语实录

如果要说一段经历是自己人生里的"转折点",同学们多数会用 It was a turning point for me. 其实这个说法本身挺不错,但用的人过多容易被考官 takes it for granted。其实还有另外两种说法在地道英文里也很常用,但国内考生几乎从来不用:It altered my lifestyle. 和 It was a watershed moment in my life.

【剑桥例句】

(1) Giving up our car has altered our lifestyle.

(2) The year 1969 was a watershed in Madison's life — she changed her career and changed her partner.

2. 体育事件

Describe a sports event.

You should say:
    what it was
    where it was held
    who went to the event
and explain why it was special.

Pat 指南

最容易准备、不需要特别的专业知识的,肯定是 the Olympic Games。因为权威的朗文词典对 the Olympic Games 的英文定义就是:a modern international sports event in which people of all nationalities... 完全符合这个题目的所有要求。而且我还专门向环球雅思的几位前任和现任考官进行了确认,大家一致认为,奥运会是符合题目要求的,关键是你怎么描述才能最清晰。由于 2012 年的伦敦奥运会还没开,所以我们目前只能先用上一届的北京奥运会了解一下描述 sports event 的关键字。

难度指数:★★★★☆

Pat 的答案

As you probably know, three years ago the Beijing Olympic Games attracted worldwide attention.

EVERYTHING was just so impressive, the torch relay, the opening ceremony, the competitions, the closing ceremony... you name it.

What I particularly liked about the Beijing Olympics was that the ceremonies had a Chinese "feel" to them, which made them so unique.

During those two weeks, Beijing was teeming with visitors. The Olympic venues like the "Bird's Nest" and the "Water Cube" were absolutely breathtaking. And the city offered an amazing variety of museums, night clubs, restaurants and shopping malls. And some traffic was ordered off the streets to keep the Beijing skies clear.

I felt proud of myself coz I volunteered for the Beijing Olympics. You know, I helped out disabled people and looked for translation errors on public signs. It felt different being a volunteer in Beijing, since the city was huge and there were already so many volunteers available. Anyway, it was fun to be part of it.

We rooted for China, of course. But we Chinese sports buffs also made some foreign athletes our idols, like Michael Phelps and Kobe Bryant.

The Beijing Olympics blended sports with culture. A totally incredible sports event!

轮到你了　　　　　　　　　　　　　　　　　　It's Your Turn.

> **▶ Word Bank on This Topic**
>
> 火炬传递 torch relay　　　　　　　　　　应有尽有 ... you name it
>
> 氛围 feel (*n.*) /atmosphere　　　　　　独特的 unique
>
> 充满了 be teeming with... / be packed　奥运场馆 venue
>
> [剑桥例句] The train was so packed that I couldn't find a seat.
>
> （作）志愿者 volunteer（这个词可以作 *n.* / *v.* / *adj.*） 残疾人 disabled people
>
> 公共标识 public signs　　　　　　　　　支持（比赛中的某一方）root for
>
> 因为 because / coz / since　　　　　　　运动员 athlete

315

体育迷　sports buff

吉祥物　mascot

[剑桥例句] The Olympic Games always has an official mascot.

难以置信的（一般是指积极的）　incredible

见证　witness

独特的　distinctive

精美的　exquisite

[剑桥例句] Anna's got a very distinctive voice.

请参考Pat的思路，并适当借鉴这个词汇表里的单词，思考如果是您会怎么说

Pat 的海外生活英语实录

"激烈的竞赛"，基础好的考生一般都知道 fierce competition 这个短语。但地道的英文口语里还有个说法，用来描述体育比赛的激烈程度属于当仁不让的好词：**cliffhanger**。想象一下被悬在悬崖上的感觉多么让人紧张，就知道这样的比赛会是多么"扣人心弦"。

【剑桥例句】

(1) It looks as if the election is going to be a cliffhanger.

(2) Netherlands beat Kenya in a cliffhanger in their 2011 World Cup warm-up match.

3. 英语课堂演讲

☆ 英语课堂活动之　presentation / an interesting speech

> Describe an activity in an English lesson.
>
> You should say:
>   what the activity was
>   what you learned from this activity
>   why you enjoyed it
> and explain whether you would like to do a similar activity again.

Do you know what amazes me more than anything else?
The impotence of force to organize anything.

—Napoleon Bonaqarte

Pat 指南

国外大学在教学形式上有很多和国内不一样，有些 Pat 一直没想清楚应该怎么翻译成中文，比如 seminar 和 term paper，还有一个很常见的就是 presentation。我把这个答案写得比较长，其实用词并不难，希望大家能预先好好体会一下国外课堂的"轻松"感觉。

难度指数：★★★☆☆

Pat 的答案

Last week, our English teacher asked us to prepare for a presentation on the differences between some British writers and their works. He told us how we should structure our presentation and then divided us into pairs.

So after class, my teammate and I went to the library and checked out a whole bunch of books on those writers. After that, we read the materials thoroughly and figured out what we would present. Then we started making visual aids. You know, we used Power Point to make the information we were going to present more memorable. We also made some note cards to guide the direction of the presentation.

During the actual presentation, my teammate did the introduction and then managed the aids while I presented our findings. At first, I was a bit nervous up in front of the class. But gradually I began to feel at ease. When I forgot what I should say next, I just glanced down at the note cards and then I remembered what I was supposed to say.

My teacher and my classmates were totally impressed with our knowledge. So after we finished the presentation, some of them approached us right away to compliment us on our performance.

I learned a lot from that experience, like preparation could really make all the difference between a good and a bad presentation.

I'm looking forward to our next presentation now...

▶ Word Bank on This Topic

课堂演讲（我只能想到这么翻译，如果您想到有更好的翻译方法请及时 text 我）

presentation

安排结构　structure（*vt.*）   作品　works

【剑桥例句】The museum has many works by Picasso as well as other modern painters.

详细的　thorough   借书　check out books

[剑桥例句] They did a thorough search but found nothing.

视觉提示工具　visual aid   想出　figure out

感到适应的　feel at ease   容易记忆的　memorable

[剑桥例句] Logan felt completely at ease.

走近　approach   低头看一眼　glance down at

表现　performance（这里不是表演的意思）   夸奖　compliment

产生差异　make the difference between... and...   准备　preparation（*n.*）

录像　videotape   团队精神　team spirit

提示自己用的小卡片　note cards（这也是在国外做 presentation 的常用技巧之一）

集体讨论　group discussion   辩论　debate

合作　cooperation（*n.*）   预先"排练"　rehearse

听众　audience

请参考Pat的思路，并适当借鉴这个词汇表里的单词，思考如果是您会怎么说

Pat 的海外生活英语实录

    评价好的 presentation 有很多标准，比如 engaging（能吸引听众注意力的），well-rehearsed（预先"排练"充分的），well-structured（结构合理的）等。但其实说到底唯一的标准就是 presentation 够不够 informative，因为做 presentation 的根本目的就是 deliver information to our target audience。

【剑桥例句】

（1）This is an interesting and highly informative book.

（2）The dietician's（营养学家）talk was very informative.

Time to Branch Out.
推而广之

Describe a success.

Describe a skill.

Describe an important letter you received / wrote.

补充弹药

rewarding　有回报的

boost my confidence　提升我的自信

uplifting　令人振奋的

When the going gets tough, the tough get going.（谚语）

这个其实很像中文的"坚持就是胜利"了。

4. 一场表演

☆ 一场表演之　音乐会

Describe a performance or a show.（such as a dancing or singing performance）

You should say:

    what kind of performance / show it was

    when and where you watched it

    who you watched it with

and explain how you felt about it.

Pat 指南

我自己从高中就开始组织车库乐队，刚回北京的时候还在三里屯的几家酒吧唱过歌。在其中一家唱了一个月后经理就找我谈话，说他们的啤酒销量那个月下降了40%。还有一家在我们唱了7天之后，酒吧倒了（went bust）。不过我仍然很热爱音乐，这里给大家写一段去看 rock concert 的经历吧，大家可以体会一下怎么用英文描述那种热烈的气氛（ambience），估计这个话题大家掌握起来比其他表演容易点。这个答案掌握一半的内容后再描述摇滚音乐会就得心应手（feel at home with it）了。

难度指数：★★★☆☆

Pat 的答案

I went to … (*Put the band's name here.*) 's concert last Friday night. It was held at the Workers' Stadium . You know, I'd long been a big fan of them so when a friend of mine got me a ticket to their concert, I was like, "WOW!" and felt like I was on top of the world.

I just couldn't wait till Friday came around . My friend and I made a huge poster with the members' names on them, to hold up during the concert.

It turned out that **not just** young folks **went there. Actually, the concert** attracted people of all ages . **One more reason for me to feel proud of the band. The stadium was totally** packed !

Then when the band actually took the stage , **we went** fanatical . **Some fans got so thrilled they** cried **and some even** passed out at the sight of the band .

They were amazing performers . **They played songs from many of their** albums , **including their latest** album , **and even played some** acoustic songs , **which was pretty much** the highlight of the concert . **The** live music **and** the thrill **of just being there were** incredible .

We knocked into one another , sang along with the band **and** screamed their names at the top of our lungs. **And you know what? The singers even** noticed our poster **and** waved at us **when they were on stage…**

It was a blast !

轮到你了 It's Your Turn.

▶ Word Bank on This Topic

体育场　stadium　　　　现场的　live (*adj.* / *adv.*)

海报　poster　　　　　挤满了人的　packed（其实口语里这个词比 crowded 更常用）

登台　take the stage　　疯狂的　fanatical / wild / crazy

[剑桥例句] Her enthusiasm for aerobics（有氧健身操）was almost fanatical.

兴奋的　thrilled / excited

昏过去了　pass out（以上三个词都是描述 rock concert 太常用的词汇了）

专辑　album

纯演奏版　（就是不用 MIDI 合成的那种，喜欢玩儿摇滚的朋友肯定能了解我的意思）
　　　　acoustic version

亮点　highlight　　　　难以置信的　incredible

[剑桥例句] Highlights of the match will be shown after the news.

尖叫　scream　　　　　大声的　at the top of our lungs

超级好玩　It was a blast !／We had a great time.

音乐的内涵信息　political messages　（这个基本是 rock concert 少不了的，比如 peace）

气氛　atmosphere / ambience　　场馆　venue

[剑桥例句] The stadium has been specifically designed as a venue for European
Cup matches.

现场音乐会　a live concert　　　嘉宾演出　guest performance

激情　passion　　　　　　　　灯光　lighting

高分贝　high-decibel levels　　不去不行　be dying to go to...

请参考Pat的思路，并适当借鉴这个词汇表里的单词，思考如果是您会怎么说

Pat 的海外生活英语实录

　　如果要说演唱会上歌手和观众之间的"互动"，基础好的同学都能想到
interaction。的确，the interaction between the singer / the band and the audience
（有时也简称为 the singer / band — audience interaction）就是这个意思。

> 但如果问您演唱会上歌迷挥的 "荧光棒" 英文怎样说您能回答么？ glow sticks 就是口语里的 "荧光棒"，而 "挥舞" 则还是 wave 那个动词。不过在英美有些歌手和 DJ 最近还联合发起了一场 *Ban the Glow Sticks* 的运动，也算是为环保做点小贡献吧。

5. 婚礼

```
Describe a wedding you have attended.

You should say:
    when it was
    who got married
    what happened at the wedding
and explain this was a typical wedding.
```

Pat 指南

William 王子的 royal wedding 在全世界获得了 20 亿观众的收视率，可见婚礼永远是一个让人向往的主题。

这道题是说中式婚礼好还是说西式婚礼好呢？To be or not to be. 那是个问题。其实这么想可能会比较清楚：如果两种都能说得很流利很明白，肯定两种都很好，而且中式的应该更好。但是如果本来英文就不流利，发音也不地道，表情还不自然，再给考官说一堆他/她根本不了解的概念，会是什么效果？如果说西式婚礼至少考官的 "听懂率" 还能高一点。

说 wedding，掌握一下顺序（sequence）的描述，还有一些专门的词汇，看完答案之后自己大致回忆一遍就差不多了，也没必要说得 "过好"，毕竟咱们谁也不是每天参加婚礼玩儿的人。

难度指数：★ ★ ★ ★ ☆

Pat 的答案

A friend of mine got married last month. I went to her wedding ceremony. It was held in a church and began at 9 in the morning. It was a typical Western-style ceremony, pretty simple but solemn.

The officiant made some opening remarks. Then the groom, in a black tuxedo, made his way to the altar with the best man and waited there.

When the Wedding March was played, the bride's attendants entered, including the maid of honor and the flower girl. My friend, you know, the bride, entered last in her white wedding dress, escorted by her father.

I was so moved watching my friend walking down the aisle. Then her father left her at the altar with the groom.

At the altar, the couple exchanged wedding vows and wedding rings. Then they kissed and were pronounced husband and wife.

After the ceremony, the couple was showered with handfuls of rice...

The wedding reception was held at the Sheraton Hotel. It was like a big party, you know, when all the guests celebrated the marriage with the bride and groom. Cocktails and food were served...

轮到你了

It's Your Turn.

▶ Word Bank on This Topic

仪式 ceremony	典型的 typical
庄严的 solemn	主持人 officiant
新郎 groom	伴郎 best man（教堂里的）
男士晚礼服（一般在最正式的场合才穿） tuxedo / tux	
神坛 altar	婚礼进行曲 Wedding March
随从 attendants	伴娘 maid of honor

[剑桥例句] The Prince was followed by his attendants.

花童 flower girl(s)

新人 the new couple / the bridal couple / the newly-wed couple

陪伴 escort (v.)	婚纱 wedding dress / wedding gown
交换 exchange	

婚礼誓言 wedding vow（就是那段 Hollywood 电影里经典的

"... from this day forward,

for better, for worse,

for richer, for poorer,

in sickness and in health,

to love and to cherish,

till death us do part...")

宣布　pronounce（这里不是"发音"的意思）

[剑桥例句] The government pronounced they were no longer a nuclear state.

祝酒　propose a toast　　　　　　　祝贺　congratulations (*n.*)

切蛋糕　cake-cutting　　　　　　　蜜月　honeymoon

扔花束（据说拿到花束的女孩就是下一个会结婚的女孩）toss the bouquet

婚宴（婚礼仪式之后）wedding reception / wedding banquet

撒米/纸片或者金属片 shower the couple with handfuls of rice / confetti

请参考Pat的思路，并适当借鉴这个词汇表里的单词，思考如果是您会怎么说

Pat 的海外生活英语实录

　　如果描述一次婚礼，每个考生估计都要说十次以上的 get married。其实地道口语里可以代替这个短语的表达不胜枚举，但是其中的多数在语义或语气上并不适合出现在 IELTS 口试的答案中。一个适合出现在考场里的替换方案是 tie the knot，用一个结把两人牢牢捆起来，可见爱得真挺瓷实的。

【剑桥例句】

（1）So when are you two going to tie the knot?

（2）Evie's going to tie the knot with her German boyfriend next June.

　　Pat 最近在一本介绍中国文化的书里看到一段英文，专门描述中国文化中人生的四大喜事，挺有意思，请看看您能不能猜出来分别是什么：

Marriage is known as one of the four happiest things in one's life. The other three are achievement in examinations, meeting old friends away from home and rainfall after

*D*o you know what amazes me more than anything else?
The impotence of force to organize anything.

—Napoleon Bonaqarte

a drought (a long period of dry weather).

BONUS（附送话题）

顺着上一个婚礼话题的结尾，其实我们可以一起把"**Describe a party.**"这个难题一起准备了。

难度指数：★★★☆☆

After the grand entrance, cocktails and food were served. People proposed toasts and gave the new couple their best wishes. I was sitting next to the groom's father and he told me lots of fun stories about his family.

Then the dancing began. The bride and groom did the first dance. They looked wonderful together and everyone could tell they were deeply in love. The music was slow and it felt soooooo romantic. The dancing went on, you know, the father / daughter dance, the mother / son dance…

A while later, my favourite part, the cake-cutting! The cake was huge and delicious and everyone got a bite…

The most exciting part was probably when the bride tossed her bouquet to the single ladies there coz the girl who got the bouquet was supposed to be the next to marry. All girls tried to become the lucky one but, you know what? A 9-year-old ended up catching it…

At the end of the reception, all of us gathered in a circle and sang happy songs…

That was a really memorable experience.

轮到你了   It's Your Turn.

▶ **Word Bank on This Topic**

新郎新娘 （英文的顺序是 the bride and groom）   到来 the grand entrance

祝酒 propose a toast   吃到一份 get a bite

扔花束 toss the bridal bouquet   值得回忆的 memorable

让人开心的 delightful

请参考Pat的思路，并适当借鉴这个词汇表里的单词，思考如果是您会怎么说

6. 节日

☆ 节日之 端午

> Describe a festival that is popular in your country.
>
> You should say:
>
> what the festival is
>
> what people do during this festival
>
> whether people celebrate this festival in the same way
>
> and explain why this festival is important.

Pat 指南

无数人描述过端午节，这是我的版本。它没有别的好处，唯一的优势是考官一定能听懂。对背景知识则没必要太"死磕"（hung up on），因为即使你说错了估计考官也不知道，英文对就是真的对。

难度指数：★★★☆☆

Pat 的答案

The Duan Wu Festival has become even more popular since it became a public holiday in China.

This festival has long been associated with a famous poet in history, who was so worried about his country that he drowned himself. On this festival, people all across China eat rice balls (*or in Chinese, zong zi*), to pay tribute to this poet. People love those who love their country, right?

Another thing often associated with this festival is the dragon boat races. It's like a number of teams rowing and competing against one another. To be honest, I've only watched boat races on TV. It seems like such races are rare in cities. But from what I saw on TV, I could tell they were very vibrant events.

As I see it, the Duan Wu Festival is about vitality, about the circle of life.

轮到你了 /// It's Your Turn.

▶ **Word Bank on This Topic**

和……联系到一起　is associated with

[剑桥例句] This brand is associated by most people with good quality.

生命的活力　vitality

[剑桥例句] According to the packet（小包装袋）, these vitamin pills will restore lost vitality.

跳河自尽　drown oneself	起源　origin
向……表示敬意　pay tribute to…	元宵节　the Lantern Festival
划船　row	中秋节　the Mid-Autumn Festival
竞争　compete	月饼　mooncake
罕见的　rare	（粽子或者元宵的）填充物，"馅儿"　stuffing

[剑桥例句] I really like the stuffing for the turkey.

有活力的　vibrant / dynamic	豆沙馅　bean paste
竹叶　bamboo leaves	历史悠久的传统　time-honored tradition

[剑桥例句] The developers dealt with the problem in the time-honoured way.

节日活动　festivity	驱难避邪　ward off evil spirits
灯展　display of lanterns	清明节　Tomb-Sweeping Festival
压岁钱　lucky money	红包　red envelope
阴历　the lunar calendar　标志着	mark / represent / symbolize (*vt.*)
许愿　make a wish　午夜倒计时	count down to midnight

请参考Pat的思路，并适当借鉴这个词汇表里的单词，思考如果是您会怎么说

7. 双语感悟之　人生里一个积极的变化

Random Bilingual Reflections on Positive Changes

Describe a positive change in your life.

You should say:
　　when this change happened
　　what this change was

> why it was positive
>
> and explain how this change has influenced your life.

Pat指南

  首先要注意的是：讲这个题目的时态一定要用过去时！然后请想一想什么样的 change 算是 positive change？比如一次 basketball game 之后你的 teammates 让你意识到自己的问题在哪里；又比如一次家长生病了，你人生里第一次真正懂得应该照顾自己的父母；还比如你学开车考驾照（driver's license/driving license），比过去更遵守交通规则了；再比如第一次离开家去别的城市上学，您不得不开始自己叠被子了（made your own bed）。以及决定出国读书后自己的种种变化也可以考虑……只要不紧张，找准话题往下讲就不会觉得太困难。有些地道的套话（clichés）是描述 change 的时候经常用的，比如：

英文	中文
This experience changed the course of my life.	这次经历改变了我的人生道路。
At first, I was really bewildered and frustrated.	刚开始我感到很困惑也很沮丧。
My teammates' encouraging words really cheered me up.	队友们的鼓励话语让我振作起来。
My driving instructor's sound advice led to a major change in my performance.	驾车教练的忠告让我的表现提高了很多。
It not only improved my skills, but solved my attitude problem as well.	这不仅仅提高了我的技术，也让我改变了自己心态上的问题。
For the first time in my life, I found my father so vulnerable and so helpless.	有生以来第一次，我感到父亲这么无助。
This experience had a profound influence on my life.	这段经历对我后来的人生有深远的影响。
I became a caring and loving son/daughter.	这件事情以后，我变成了一个更关心父母的孩子。

（续表）

英文	中文
It prompted me to start working on my agility and team spirit.	这件事促使我提高了我的灵敏程度和团队精神。
That was pretty much a milestone in my life.	这段经历可以说是我人生道路上一个新的里程碑。
It made me tougher and more determined.	这让我变得更坚强，更有决心。
Nothing endures but change.	（这是古希腊哲学家 Heraclitus 的名言，在英美生活中仍然经常被大家引用）世界上唯一不变的是改变。
I saw the light at the end of the tunnel.	（困难时）我终于看到一线光明。

更多本类相关句型　Bonus Sentences（高分内容）

At first everything seemed so tough.

But little by little（=gradually），I got the hang of it（掌握诀窍）.

It was indeed a memorable experience.

All my hard work paid off（有回报）.

Looking back that experience was special indeed.

It was really an eye-opener（让人大开眼界）.

I was so disappointed /frustrated.

But in the end，everything worked out just fine.

临时抱佛脚

有个卡片话题由于内容不好想一直被视为难点中的难点：

Describe an important letter you wrote.

可 Pat 真觉得准备这道题最不需要花时间：既然申请留学或者申请移民当然是要递交申请信的（申请信的英文说 application letter 或者 letter of application 都行，但现在也很时髦在申请资料里单独再写一封 covering letter ）。即使这封申请信并不是您自己写的那么找 agent 把信要一份过来看两遍也就熟悉了，而且今后万一大学或者移民官要面试您也会更清楚应该怎么说，是一举两得的好事不是么（kill two birds with one stone)？

不管你的申请信是如何写的，在描述时都一定能够用到下面几个单词和句型：

I'd like to talk about an application letter / a cover letter I wrote to...

My letter was made up of / consisted of... parts. 这封介绍信包括几个部分……

I explained how and where I learned about （了解到） their program / the position and the reason for my application. 接下来还可以大概说说你申的到底是哪个 program 或者什么 position，即使英语再不好介绍一下自己申的相关专业或者职位肯定还是能扯几句的；

I described my personal and educational / professional qualifications. 这里也可以大概说说自己的教育背景或者工作经历，比如自己的 experience, skills, major... 等。而这些都是国内孩子们在去 English corner 的时候最爱聊的内容，肯定能说得很流利。"最高学历" 的英文叫 highest academic qualification，比如 I hold a Master's Degree in...；

I expressed my desire （在书信里是愿望的意思） for an interview.

I indicated （给出了） how I could be contacted.

I then thanked the reader for reviewing my application and expressed my interest in getting a reply even if it was not what I hoped for.

在结束对这个卡片题的描述之前你还可以再谈谈这封信可能将带来的结果。如果申请结果根本无法确定则可以告诉考官 But everything is still up in the air...

Pat 的海外生活英语实录

如果问我 "班长" 这个词英文怎么说，我只能很老实地回答： "Beats me." （答不上来。）因为在英国和北美的中学里根本就没班长。让老师指定（appoint） 一个学生当班长的做法，即使学生不提出抗议（protest），家长们肯定也不干（They will be up in arms about it.），因为如果这样的话老师的权力（authority） 就太大了，

─────────────

（※申请材料中放入的简短自我介绍信在英国叫 covering letter，而在美国则被称为 cover letter）

在 PTA meeting（家长会，北美的 PTA meeting 在很多中学里每两到三个月就开一次）家长们肯定要向校方直接提出投诉了（file a complaint）。

在英美比较被接受的方式是 student council，这其实并不是学生会，中文大约翻译成"学生政府"比较适合。它是一个很完整的机构，设有 president, vice president, secretaries, treasurer（有点像财政部长，负责管钱的，防止 student council 里的 president 出现经济犯罪）等职位（posts）。

【剑桥例句】

(1) They didn't have the authority to examine the company's records.

(2) We received several complaints about the noise.

(3) Teaching posts are advertised in Tuesday's edition of the paper.

下面这段简单的英文，可以让大家更深入地明白这个 student union 的 "ins and outs"，并且进一步领略"小词"在真实国外生活里的表现力。

Reasons to Run for Student Council

Student government might be a good activity for you if you:

- Like to bring about change.

- Would enjoy a career in politics.

- Enjoy planning events.

- Are outgoing and sociable.

- Have time to attend the meetings

Steps to run for student council:

- Read all the campaign rules carefully. They will differ from school to school.

- Make sure you meet academic requirements.

- Complete the application in a professional way. No messy handwriting or lazy answers. Teachers and advisors will be more supportive if they think that you are serious.

- You may be required to collect a number of signatures from fellow students, teachers, and administrators .

- Find a certain problem or policy that is meaningful to your classmates and make it part of your points. Create a catchy (=easy to remember) slogan .

- Find a friend who can help you create material. Just be sure to follow school rules.

- Prepare a campaign speech .

- Remember to play fair. Don't destroy, or cover over other students' posters .

- Use the Internet and email in your campaign.

都是很简单的英文不是吗？如果对国外学校中的 student union 还想了解更多，请记得一定要看看 *Election* 这部电影，Matthew Broderick 的表演绝对 phenomenal，Reese Witherspoon 演的 Tracy Flick 也真够强势的（pushy），而最神的（wacky）却是它让人没想到的结尾（unexpected ending）…

超短线
The Ultra-Short Track

刚开始在国外大学上课时，很多中国孩子都注意到国外的"叫兽"们布置各种论文时经常会明确地交待写论文需要遵守的 format（排版格式），但由于大家在国内时从未接触过这类英语经常会看不懂要求。而且近期的一道口语新题：Describe something you did on a computer. 也需要运用这方面的知识。www.baycongroup.com/tutorials.htm 是个在这方面很有用的网站，因为它提供了所有常见电脑软件英语操作的免费教程。点击 Word，Excel，PowerPoint，Macromedia Flash 8.0 等之后就可以开始学习了。不仅可以用它来准备好这道考题，而且也可以为大家了解国外大学里常用的论文排版术语打下基础。

Day 9

 激辩 **Part 3**

Don't let it become your Achilles' heel.

Pat's Guide
To the Speaking Test

I talk of freedom
You talk of the flag
I talk of revolution
You'd rather brag
and as the final sunset rolls behind the earth
and the clock is finally dead
I'll look at you, you'll look at me
This will be what we said
Yes, this will be what we said

http://www.btinternet.com/ ~ ted.power/discuss.html *

　　口语 Part 3 的话题比较正式，和雅思写作的作文话题有某些相似之处，但用词仍然还是没必要像写作那么大，像 involve（涉及到），concern（关注）和 participate in（参与）这些常用词对于口语第三部分来说难度已经足够。

　　大家可以经常看看本页上方的这个网站，基本覆盖了 Part 3 的常见话题，而且对话部分的英文风格很接近 Part 3 高分答案的风格：用词略显正式，但也并不是大得吓人。

▶ *We just have adopted a laid-back approach, even though we take the test seriously.*

准备 Part 3 应该做什么？

考前的"蹲点儿"（the stakeout for getting the scoop on the test questions）是准备 Part 3 最省力的方法，或者如果不方便"蹲点儿"，至少也应该争取看看在考试那一天网上的考生回忆。如果可以提前知道考题，Part 3 就肯定不会有大问题（It'll be a cinch.）。但是如果你碰巧被安排在上午或者下午口语考试的第一个或者非常靠前，那么"蹲点儿"就只能是幻想（a fantasy）了。

但即使不知道考题，我们也完全可以在短时间内突破 Part 3。

Part 3 的 7 分答案长什么样

总体来说，Part 3 的话题要比 Part 1 的话题"大"一些，相应的用词也会略难一点。

请认真体会下面的《剑 8》Test 2 Section 3 的 7 分水平答案：

> **Do you think there will be a greater choice of food in shops in the future，or will there be less choice?**
>
> *It seems the general trend is there'll be more options for us consumers，not just in terms of food，but almost any products，because the demand is increasing. Then the food production industry and the shops will try to keep up with the demand.*

可见与口试的第一部分相比，Part 3 的答案略有点"打官腔"的味道，但用词还不算恐怖。

而下面的《剑 8》Test 3 Section 3 问题则已经涉及到了全人类的命运：

> **Do you think that meetings between international leaders will become more frequent in the future?**
>
> *Hopefully，they can meet up more frequently as new problems keep coming up，like climate changes，earthquakes and financial concerns. The effort would be much more effective if countries could join forces and support one another.*

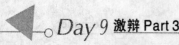

《剑8》里这种"高大全"问题的 7 分答案虽然用了些大词,但也绝没有达到"G-20 联合公报"的难度。而且答案依然带有清晰的层次感,并没有因为片面追求用大词而变得令人费解。

对于需要口语 7 分的那部分考生来说,今天后面您即将学到的"284 个 Part 3 高分词汇"可以满足回答 Part 3 问题的全部用词需求,而且对各位今后的海外留学经历也将颇有裨益。

有效提高 Part 3 实力的 7 步
(Seven Steps to Hone Your Skills and Improve Your Competence in Part 3)

Please read the following text thoroughly.

A 回答"比较区别"的题目有哪些必备句型?

为了把比较题准备熟练,请一定熟记下列句型,但是每组最多只要记 1 ~ 2 句即可,"大牛"们看看就行,自己能说最好。

> There are quite a few differences between them.
>
> Well, actually, there are a variety of differences between them.
>
> It seems to me like they are just totally different.
>
> I would say there are a whole lot of distinctions.
>
> There're a couple of differences between them.
>
> The main differences I can think of now are...

如果你真感觉考官让你比较的两种东西根本"风马牛不相及",英文怎么说呢?那么请用地道的英文告诉他/她你的这种感觉,然后再讨论,"That's like comparing apples and oranges. But basically, ..."像这样有针对性的评价是具有沟通的实际意义的,而非 Pat 在国内见到过的大量"自说自话"的口语模板。我们在 Day 1 里已经综合了多位真实剑桥考官的看法充分证明了考官们的核心任务是测试你的英语。你完全可以有和考官不一致的看法,但却不可以根本就没有能力用英语去表达自己的看法。

> The most fundamental one is...
>
> The most significant one is...

The most essential one is...

The most obvious one is...

Unlike..., ...

Compared with..., ...

Also, ...

Besides, ...

Apart from that, ... Additionally, ...

A second difference would be... (请注意这里不要说 The second difference...)

> 另外，我们在 Day 4 里学过的 while / by contrast / in contrast / whereas / on the other hand / compared with... / unlike... 这样的连词也可以用在对两种事物的描述句中间，表示这两种事物的对比。这些词组的语气用在 Part 3 相当合适，并不会显得过于正式，请放心使用。

So, you see, they are totally different.

Those are the main differences between them.

There are other differences as well, but basically these are the main ones.

I guess that's it.

对于比较现在 vs 过去，或者比较现在 vs 将来的题目，一定要注意时态的变化，而且你将会发现下面的词组也很有用。

In the past, ...

Traditionally, ...

Historically, ...

In the previous centuries, ...

People used to...

In the future, ...

In years to come, ...

20/30/40 years from now, ...

It's very likely that in the future...

Who knows, maybe in the future, ...

Hopefully, ...

These days,

Today,

Now,

Currently, ...

At present, ...

口语里说"现在"请不要频繁地使用 nowadays。

如果感觉考官要求比较的两方真的很相似,那么也完全可以用下面的句型如实回答:

Actually, they have a lot in common.

Well, it seems they are very similar.

Honestly, I don't think there's much difference between them.

描述将来的目标时常会用到一个动词:

fulfill(实现):

e. g. fulfill their dreams / fulfill our potential(潜力) / fulfill their promise / fulfill their aspirations(志向) / fulfill our tasks / fulfill our responsibilities...

B   回答 causes/Why 原因类问题应该熟悉的句型

要求仍然是每组最多知道 1 ~ 2 句就好了。

As I see it, several factors contribute to... （请大家注意这里的 contribute to 不一定是 "做贡献" 的意思。<u>其实这个词组后面完全可以跟坏现象</u>，而当这样用时 contribute to 就变成 "导致……" 的意思了）

In my view, the causes of... are complicated （复杂的）.

Actually, I believe more than one factor lead to this trend.

There's a combination of factors.

I think a number of factors are involved here.

There could be a number of explanations.

That's due to （因为）the fact...

The most significant one may be...

The chief contributing factor is...

The most obvious one would be...

A secondary one may be...

A subsequent factor could be...

As a result, ...

As a consequence, ...

Consequently, ...

Thus, ...

Pat 指南

回答原因类 题目有三个很常用的词组：

☆ **to the best of my knowledge** 这个词组可以很客气地帮助你逃避你不太了解原因的现象：

e. g. Hmm, **to the best of my knowledge**, the dying out of many languages is due to （因为）the fact English is so commonly-used today.

☆ **The underlying problem is** 意为潜在的问题是……讨论（貌似）深层的原因时很有用

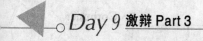
☆ **is closely linked to** 这个词组可以表示"和……联系密切"

e. g. This financial crisis(金融危机) **is closely linked to** the subprime loans(次贷).

C　回答"solutions/How should...?"类问题的常用句型

I guess that requires(需要)……

I guess that calls for(需要)……

To solve this problem, the government should…

I guess it will take some integrated measures(综合的措施) to solve…

I believe a series of(一系列的) steps should be taken, you know, such as…

Things should be done step by step. The initial thing that should be done is…Then, … And probably most importantly, …

That will involve a wide range of efforts, such as…

The most effective way to tackle(解决) this problem would be…

A number of actions should be taken.

In reaction to…(作为对……的回应), the government should…

The most sensible(明智的) way to confront(应对) this would be…

Pat指南

回答解决方法类题目一个极度好用(但国内同学基本从来不用)的词是 otherwise(否则)。试想:当提出你的解决方法之后,再说一下如果不这么做就会有什么可怕的后果,是不是让你的解决方法显得更加有效(can work wonders)呢?

e. g. All the governments on this planet(星球) should start limiting the car emissions(尾气排放). **Otherwise**, the global warming will get totally out of control.

回答解决方法类的问题还有一个很强大却从来没听到同学们用的句型是:**Ideally**, … **But in practice**, …(理想状态应该是……可实际上……)。听到你这么真诚(sincere),正常的考官也会是一声叹息(sigh with sympathy)。

e. g. Ideally, all cars should be eliminated from this world coz they are causing headaches for us. But in practice, the number of cars simply can't be controlled.

类似功能的地道英文句型还有三个，一旦有机会用到，必定拿分：

(1) In theory, … But in practice, …

(2) Hypothetically speaking, … But in practice, …

(3) Theoretically, … But in actuality, …

D 回答 advantages 常用的词汇和句型

在 Part 3 的答案里，一旦考到 advantages 就必然要多次用到此含义，所以 advantage 宜用下面的词汇替换以避免重复用词benefit / merit / favorable aspect / positive feature / strong point / strength。

下列句型经常用来回答和 advantages 有关的问题（要求仍然是只要记 1~2 句）：

There are a number of benefits.

Clearly, the advantages include (but are not limited to)…

That is beneficial primarily because…

It is beneficial for a variety of reasons.

Its most obvious advantage is…

And it's advantageous because… as well.

It's valuable also because…

And of course, it's positive also due to the fact…

Pat指南

在回答 advantages 类的题目时，经常会用到 and better still, …（更棒的是）这个词组。

e. g. That restaurant has great food and better still, offers flawless（无懈可击的，口试时代替 perfect 的好选择）service。

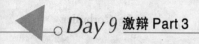
E 关于 **disadvantages**，我们经常需要用下面的词汇和句型

disadvantages 的 替 换 说 法：shortcomings / negative aspects / drawbacks / weaknesses / weak point / unfavorable quality / limitations。

下面的句型可能会有用的(come in handy)：

There may be some risks involved.

Apparently, some hazards(危险)may be involved.

One major concern about this issue is...

This is very disturbing(让人担心的) because...

This is definitely alarming(让人警觉的) simply because...

What makes this really perturbing(困扰人的) is...

The main problem associated with(和……联系到一起) this trend are...

Pat指南

and worse still, ...(更加糟糕的是)这个词组经常用在回答 disadvantages 类的题目里。

e. g. Economic problems bring layoffs(裁员) and worse still, lead to more crimes.

 如果一个现象既有利又有弊,如何评价它呢?

Every coin has two sides. 是一个在 1980s 年代的"老托福"里就已被考生用滥的句型,可 21 世纪的"新雅思"考生们却还在前仆后继地用着。

请坚定地跟考官这样说,"It cuts both ways — ··· but on the other hand, ···"

F 口语 Part 3 必备的高分词汇

☆ 这个词汇表里的多数单词其实大家都已经认识了,但是不一定会想到去用。对于确实想说出有一定复杂程度答案的考生,花些时间熟悉这些词汇是一定不会让你后悔的。

☆ 对口语词汇来说熟练特别重要,如果只是像 reading 的词汇那样看见之后才认识的单词在口试里面是一点用处都没有的。熟练掌握词汇最好的方法就是多复习并且积极地使用。Keep in mind that if you see a word three times in your life, it's yours forever.

☆ 即使在第三部分难词也不要用得太多。这些加分词汇在回答 Part 3 问题时,如果能用到 5 ~ 8 个,你的 Part 3 答案就已经有绝对足够的难度了。

☆ 过去 8 天学过的 cute words 还可以继续用,这些词只是对大家现有词汇的继续补充。

Pat 归纳出的 284 个 Part 3 拿分词汇(7 分词汇)
284 Words that Help You Build a More Educated Vocabulary for Part 3

1	abstract	*adj.*	抽象的(回答和 art 有关的题目用,反义词是 concrete / realistic)
2	abuse/mistreat	*v.*	虐待
3	accurate	*adj.*	准确的
4	achieve	*v.*	完成,实现 = fulfill
5	acid rain		酸雨
6	acquaintance	*n.*	认识的人(感情色彩上没有 friend 那么亲近)
7	adequate/sufficient	*adj.*	足够的,充足的(在 Part 3 经常用来代替 enough)
8	adopt	*v.*	接受,采纳(很多时候可以代替 accept)
9	a double-edged sword		这个应该不用解释了吧,写作里面用这个表示有利有弊太俗了,但是雅思口语里面用还是挺精彩的
10	affluent	*adj.*	有钱的 = wealthy = rich(反义词 needy / impoverished)
11	a healthy diet		健康的饮食
12	ambience	*n.*	气氛,氛围(Part 3 中经常用来代替 atmosphere)
13	ancestors	*n.*	祖先(一般用复数)
14	animal rights		动物权益
15	approach	*n.*	做某事的方法(Part 3 中很多时候可以代替 method)
16	appropriate	*adj.*	恰当的,合适的 = proper
17	approximately	*adv.*	大约 = about

（续表）

18	aspirations	*n.*	志向,理想 = ambitions
19	attempt	*v. & n.*	努力尝试 = effort
20	attractive/appealing	*adj.*	有吸引力的,诱人的
21	available	*adj.*	可以使用的,可以利用的
22	avoid	*v.*	避免(后跟 noun/verb-ing,但是不要说 avoid to do sth.)
23	backstabbing	*n.*	出卖朋友(经常用来回答 friends 类题目,"为朋友两肋插刀"英文则是 would you the shirt off his back)
24	barrier	*n.*	障碍
25	be concerned about		关注(后面跟某种不太好的事情,Part 3 中很多时候可以代替 pay attention to)
26	behavior	*n.*	行为(经常在说 children 时用到)
27	biased	*adj.*	有偏见的(描述 media 时常用)
28	blockbuster	*n.*	大片儿
29	boost	*v.*	提升,促进(可以跟 efficiency / the standard of living / economy 等等)
30	budget	*n.*	预算
31	burden	*n.*	负担
32	candidate	*n.*	候选人
33	casual	*adj.*	随意的,休闲的(比如 casual clothing)
34	celebrate	*v.*	庆祝
35	celebrity	*n.*	名人 = famous people
36	characteristics	*n.*	特征(这个词很常用但是发音比较难,如果练习多次还是搞不定那就忘了它吧,或者改说 features)
37	charities	*n.*	慈善组织(这个词多数时候用复数)
38	cherish	*v.*	珍视,珍惜
39	chronic/persistent	*adj.*	长期存在的(后面跟某种坏现象,比如 pollution, poverty)

（续表）

40	clash	n.	冲突（性格上的冲突也可以叫做 personality clashes）
41	cloning	n.	克隆
42	combine/blend	v.	结合（经常用来回答 Western culture/Chinese culture 的题目）
43	commonly-used	adj.	被广泛使用的（经常跟某种工具或者语言）
44	communicate with		沟通，交流
45	community	n.	社区，经常会和 individuals（个人）一起用到
46	compete	v.	竞争（极度常用，和反义词 cooperate 合作都要背熟）
47	complicated/complex	adj.	复杂的
48	comprehensive	adj.	广泛的，覆盖面广的
49	computer-savvy	adj.	精通电脑的，(...-savvy 都是精通……的)
50	concentrate on/focus on		集中在……上面
51	confident	adj.	自信的
52	consequence	n.	后果，结果（Part 3 中经常用来代替 result）
53	conservative	adj.	保守的（作名词当保守派讲时比 the elderly/young people 常用）
54	constantly	adv.	持续不断的（Part 3 中经常用来代替 always）
55	contemplate	v.	考虑（Part 3 中很多题目可以用来代替 consider）
56	conversation	n.	谈话（比 chat 范围更广，不管轻松的还是严肃的谈话都可以叫 conversations）
57	corruption	n.	腐败
58	cultural heritage		文化遗产（有时也说 national heritage）
59	curious	adj.	好奇的（+ about something）
60	customs	n.	风俗习惯（经常和 traditions 一起用）
61	cut down on/curtail	v.	削减

（续表）

62	decorate	*v.*	装饰（名词为 decoration，回答建筑题目时也很常用）
63	delightful	*adj.*	令人高兴的，可爱的
64	democratic	*adj.*	民主的
65	desirable	*adj.*	好的，积极的，值得拥有的（这个词很多时候可以用来代替 good / positive，相当好用）
66	determine	*v.*	决定（很多时候可以代替 decide）
67	detrimental	*adj.*	Part 3 里完全可以代替 harmful 这个词
68	devastating	*adj.*	毁灭性的（语气比上面的 detrimental 强十倍，经常用来说 environmental issues）
69	digital	*adj.*	数码的
70	discipline	*n.*	纪律
71	discover	*v.*	发现
72	dishonest	*adj.*	不诚实的
73	distinction	*n.*	差异（Part 3 中经常用来代替 difference）
74	distraction	*n.*	干扰（动词是 distract sb. from…）
75	disturbing	*adj.*	困扰人的，让人很烦的（很多时候这个词可以用来代替 bad / negative / annoying，非常实用）
76	domestic	*adj.*	国内的（反义词是 international）
77	durable	*adj.*	耐用的（经常说某种工具）
78	dynamic	*adj.*	有活力的 = active
79	eco-friendly	*adj.*	有益于生态保护的（the ecosystem 是生态系统）
80	economical	*adj.*	省钱的
81	economy	*n.*	经济（一定要区分这三个词：economy 经济，economic 和经济有关的，economical 省钱的）
82	effective	*adj.*	有效果的，效果好的
83	efficient	*adj.*	效率高的
84	electronic	*adj.*	电子的
85	eliminate	*v.*	消除（后面经常跟 poverty 或者 barriers）

（续表）

86	embarrassed	*adj.*	不好意思的，丢脸的
87	encourage	*v.*	鼓励（经常用来回答 children 有关的题目，名词 encouragement，形容词 encouraging 也很常用）
88	encouragement	*n.*	鼓励（经常在回答和 children 有关的题目时用到）
89	enigmatic	*adj.*	神秘的 = mysterious
90	enjoyment	*n.*	享受，乐趣 = pleasure
91	entertaining	*adj.*	娱乐性强的
92	entire = whole/ entirely = wholly	*adj.*	Part 3 的 whole 和 wholly / completely 经常可以用 entire / entirely 代替
93	equality	*n.*	平等（形容词是 equal）
94	essential	*adj.*	非常重要的（代替 important 很棒）
95	establish	*v.*	建立（Part 3 中回答解决方法类题目的一个句型是 establish a mechanism for... 建立……的机制）
96	establishments	*n.*	这个词非常常用，基本上等于中文的"场所"，比如 eating establishments, entertainment establishments, business establishments, retail establishments，真可惜我们的考生用得太少了
97	exception	*n.*	例外
98	exchange	*v.*	交换(+ ideas / thoughts)
99	exhaust fumes	*n.*	汽车尾气（可以用复数）
100	exhausting	*adj.*	让人精疲力尽的（可以说 sports / work）
101	experience something vicariously		间接地体验某事（经常用来回答和 media 或者 future 有关的题目）
102	experienced	*adj.*	有经验的（经常用来描述谁给你 advice 的题目）
103	experiment	*n.*	实验
104	expert/specialist	*n.*	专家（反义词 lay-people，外行）
105	explore	*v.*	探索（说 traveling 或者 future）
106	extended family		几代人合住的大家庭
107	exterior	*n.*	外观（Part 3 里面经常用来回答与建筑相关的题）

（续表）

108	extravagant	*adj.*	奢侈的(这个词很不错,但是如果实在记不住那就说posh,意思差不多但是更口语化)
109	facilities	*n.*	设施,这个词多数时候用复数,注意和equipment(设备)区分,一般来说equipment规模体积比较小
110	factor	*n.*	因素(关键因素叫key factors)
111	family bonds		亲情
112	family reunion		家庭团聚(常用来说festivals)
113	fireworks	*n.*	焰火(回答跟festivals有关的题目时常用,啪啪响的鞭炮叫firecrackers,燃放焰火/鞭炮叫set off fireworks / firecrackers)
114	flexible	*adj.*	灵活的,机动的
115	foster	*v.*	培养(后面一般跟某种素质,比如students' creativity / the public awareness about…)
116	freedom	*n.*	自由
117	frugal	*adj.*	俭朴的(回答与老人相关问题时常用)
118	frustrated	*adj.*	失望的,沮丧的(名词是frustration)
119	fulfill	*v.*	实现,完成,发挥
120	function	*n.*	功能
121	generation gap		代沟(回答the elderly / children的题目时极度常用)
122	genetic engineering		基因工程
123	genetically-modified food		转基因食品
124	global warming		全球变暖
125	gradually	*adv.*	逐渐地
126	green	*adj.*	这个形容词在西方已经成了"eco-friendly"的同义词,非常常用
127	greenhouse effect		温室效应

128	guidelines	*n.*	指导原则
129	habitat	*n.*	动物的栖息地
130	handle	*v.*	处理,解决
131	harmonious	*adj.*	和谐的(名词是 harmony)
132	have a yearning for	*v.*	非常渴望得到…… = be dying for
133	hazard/risk/danger	*n.*	危险
134	health-conscious	*adj.*	关注健康的,健康意识强的
135	homeless (people)		无家可归的(人们)
136	humdrum/mundane	*adj.*	无聊的,没劲的(Part 3 中代替 boring 极为常用)
137	identify	*v.*	确认,确定,找出(很多句子中可以代替 find)
138	ignore / overlook	*v.*	忽视
139	illegal	*adj.*	非法的,违法的
140	imitate	*v.*	模仿……(经常在说到 children 的时候用到)
141	immediately	*adv.*	立刻 = right away
142	impair	*v.*	后面只能跟 health 或者 eyesight, 其他的破坏不要用这个词
143	incentive	*n.*	(物质的)动力和 motivation(精神的动力)区别
144	inconvenient	*adj.*	不方便的
145	independent	*adj.*	独立的(反义词是 dependent 依赖的)
146	indispensable	*adj.*	不可或缺的
147	inferior	*adj.*	劣质的,落后的
148	influential	*adj.*	有影响力的
149	information highway		很多时候用来代替 the Internet
150	informative	*adj.*	信息量大的(说 media 时常用)
151	ingredients	*n.*	原料,说 food 时常用
152	inhumane	*adj.*	不人道的(经常用来回答和 animals 有关的题目)
153	integrity	*n.*	正直(请注意它是名词)
154	intelligent	*adj.*	聪明的

（续表）

155	interaction	*n.*	交流,互动(很多时候可以代替 communication)
156	interactive	*adj.*	互动的(很多时候可以描述未来的工具)
157	isolated	*adj.*	孤立的(说 globalization 或者 individuals 话题时常用)
158	lack	*v. & n.*	缺乏
159	layoffs	*n.*	(大规模的)裁员
160	layout	*n.*	布局(说建筑,城市或者 media 题目时常用)
161	legislation	*n.*	立法(注意是名词,基本就是 law 的意思了)
162	loyal	*adj.*	忠实的(经常在回答与 friends 有关的题目时用)
163	malnutrition	*n.*	营养不良
164	media hype	*n.*	媒体炒作
165	metropolis	*n.*	大都市
166	misleading	*adj.*	有误导性的
167	monitor/supervise	*v.*	监督
168	multimedia	*adj.*	多媒体的
169	natural resources	*n.*	自然资源
170	non-governmental organizations (NGOs)		在英美很重要的一个概念,非政府组织,很多国际问题的解决,包括 environmental issues, poverty, online pornography 等等都需要 NGOs 的努力
171	normally	*adv.*	通常 = usually
172	nostalgic	*adj.*	怀旧的(经常用来回答与 photos 有关的问题)
173	nuclear family		只有父母和孩子的小家庭(反义词是 extended family, 好几代人住一起的大家庭)
174	nutritious	*adj.*	有营养的
175	obligation	*n.*	Part 3 中经常代替 responsibility
176	obtain	*v.*	获得(Part 3 中经常代替 get)
177	obvious	*adj.*	明显的 = evident
178	occupation	*n.*	职业(注意和 employment 就业的区别,就业机会要说 employment / job opportunities)

（续表）

179	offender/criminal	*n.*	罪犯
180	old-fashioned	*adj.*	老实的,过时的
181	opportunity	*n.*	机会
182	optimistic	*adj.*	乐观的(反义词是 pessimistic 悲观的)
183	option	*n.*	选择(代替 choice 的好选择)
184	organised	*adj.*	说事物是指"整齐的,有秩序的",说人是指"做事有条理的"
185	overweight	*adj.*	肥胖的,超重的
186	ozone layer		臭氧层
187	paparazzi	*n.*	(复数名词)狗仔队
188	parenting	*n.*	家庭教育(反义词是 schooling 学校教育)
189	participate in		参与 = join
190	pastime	*n.*	业余爱好(Part 3 中经常可以代替 hobby)
191	pattern	*n.*	模式,方式
192	pessimistic	*adj.*	悲观的
193	performance	*n.*	表演
194	personalized	*adj.*	个性化的,专为个人设计的
195	poisonous/toxic	*adj.*	有毒的
196	policy	*n.*	政策
197	portable	*adj.*	方便携带的,便携的
198	potential	*n.*	潜力(也可以作形容词,"潜在的")
199	poverty	*n.*	贫困
200	practical	*adj.*	实际的,实用的
201	precious/valuable	*adj.*	珍贵的,宝贵的
202	preference	*n.*	偏好,偏爱的东西
203	preserve	*v.*	保护(后面可以跟资源、建筑、传统等等)
204	prevent	*v.*	防止(prevent sb. from doing sth. 或者 prevent sth.)

（续表）

205	primary /principal / chief	adj.	首要的,最主要的
206	prior to		Part 3 中很多时候可以代替 before
207	priority	n.	首要任务
208	process	n.	过程
209	proficient in = well-versed in	adj.	很熟悉的……
210	promote	v.	促进
211	psychological	adj.	心理的
212	radiation	n.	辐射
213	rare	adj.	稀有的,珍稀的
214	real-time communication	n.	实时交流(比如 MSN、QQ 都是)
215	recipe	n.	某个菜的做法(e. g. a recipe for hot and sour soup)
216	recreation/leisure	n.	休闲
217	recycle	v.	循环使用(经常用在跟 environment 有关的答案里)
218	reflect / embody / symbolize	v.	反映,体现
219	relieve	v.	减轻(后面可以跟 traffic congestion, poverty 或者 stress 等等)
220	repercussions	n.	影响(Part 3 中经常代替 influence)
221	replace/supplant	v.	代替(经常用来回答 future 和 Western culture / Chinese culture 的题目)
222	represent	v.	代表,体现
223	reputation	n.	名誉,声望
224	require	v.	需要(主语是事物的时候这个词完全可以替换 need)
225	retirement	n.	退休(动词为 retire)

（续表）

226	reward	*v.*	奖励,回报（它的形容词 rewarding "给人回报的"也很常用）
227	ridiculous	*adj.*	荒唐的,荒谬的 = absurd
228	rules and regulations		这两个词经常可以连在一起说,表示"规章制度"
229	satisfy the need of / meet the need of...		满足……的要求或需要
230	scandal	*n.*	丑闻（经常用来回答和 media 或者 famous people 有关的题目）
231	schedule	*n.*	时间安排,时间表
232	seek	*v.*	寻求
233	seniors/the elderly	*n.*	老年人
234	separate	*adj.*	单独的,分开的（副词形式是 separately）
235	settle	*v.*	解决
236	shortage	*n.*	短缺 = scarcity
237	siblings	*n.*	一个人的兄弟姐妹的总称
238	significant — essential — vital	*adj.*	三个词的语气一个比一个强,基本等于是 important — very important — extremely important
239	sleep-deprived	*adj.*	睡眠不足的
240	snobbish	*adj.*	势利的（贬义词）
241	source of energy		能源
242	souvenir	*n.*	纪念品
243	spacious	*adj.*	宽敞的
244	species	*n.*	物种（注意它的复数也是 species）,濒危物种 endangered species
245	staff	*n.*	员工（需要注意这个词是员工的总称,一般不加复数,员工个人叫 staff members）
246	standard of living		生活水平
247	staple food	*n.*	主食
248	state-of-the-art	*adj.*	先进的,最尖端的（这个词和 art 其实没有关系）

（续表）

249	status symbol	n.	身份地位的标志（比如 Mercedes, 奔驰其实可以这么说）
250	steady	adj.	稳定的
251	stressful	adj.	压力大的
252	strive for	v.	努力争取……（后面加名词）
253	subsidize	v.	补贴（经常用来说 government 话题）
254	supervise	v.	监督
255	sympathy	n.	同情心
256	tabloid	n.	小报儿（经常回 famous people 题目时用）
257	tackle	v.	解决（可以代替 solve）
258	target / objective	n.	目标
259	tax revenue		税收
260	taxpayer	n.	纳税人（在西方 tax 是非常重要的概念 Only two things in life are certain: tax and death.）
261	temptations	n.	诱惑
262	tension	n.	紧张感（也可以描述国家间的关系）
263	the population boom		人口爆炸 = the population explosion = overpopulation
264	the unemployment rate		失业率
265	Third-World countries		第三世界国家（基本等于 developing countries, 反义词是 industrial countries/developed countries）
266	time-consuming		消耗时间的
267	traffic congestion		交通堵塞
268	tranquil and serene		宁静的, 安静的 = peaceful
269	typical	adj.	典型的
270	undermine	v.	破坏（后面跟抽象的概念, 比如 relationship between countries, 但对具体物品的破坏不要用这个词）

（续表）

271	unethical	adj.	不道德的
272	unwind	v.	= relax
273	user-friendly	adj.	好用的,方便的
274	values	n.	价值观(复数名词,经常用来对比 the past 和 the past)
275	vehicle	n.	交通工具
276	veterinarians(vets)	n.	兽医(这个词要能听懂,09 年真题出现过)
277	victim	n.	受害者
278	violate	v.	侵犯(后面常跟 privacy, the law 或者 rights)
279	violence and pornography		暴力与色情
280	virtual reality		虚拟现实(很多时候回答与 future 有关的题目会用到一些 virtual-reality equipment)
281	virtue	n.	美德
282	westernized	adj.	西方化的
283	worthwhile	adj.	值得的
284	yet another		又一个,再一个,经常在 Part 3 用来引出另一个原因或者解决方案,比如 This is yet another reason why we should be cautious (谨慎的).

Pat 指南

　　下面的四个名词在 Part 3 中经常用到,如果用到一定不要加复数,因为它们都是不可数名词:knowledge, research, equipment 和 information。

G　口试 Part 3 的最常用句型(高分内容)

积极方面的句型	译文
take measures… = take action… = take steps…	采取措施(其中的 action 也可以用复数)
is a main driving force behind…	是……的主要推动力

（续表）

积极方面的句型	译文
establish a mechanism for...	建立……的机制
it's worthwhile to...	做某事是值得的 [剑桥例句] If we need more citizens on this project, we've got to make it worthwhile for them.
create job opportunities...	创造就业机会
show one's respect and appreciation for...	表示对……的尊重和欣赏（比如回答关于 traditional festivals 的问题）
is beneficial to...	对……有好处
it enables sb. to...	让……有能力去……（比如回答和 future / technology 有关的问题）
give priority to...	把……当成首要任务（比如回答 government 类题）
meet / satisfy the need of...	满足……的要求
should ensure that...	应该确保……
is a passport to...	是……的必要条件（这里的 passport 跟护照没关系，但挺形象的）
There's no substitute for...	……是不可替代的 [剑桥例句] You can work from plans of a garden, but there's no substitute for visiting the site yourself.
reverse the damage to...	消除已经对……产生的破坏
raise the public awareness about...	提高公众的……意识
It's absolutely essential for... to...	必须要……（经常可以用来在 Part 3 中代替 must）
If everyone pitches in, ...	如果每个人都参与，那么……
plays a key role in...	在……中起关键作用
enjoy high social status	社会地位很高（比如说与职业 occupation 有关的题目）

（续表）

积极方面的句型	译文
have a large following…	受到追捧（说 celebrities, technology 或者 a new trend 都可以用） [剑桥例句] The shop has a small but loyal（忠实的）following.
I can't imagine life without it.	无法想象没有……的生活
motivate / inspire sb. to…	给某人动力去……（特别是常说 children）
release pressure…	释放压力
is / are sweeping…	席卷…… [剑桥例句] A 1970s fashion revival（时尚怀旧风潮）is sweeping Europe.
shift more resources to…	把更多的资源用在……
promote sustainable development…	促进可持续发展（其实就是不破坏 the environment 的发展了）
take part in / get involved in / make (a) contribution to…	参与……，为……做贡献
boost the efficiency of…	提升……的效率
lower the rate of…	降低……的发生率（crime / pollution…）
offers us a wealth of knowledge…	丰富我们的知识（是不是比 broaden our horizons 新鲜点？）
is a real eye-opener…	真让人大开眼界（这是地道的英文，而且比 enrich our knowledge 可爱多了） [剑桥例句] Living in another country can be a real eye-opener.
exchange ideas…	交流思想
place emphasis on…	把重点放在……上面
hold on to our traditions…	保留传统
get along with…	跟……合得来

消极方面的句型	译文
is / are caused by...	是由……产生的
A potential problem would be....	一个潜在的问题可能是……
drive up the crime rate...	导致犯罪率上升
be addicted to...	对……上瘾
be incompatible with ... = be at odds with...	与……不协调, 不一致 [剑桥例句] Any new video system that is incompatible with existing ones has little chance of success.
at the expense of...	以……为代价 [剑桥例句] Sometimes pets take up too much of our attention at the expense of our family members.
cause psychological strain...	产生心理压力
be awash with blood and nudity...	充满了暴力和色情
be in a mess... / be in chaos...	处在很混乱的状态中
lose sight of...	无视, 忽视
is a hindrance / hurdle to...	对……构成障碍
pose a threat to...	对……构成威胁 [剑桥例句] Nuclear weapons pose a threat to everyone.
are going extinct / are vanishing / are dying out	正在逐渐灭绝
is / are to blame = should be held responsible	……应该对某事负责任
The competition is so fierce.	竞争很激烈。
The standards of... are falling.	……的水平正在下降。
The gap between... and... is widening.	差距正在扩大。
We are confronted with...	我们面对……(危机, 挑战, 困难等) [剑桥例句] It's an issue we'll have to confront at some point.

（续表）

消极方面的句型	译文
restrict our freedom...	限制他们……的自由
be concerned about...	很关注……
Spoil their kids rotten.	把他们的孩子宠坏了。
pay lip service to...	只对某事进行敷衍（不要理解成"嘴唇服务"） [剑桥例句] Sarah claims to be in favor of training, but so far she's only paid lip service to the idea.
Spoil the cityscape.	破坏市容。
The pace of life is speeding up.	生活节奏越来越快。
Individuals are so alienated from one another.	人们彼此越来越疏远。
under intense stress...	压力很大
Resources are being depleted.	资源正在被消耗。 [剑桥例句] If we continue to deplete the Earth's natural resources, we will cause serious damage to the environment.
interfere with...	干涉……
calls for joint effort from...	需要……共同的努力
fine sb.	当 fine 作动词它可一点都不"好"，在这句里指罚款，可以用来回答很多问题的解决方法对吧？
irreversible damage has been done to...	已经对……产生了无可挽回的破坏
breed crime...	滋生犯罪

不好也不坏的句型	译文
That involves...	这涉及到…… [剑桥例句] I prefer teaching methods that actively involve students in learning.
This can be attributed to...	这可以归因于……

（续表）

不好也不坏的句型	译文
It's no exaggeration to say that...	毫不夸张地说，……
And... is no exception.	而……也不是例外。
The repercussions can be really serious.	影响将会很严重。 [剑桥例句] Any decrease in tourism could have serious repercussions for the local economy.
You know, it's like ... a supply and demand kind of relationship.	你知道的，这就像一个供求关系的问题。
is a symbol of... = symbolise...	是……的象征
Statistics show that...	统计数据显示了……，用现在时态 [剑桥例句] **Statistics show that** in most countries, women live longer than men.
support... = be in favor of...	支持
be opposed to... = be against...	反对……
In theory, / Ideally... But in practice, ...	理论上说，……但实际上，……
I would assume that...	据我猜想…… [剑桥例句] **I would assume that** you knew each other because you went to the same school.
is regarded as...	被视为是……
Plenty of evidence has shown that...	充分的证据已经表明……（也可以改用一般现在时）

超短线
The Ultra-Short Track

从开始教 IELTS 那一天起，Pat 就一直坚信充分领会 Cambridge ESOL 的真实官方要求是一切备考者和辅导者的核心任务。对于时间紧却面对 L. R. W. S 四座大山的考生们来说,如果实在找不出时间去充分准备 the Speaking Test 的 Part 3 了,那么至少要好好听听剑 4~剑 8 官方真题里每套 Listening 的 Section 4 吧,你会发现其风格酷似口语 Part 3 的答案。例如剑桥官方真题里这个关于 recycling 的段子的和近期口语 Part 3 中关于 recycling 的考题何其相似:

This high quality comes at a cost in terms of the waste produced during the process. Plastic causes problems because there're so many different types of plastic in use today, and each one has to be dealt with differently. One of the most successful activities is recycling plastic bottles to make containers which are used all over the country.

其中标出颜色的部分全都是我们在本书中学过的高分口语表达。

或者如果您连通过听力 Section 4 来提高口语 Part 3 的时间都没了,那么最后的一道防线就是直接利用你的 Writing 基础来准备口语 Part 3 的问题。虽然这两个考试还真有不少话题是相似的,比如 Environment, Animals, Culture, Government 等,但全凭写作功底回答出来的 Part 3 会显得有点过于正式了,所以只可以作为 last resort 的应急之选。

Day

黯然消魂者
Never Say Farewell.
Say Bye.

Pat's Guide
To the Speaking Test

The play is done; the curtain drops
Slow falling to the prompter's bell
A moment yet the actor stops
And looks around to say farewell

关于 IELTS 有很多好网站，但是最靠谱儿的网站永远是 http://www.ielts.org/。任何小道消息，无论是关于变题的还是评分标准变化的，只要这个网站不证实，您就别太当真。

▶ We just have adopted a laid-back approach,
even though we take the test seriously.

最后一天了。

江淹的《别赋》说："黯然消魂者，唯别而已矣。"

其实除了离别，还有 10 个口语的超难卡片题，也是一样消魂的，留到最后一天来强势推出。不过在正式启动前，先给大家吃点镇静剂（tranquilizer）吧。

今天（上）部分给大家看的 10 个题，难度都只有★☆☆☆☆甚至只有 0 星。这 10 个题也是最近常考的话题，包括近期常考的 a good law 的话题，而且把它们搬到其他题目去也相当容易搬。想展示给大家的是：即使是简单得让人难以置信的词句，也能描述清楚很难的话题。

这就是——口语 10 大弱智卡片题。

（上）雅思口语卡片 10 大弱智话题

1. Describe an occasion（场合）that you were late for. / Describe a traffic jam. 一次迟到的场合/一次交通堵塞

Let me talk about an important occasion that I was late for. A couple of days ago, I got an email from a company, inviting me to a job interview. I applied for that job last month and really hoped I could get it. At first I felt excited. But then I got nervous. I slept little that night. So the next morning, I woke up late, like 8: 30 or something. They asked me to get to the company at 9 am. In a great hurry, I took a taxi and told the driver to drive as fast as possible. But there was a serious traffic jam then in the city and we got stuck in traffic. We moved so slowly I got totally mad. I yelled at (= shout something in an angry manner) the driver but he told me there was really nothing he could do about it. I had no choice but to call the manager of that company and told him that I would probably be late for the interview and really felt sorry about it. To my surprise, that gentleman was so nice and calm and told me not to worry about it. They would just wait for me. He even asked me to tell the taxi driver to drive safely. Finally I got there and had the job interview. I answered all their questions about myself and about my past experience very fluently and clearly. They were impressed by all my answers and... I got the job! I was totally excited. That experience was really special coz I felt I was lucky. But looking back, I guess I·should have said sorry to that taxi driver. I shouldn't become mad at him even though I would be late for an important occasion.

2. Describe an interesting subject.

一个有趣的科目

Let me talk about my favourite subject — English. I'm fond of this subject for a couple of reasons. You know, I'm keen on it primarily because it helps me understand the Western culture better. English abilities enable me to read English novels, to understand Hollywood movies and even to appreciate English songs. Another reason I like this subject is that English is a beautiful language and I really enjoy the pronunciation of English words and their spelling as well. Most importantly, English helps me make more friends. You know there are tons of English learners in my university. We often chat with each other in English and we sometimes read English books and magazines together, which is totally fun.

I learn this language primarily through the help of my English teachers. They are nice and patient. They often organize discussions in class. Through these activities, we get more used to speaking this foreign language and thinking in English. Also, I listen to English songs to practice my listening ability. Watching Hollywood movies also helps me a lot. You know, these days if you can't speak English, it's totally hard for you to get a job in big cities in China and I guess that's also a reason why I spend so much time learning this language.

3. Describe a big decision. / an important conversation.

一个重大的决定 / 一次重要的谈话

Well, I guess the biggest decision I've made so far was the decision to go abroad.

Actually, it was a very tough decision for me coz things in my life had been pretty organised (= well-planned) before I decided to go study in a British / Australian university. You know, I was studying in a top university back then. And I had tons of friends here in China. I was sure I would miss them a lot if I went abroad. But the problem at that time was that I felt bored with all those things. You know, my life was in a rut (=a situation that never changed) and I just wanted to get out of it. I felt it was time for a change. I hoped I could experience something new and exciting, maybe a foreign culture. So I just asked my parents and my friends for advice. My parents had an hour-long conversation with me and they were obviously concerned about me. They thought it wouldn't be worth it if I put a steady (=dependable) path of life at risk simply because I wanted a change. And they were worried that I would feel lonely if I were so far away from them. Some friends of mine were also against my plan coz they thought I

Civilization is the art of living in towns of such size the everyone does not know everyone else.

—Julian Jaynes

would have to make a lot of effort for it and lose many things. But I was determined to pursue my dream (=to make my dream come true). No one could talk me out of it. I started preparing for the IELTS test and went to the university English corner every weekend to improve my speaking ability. Also, I read English novels to practice my reading skills. Little by little, I felt my English was getting better. This decision is really important coz I'm sure it changed my life positively. As for the conversations I had with my parents and friends, of course they just wanted to help me but I believed the only person to depend on was myself. Advice is something that helps people to see things more clearly, not something for us to follow blindly.

Time to Branch Out.
推而广之

Describe an important stage of your life.

补充弹药

| be torn between A and B 左右为难 | be in a dilemma 处在两难的境地 |

[剑桥例句] The Prime Minister is clearly in a dilemma about how to deal with the crisis.

see the light at the end of the tunnel （很困难的时候）看到了一线光明

alter the course of my life 改变了我人生的道路

full of uncertainties 充满不确定性

[剑桥例句] Nothing is ever decided, and the talks are still full of uncertainties.

weigh the pros and cons 比较利弊   face up to the challenge 迎接挑战

Extra Ammo

4. Describe a festival.

一个节日

Let me talk about the Spring Festival in China, you know, *Chun Jie*.

It's by far the most important festival in the Chinese culture coz it marks the beginning of a whole new year. On that day, young people return to their parents' home and celebrate this festival. On the eve of Chinese New Year, people have big meals and drink a lot. They prepare tons of food to show their hope that the next year would be really promising. Not only food, the clothes people wear on the Spring Festival are also special. Some men wear traditional Chinese coats called Tang Suit and ladies wear chipao, a traditional Chinese dress. Children are totally excited on the Spring Festival coz they can get boxes of candy and new clothes. Many kids set off firecrackers to celebrate this festival. These days, the Spring Festival is not as important to Chinese as it used to be coz people today have more ways to get relaxed, like partying and clubbing. Besides the Western festivals like Valentine's day are more popular now. But as I see it, it's still one of the key things that make us Chinese.

5. Describe a good law in your country.

一部好的法律

Well, I'd like to talk about the marriage law in China. I'd like to get started by talking about the history of this law. It was first passed in 1955 in by the National People's Congress but then it was changed many times. The latest change to this law, as far as I know, took place in 2002, which was about the marriages between Chinese citizens and foreigners. Then, let me talk about the contents (内容) of this law. It is made up of six parts, or six " chapters", which are the general principles, the rules about family relations, the rules about marriages, divorces and responsibilities and also some recent changes to the rules. This law is so essential coz there are many people marrying or divorcing each year. So we really need a law to control such activities. For example, as you may know, many young people marry in some rural areas before they reach the legal age to get married, and that has brought many problems such as family violence or bad treatment of their kids. So you see, we need such a law. On the other hand, I guess there are still some problems with this law. You know, a friend of mine married last year but he didn't get along with his wife. So they divorced. But they now had problems dividing their property (= things they own) and debt. So I suppose we still have a long way to go before we get a really effective and efficient marriage law in China.

6. Describe a foreign culture.

一种异国文化

Let me talk about the Korean culture. You know, Korea is very close to China and basically its culture is similar to the Chinese culture. But there are still many differences between them. The Korean culture is exciting. You know, there're many talented Korean singers and songwriters and their music is very creative. Also, a host of world-class directors and actors work there. The Korean movies have quite a large following in China. My favourite Korean movie is called "*My Sassy Girlfriend*". Korean food is tasty. My favourite Korean food is the Korean barbecue and kimchi (韩国泡菜). Koreans are into sports. There are tons of soccer nuts and taekwondo buffs in that country. Besides, I guess the Korean architecture is pretty unique too. It blends the traditional Asian architecture and modern architecture, very beautiful.

7. Describe your favourite room in your flat.

公寓里的一个房间

I live in the northeastern part of Beijing and my flat is on the fourth floor of an eight-storey building. It's kind of worn-out (= old and damaged by countinued use). My favourite room in this flat is the bedroom. It's not big, you know, just like 10 square meters. There's a single bed in the corner. The bed pillows are fluffy and comfortable. There's a bedside table next to it and it's brand-new. I bought it last week. There's also a wardrobe in my bedroom and I put all my favourite clothes in it. Besides, there's a desk in this room. Sometimes I read fun books in my bedroom or surf the Internet. My favourite part of this bedroom is the potted plants. These plants are gorgeous and they smell good, too. By the way, I decorated this room all by myself.

The reasons I'm fond of this room are that, you know, it's my own space. I can really enjoy my privacy there. Also it's relaxing. I can enjoy the peace and quiet of the night in my bedroom. Sometimes I even spend the whole weekend daydreaming there. If you see it for yourself, you'll know how lucky I am to have such a room.

8. Describe an old piece of furniture. / Describe an antique.

一件老家具 / 一件古董

Let me talk about an old chair in my living room. This chair is special because of its long history — you know, it was made in the Qing Dynasty and was handed down in my family from my great-grandparents (= grandfather's/grandmother's parents). This chair is dark red and the paint is a little fading (= losing colour) now. It has four legs and a backrest. There are some cracks in the chair, coz, it's just so old. It makes some noise when someone sits on it. But I think it's gorgeous and perfect for my living room. That's because there are many old things in my living room, like old Chinese paintings and old desks. This chair is valuable also because it reminds me of my great-grandparents. They were kind of famous in their time and many people admired them. This chair was their only gift for their great-grandchildren. It looks unique. I guess it must have cost them a lot. Now it's worth like 10,000 RMB or something like that but I just won't sell it. I'll keep it in my living room to show my respect for my great-grandparents.

9. Describe an unhappy shopping experience.

一次不愉快的购物经历

Let me talk about one of my recent shopping experiences. A couple of days ago, I went to a supermarket to buy some food. I saw some apples that looked great. I paid for them right away and went back home. But then I was so surprised to find that the apples tasted so bad. Actually they were totally gross. So I returned to the supermarket and wanted them to give my money back. But the salesclerks just didn't give me my money and they were like, "Well, you should have tasted them before you paid." I got so mad coz the service was terrible and the food was so unbelievably bad. I complained to the customers around me. But those salesclerks still refused to give me my money. I was left with no choice so I called the Consumers' Association and complained to them about this matter. They promised me they would look into the whole thing. Yesterday I got a phone call from the supermarket and they told me they would give me the money. That was a totally unhappy shopping experience. But I learned a lesson from it. Now I know that I shouldn't be fooled by the look of things in stores.

10. Describe an open-air market.

一个露天市场

Let me talk about my favourite open-air market. It's located in the eastern part of my hometown. It's very big, you know, huge. Its history goes back all the way to like fifty years ago and it's very famous in my hometown. Actually, everyone can tell you something about this market in that city. The market is made up of many parts, like the food section, the toy section and the clothing section. Many people go there every day. Some of them buy things and some others just look around. Also, many people from out of town visit this market. They heard a lot about this open-air market and hope to get some exciting shopping experience. This market never gets them disappointed. You know, tons of stuff there and everyone can find the thing he or she wishes to get. Some others just enjoy chatting and bargaining there. That's exactly why sometimes it's pretty noisy out there. My favourite part of this market is the clothing part. I can find many different kinds of clothes, like casual clothes, formal clothes and sporty clothes there. Most importantly, the price is always reasonable. In fact, I can always get a discount coz I know all the salesclerks there. The atmosphere in that market is very laid-back. It feels busy but people are friendly to one another. They always wear a smile on their face and enjoy the experience of buying or selling things. This market is totally amazing in that although it's so big, it's very well-run, just kind of noisy but that's perfectly natural for an open-air market. I'm sure if you go and visit that market yourself, you'll just agree with me.

（下）雅思口语 10 大消魂卡片

下面这 10 个题目确实需要不少专门的词汇，所以往往导致考生一旦被问到那么回家之后就立马准备报名下一次的考试了。但相应地，如果你能好好准备，反而能让别人的弱势变成你的优势不是么？

这十个考题分别是：

Describe a museum / art gallery.

Describe a sculpture.

Describe a small business.

Describe a concert hall.

Describe a special meal.

Describe a party you prepared for another person.

Describe a naughty thing you did when you were a child.

Describe something in your home that was broken or didn't work.

Describe a place with a lot of noise.

Describe things that you can do to help improve the environment.

面对这么诡异（bizarre）的题目，Pat 仍然坚信，"There's nothing to fear but fear itself."

Killer A

1. 美术馆　Describe a museum / art gallery.

Pat 指南

准备一个美术馆吧，就能把这两个很难的题一起都准备好了。

难度指数：★★★★☆

Pat 的答案

The museum I like best is the Modern Art Museum in... (*Put the city name here.*)

371

The museum is situated in the city center. It's enormous, you know, and pretty blocky with very few windows. The interior is spacious and is divided into various sections, like Asian art, Middle-East art, European art and North American art. My favourite part is Sculpture Garden where there are hundreds of sculptures on display.

This museum has a fascinating collection of modern artworks. And it always has some temporary exhibitions going on. Last week, it held an exhibition of Andy Warhol's Works, which attracted many visitors. On weekends, it holds special events for kids, such as cartoon exhibitions and videogame festivals.

Thousands of people pass through its doors every day. But what makes this museum really special is that unlike many other museums, the staff there encourage non-flash photography coz they think that will make the viewing experience even more fun. So you see, this museum is pretty visitor-friendly.

This art museum is so famous that it receives millions of renminbi in government funding each year. All this money has been put to good use, I'm sure.

The admission fee is like … 15 yuan for adults and 5 yuan for children. Pretty reasonable, huh? It feels cool. Be sure to check it out!

轮到你了　　　　　　　　　　　　　　　　　　　　　　　It's Your Turn.

▶ Word Bank on This Topic

很大的	enormous/vast/gigantic	一整块儿的	blocky/blockish
室内	interior	部分	section

[剑桥例句] They had pictures of the house from the outside but none of its interior.

雕塑	sculpture	专门针对……	specialize in
迷人的	fascinating	收藏	collection
艺术品	artwork/ work of art	临时的	temporary
宽敞的	spacious	展览	exhibition

展品 exhibit

[剑桥例句] The museum has a fascinating collection of exhibits.

安迪·沃霍 Andy Warhol（the Pop Art 最著名的代表人物）

艺术作品 works（可以加复数）不用闪光灯的摄影 non-flash photography

构图 composition 　　　　　色彩搭配 colour scheme

审美的 aesthetic 　　　　　体验 experience

[剑桥例句] The new building has little aesthetic value.

笔触 strokes 　　　　　人像画 portrait

风景画 landscape painting 　　　　　静物画 still life

[剑桥例句] We went to an exhibition of 17th century Dutch still lifes（请注意静物画的复数要直接加 s）.

会议 conference 　　　　　方便观众的 visitor-friendly

（很多常用的英文词这样构成，还有一个更常用的就是 user-friendly）

公众讲座 public presentation 　　　　　入场费 admission fee / admission charge

[剑桥例句] The admission charge/fee 3 is £2 for the museum.

给人启发的 enlightening 　　　　　娱乐性强的 entertaining

信息量大的 informative 　　　　　当代艺术 contemporary art

漫步 wander around / stroll around

[剑桥例句] We spent the morning wandering around the old part of the city.

由……组成 consists of / be made up of

> 请参考Pat的思路，并适当借鉴这个词汇表里的单词，思考如果是您会怎么说

Pat 的海外生活英语实录

　　多数博物馆和美术馆的采光都不是靠太阳光，因为同一天里阳光的强度变化很大，视觉效果不够稳定。相应的博物馆和美术馆里的光线就不可以叫 sun ⊠，而是要叫做 lighting（照明）。

　　【剑桥例句】Don't strain your eyes by putting up with（容忍）poor lighting.

Killer B

2. 一件雕塑　Describe a sculpture. / Describe an educational visit.

Pat指南

　　这个题目要想不跑题确实得用一堆专业术语，不信你用中文试试。不过其实也好办，实在不行就把一堆术语堆给考官也能拿些分了。如果准备一个雕塑展上的某一个雕塑，就可以用一个答案同时搞定"Describe an exhibition"的话题. 所以还是比较值的（worth it）。

　　难度指数：★★★★★

Pat 的答案

I went to a sculpture exhibition last weekend. Actually I took many pictures there. But anyway, I'll try to describe the whole thing just with words.

It was held at the garden of the Modern Art Museum and showcased artworks by more than 50 sculptors. Most of the works were along the theme of "The New Challenge". And the plants in the garden provided a good backdrop to these works.

What was really special about this exhibition was it not only displayed the sculptures, it showed the artists' sketchbook ideas and working drawings as well.

The sculpture I liked best was a piece dealing with the subject of the environmental issue.

It was a reclining figure which exuded peacefulness. But when looking more closely, I noticed the form was pierced was some strange openings. Through the contrast between the solid elements and these openings, the artist expressed concerns about the conflict between human development and nature.

I adored the symbolism of this sculpture. It was very meaningful, not just something for the "shock value". I can't recall the title, though. Anyway, titles are not really that important to abstract stuff, right? ...

The exhibition was pretty educational too coz lots of brochures were handed out to the viewers.

轮到你了 | It's Your Turn.

▶ **Word Bank on This Topic**

雕塑家	sculptor	展示	showcase / display
速写本	sketch	主题	theme

[剑桥例句] The theme of honour runs through most of his novels.

背景	backdrop / background	关于……	deal with... / be concerned with...
躺着的	reclining	洋溢着，散发着	exude (v.)

[剑桥例句] Carlos exudes confidence and enthusiasm.

洞口	opening	对比	contrast
元素	element	比喻的	figurative
关注	concerns (n.)	冲突	conflict
自然界	nature	非常喜欢	adore
象征	symbolism (n.)	轰动效应	shock value
穿破	pierce / penetrated	回忆	recall / remember
抽象的	abstract	小册子	brochure
分发	hand out / distribute	具象的	representational
比喻的	figurative	体量	mass
空间	space	现实主义的	realistic
自然写实主义的	naturalistic	三维的	three-dimensional

[剑桥例句] This picture has a three-dimensional effect.

青铜	bronze	石膏	plaster
粘土	clay	大理石	marble
探索	explore	题材	subject matter

[剑桥例句] The programme's subject matter was quite improper (不适合的) for children.

标题	title

请参考Pat的思路，并适当借鉴这个词汇表里的单词，思考如果是您会怎么说

Pat 的海外生活英语实录

Pat 在国外的业余时间大约有四分之一是花在博物馆和美术馆里的，最爱就是 MoMA 里那些应接不暇的现代艺术展。classical art 和 modern art 的本质区别就是古典艺术是为别人做的而现代艺术是为自己做的，所以口试时承认你并不理解某个艺术品相当正常而且真实，只要英语对就没什么好怕的。但是"难于理解的"用地道英文到底该怎么表达呢？除了 It's hard to understand. 外，基础好的同学也许还知道 incomprehensible，unintelligible 等多音节大词，前者与听力（listening）comprehension 是同源词，后者则与 intelligent 同根。不过在考试的时候说这些大词存在舌头转不过来的可能。其实在国外真实生活里 **It's beyond me.** 才是说某事物令你费解的最常用表达，人人都能懂。

【剑桥例句】I'm afraid theoretical physics is totally beyond me.

Killer C

3. Describe a small business.

☆ 小生意之 一家餐馆（a restaurant）

Pat 指南

英文里面有两句著名的谚语叫 "Small is beautiful." 与 "Less is more." —— "小就是美，少即是多"。

说实话，国外的中餐馆里面"压根儿"就没有地道的中国菜（authentic Chinese cuisine）。因为白人比较喜欢口味重的菜（savory dishes），我们中国人喜欢的口味他们反而会觉得太淡了（bland）。反倒是 Sweet and Sour Chicken, Mongolian Beef 这样在国内很少见到的菜，在老英老美们眼里都总以为就是地道的中餐（authentic Chinese cuisine），上当了还吃得特起劲儿。在英美吃中餐见得比较多的是 Cantonese Cuisine 和 Szechwan Cuisine，后面一个是 Sichuan 的另一种拼写方式。虽然"老外"们熟悉的中国菜在国内并不是最流行的菜，不过建议大家考雅思还是多说考官们肯定能听懂的菜名吧，比如 sweet and sour soup（酸辣汤），Kung Pao chicken（宫保鸡丁），Ma Po tofu（麻婆豆腐），braised pork（红烧肉）stir-fried string beans（干煸四季豆），Wonton Soup（馄饨），General Tso's Chicken（这个左宗棠鸡很多海外中餐馆都有，但是在北京的餐馆里还真是没找到）。

难度指数： ★ ★ ★ ★ ☆

[Pat 的答案]

My favourite restaurant is a Chinese restaurant on Nan Hu Street. I'm a regular there.

It's small… you know… tiny, not obvious at all until you pass it. But it offers a great selection of Chinese food. The chef is simply awesome.

Just order some dishes there like General Tao's chicken and braised pork and you'll understand what I mean. And the portions are soooooooo BIG.

But we're attracted to this restaurant by more than just good food. It proves that "Small is beautiful." The owner knows most customers on a first-name basis. The clean tablecloths and the neatly-set tables make it so different from many other restaurants. The seats are comfortable. The waiters and waitress are pleasant and helpful. You can always count on them. They even give customers free fortune cookies.

Oh, by the way, the lighting in the restaurant is pretty and the background music is all laid-back pieces.

It's cozy, especially on a freezing winter day…

轮到你了 ///   It's Your Turn.

▶ **Word Bank on This Topic**

常客　regular

[剑桥例句] He's one of the regulars at the Rose and Crown pub.

提供很好的……选择　offer a great selection of…（描述服务行业非常常用的表达）

餐馆的厨师　chef　　　　　　　　菜量　portion

[剑桥例句] The portions are very generous in this restaurant.

吸引　attract　　　　　　　　　　老板　owner

和……很熟　know… on a first-name basis

[剑桥例句] Isabella is on a first name basis with the boss.

桌布　tablecloth　　　　　　依靠　count on / depend on

幸运饼　fortune cookie（这个也是国外的中餐馆才有的东东，是一个小饼干里面放一
　　　张小纸条描述你未来的运气）

灯光　lighting　　　　　　　柔和的　gentle

轻松的　laid-back　　　　　　舒适的　cosy

[剑桥例句] This room is nice and cosy in the winter.

室内装饰　interior décor（这个词请特别注意听 CD 的录音）

精致的　exquisite　　　　　　无可挑剔的　impeccable

[剑桥例句] The standards of service are impeccable.

饭菜的香味儿　aroma　　　　挤满了人的　packed（口语里比 crowded 更常用）

[剑桥例句] The restaurant was so packed that I couldn't find a seat.

美食家　gourmet　　　　　　推荐　recommend

地毯　carpet　　　　　　　　饮食体验　dining experience

请参考Pat的思路，并适当借鉴这个词汇表里的单词，思考如果是您会怎么说

Pat 的海外生活英语实录

　　每个在餐馆吃饭的人都可以叫做 a diner（请注意这个词里 i 的读音不是像 dinner 里面的 i，而是要读成/ai/），但却不是每个在餐馆吃饭的人都可以称为"美食家"。作为巨蟹座的代表，Pat 一直被身边的朋友们叫做"吃货"（foodie），而且深感美味的食物难以抗拒（irresistible）。"美食家"在地道英语里可不是 eating expert ☒，而是 **gourmet**（请注意结尾的 t 不发音，这个词的正确发音是/ˈɡɔːˌmei/）。口试时一旦考到跟"吃"有关的话题，当用出这个单词的时候，你得到的绝不会是考官对于贪吃者鄙视的眼神，而是他/她对于你地道口语的敬意。

　　【剑桥例句】A gourmet is someone who knows a lot about food and cooking and enjoys eating high-quality food.

☆ 小生意之　一个食品店（a small business）

Pat 指南

食品店比较好说，不过请注意社区附近的小食品店在地道英文里并不是叫 food store ⊠，而是叫 grocer's 或 grocery shop（BrE）/ grocery store（AmE），这些店通常也会卖些小的日常用品（daily necessities）。

难度指数：★★★★☆

Pat 的答案

Let me talk about our neighborhood grocery shop. I often buy groceries from that store coz it's so close to my place.

The owners are a couple from HongKong and I have to say although the store is small, it's pretty well-run. You know, clean and tidy and the staff is very friendly. They are all hardworking younger people. I often see some folks sweeping or mopping the floor when I'm there.

The shelves are always well-stocked and look neat.

That store offers a great selection of groceries, like dairy, seafood, produce like vegetables and fruits, packaged food and deli food. The stuff sold is always fresh. And the coolest thing is it has some rare items that I can't find in bigger stores, such as baked potatoes. I guess I don't really care for their cookies, though.

I love it. It really proves that "Small is beautiful."

轮到你了　　　　　　　　　　　　　　　　　　It's Your Turn.

▶ **Word Bank on This Topic**

社区　neighborhood

我家　my place（地道口语里面很多时候会用它来代替 my home）

管理得很好的　well-run / well-managed　　　干净的　tidy / neat / spotless

[剑桥例句] Put your clothes away tidily.

员工　staff （注意这个一般不加 s，是员工的总称，动词用单数或者复数则都经常能听
　　　　到）

扫地　sweep the floor　　　　　　　　　擦地　mop the floor

货架　shelf　　　　　　　　　　　　　　货源充足的　well-stocked

[剑桥例句] I always stock up the fridge before my parents come to stay.

走道　aisle　　　　　　　　　　　　　　收银员　cashier

交款台　checkout counter　　　　　　　蛋奶制品　dairy (products)

蔬菜水果　produce （这个 produce 在这里不是动词生产的意思了，而是名词，指新鲜
　　　　　　　蔬菜水果的总称，重音也要跑到第一个音节上面）

[剑桥例句] Local people come to the farmers' market each day to sell their produce.

包装　package　　　　　　　　　　　　熟食　deli food

稀有的　rare

物品　item （这个经常用来指商店或餐馆里的某一个"东东"，在地道口语里的出现频
　　　　　率不亚于 thing）

[剑桥例句] The restaurant has a long menu of about 50 items.

烤　bake　　　　　　　　　　　　　　　不是很喜欢　I don't really care for...

医疗用品　medical supplies　　　　　　指甲刀　finger nail clippers

牙刷　toothbrush　　　　　　　　　　　牙膏　toothpaste

洗面奶　cleansing foam　　　　　　　　防晒霜　sunscreen

调味料　sauce / seasoning　　　　　　　夹心饼干　cookies

> 请参考Pat的思路，并适当借鉴这个词汇表里的单词，思考如果是您会怎么说

Pat 的海外生活英语实录

　　small business 的特点就是老板通常都是"白手起家"的。要表达这样的意思，除了有个地道但比较难的英文词 entrepreneur，还有 a self-made man / a self-made woman 这样很好理解也很容易在口试时说出来的表达。

【剑桥例句】

（1）He was one of the entrepreneurs of the 1990s who made their money in dotcoms.

（2）Self-made men and women are rich as a result of their own work and not because of their family wealth.

除以上的答案外，也挺"消魂"的两个题 Describe a small company. 和 Describe a friend of yours who is a business leader. 还可以通过 smallbusiness. aol. com/success-stories/ 上近百个小企业家的故事轻松过关。

Killer D

4. 音乐厅 Describe a concert hall.

Pat 指南

对于不喜欢 classical music 的人来说，这个题目考的根本就不是能力（skills），而是考耐力（endurance）。不过如果你能把我编写的这个答案掌握差不多50%左右的话，那么有两个最近经常出现的题目 "Describe a place where you listen to music / Describe a leisure center." 就可以一起准备好了。出国之后你会发现那边儿喜欢 classical music 的人可真多，而且其实如果经常听，还真的会发现它确实具有 pop music 所没有的深度（depth）。

建筑的 location 和 exterior（外观）这里 Pat 就不再赘述了，直奔音乐厅最有特点的 interior design（室内布置）吧。

难度指数：★ ★ ★ ★ ★

Pat 的答案

I've watched a wide range of concerts there, from classical to jazz to contemporary stuff.

The hall is pretty big, like more than 1,000 seats in the hall. But the vaulted ceiling makes the ambience pretty intimate.

The all-wood walls and the carpeting look gorgeous and make the acoustical experience fascinating. The illumination is great as well.

This concert hall is PERFECT for both symphony orchestras and small chamber groups to play in. I also listened to some classical recitals there. Amazing…

I've watched many performances there, you know, like tenors and baritones in tuxedos and sopranos and altos in black, floor-length skirts…

Everything is good. And the ticket price is normally pretty reasonable (like 80 renminbi apiece)…

轮到你了

It's Your Turn.

▶ **Word Bank on This Topic**

外观	exterior	室内	interior
当代的	contemporary	弯曲的屋顶	vaulted ceiling
气氛	ambience / atmosphere	亲密的	intimate
地毯	carpet / carpeting	音质	acoustics/acoustical effect / sound effects
灯光	illumination / lighting	交响乐团	symphony orchestra
室内乐团（一般规模比较小）	chamber group		
独奏	solo / recital	男高音	tenor
男中音	baritone	男低音	bass
最正式的男礼服	tuxedo / tux	女高音	soprano
女中音	mezzo-soprano	女低音	alto
通常	normally	每张	apiece (*adv.*)
音乐剧	musical	咏叹调	aria
指挥	conductor	乐曲	music / compositions
辉煌的	glorious	激情的	passionate
精彩的	phenomenal	观众	audience
鼓掌	applaud	谢幕	take curtain calls
极大的成功	a smash		

请参考Pat的思路，并适当借鉴这个词汇表里的单词，思考如果是您会怎么说

Pat 的海外生活英语实录

音乐"令人陶醉的",绝对不要说 The music made me drunk. ☒ 英文里有 appealing / attractive / fascinating 等单词都可以表示有吸引力的,但对音乐来说最准确的则是 **enchanting** 这个词。

【剑桥例句】The audience was clearly enchanted by her performance.

Killer E

5. 双语感悟之 一顿特殊的饭 Describe a special meal / someone's cooking skill.

Pat 指南

准备过这个题目的孩子一定感受过用英文"报菜名儿"的苦恼。描述自己 cooked a meal 的过程应该是个好主意,但要特别注意真没必要说得太多,1'30"~2' 其实并不需要很多内容。

老外做菜最常用的工具是 roaster(烤肉的烤箱)、toaster & oven(烤面包和蛋糕用的烤箱)和 microwave(微波炉,全称叫 microwave oven)。而使用 gas stove(燃气灶)时则通常是煮菜(boil),而炒菜(stir-fry)却不常见,因为国外房子里面的警报器过于敏感,炒菜的油烟就能让它响(go off)。

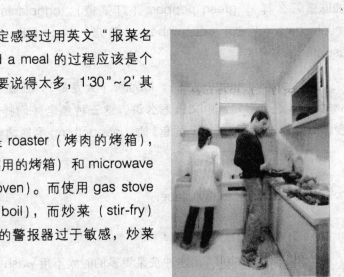

下面给大家介绍一下做菜的常用词吧,知道50%就够,不用说得"过好",否则那就不是描述一顿特殊的 meal 而是一个 cook 的求职简历了。看完这段咱就去吃饭,看着桌上的菜顺便复习。

☆ 可以先介绍一下吃这顿饭的"场景",比如:

A friend of mine visited me a couple of weeks ago.

☆ 说说为什么做饭:

At first, we just chatted / did some catching up(这个我们 Day 2 已经学过了,"叙

旧"的意思).

But then we got hungry.

Actually, there was some ready-made stuff in the fridge（冰箱）.

But I decided to cook a meal for him/her coz he/she was my special guest

☆ 去哪里买原料（ingredients）

So we went to a grocery store / a supermarket and bought lots of stuff.

☆ 买了哪些东东（挑几个就可以了，两个正常人吃不了多少吧）

meats like pork, beef, lamb, chicken（注意表示不同种类的时候 meat 可以加复数）

vegetables like tomatoes, onions, potatoes, broccoli（西兰花，西方人认为吃这个非常 healthy，甚至在加拿大餐馆 Pat 还见过有人吃 steamed broccoli 清蒸西兰花的，不知味道怎么样），green peppers（灯笼椒），eggplants（茄子），carrots（胡萝卜），mushrooms（蘑菇），cucumbers（黄瓜），spinach（菠菜），还有我的蔬菜最爱asparagus（芦笋）…

seafood like shrimp（虾），lobster（大龙虾），tuna（金枪鱼），salmon（三文鱼），snapper（这个不知道中文该怎么讲，这三种鱼老外们特爱吃，因为它们 bone（鱼刺）少，而很多老外感觉餐桌上的鱼刺是 unappetizing 会影响食欲的）

☆ 回家了

We went back to my place.

☆ 开始洗菜

rinsed all the stuff（用水冲洗菜更多的时候不用 wash 而用 rinse）

☆ 切菜方法大全：

sliced the tomatoes and cucumbers（切成片儿）

peeled the carrots（削皮儿）

chopped some broccoli（这个还是西兰花）into chunks（切块儿）

shredded the pork（切丝儿）= cut the pork into fine strips

diced an onion（切丁儿）= cut the onion into cubes

☆ 如果是做沙拉还可以说搅拌

mixed the cucumber and tomato in a salad bowl

如果烤蛋糕可以说 baked a cake

☆ 两种"打鸡蛋"

break / crack an egg 是把蛋壳打破的动作而 beat / whip eggs 是把鸡蛋在碗里打匀的过程

☆ Pat "吐血"奉献所有常见的做菜方法：

lit the burner（点燃 gas stove 燃气灶上的加热器）

boiled（水煮）and steamed（清蒸）the vegetables（国外吃蔬菜经常是吃 salad 或者清蒸）

stir-fried（炒）the onion with the ground beef（切碎的牛肉，我已经饿了⋯⋯）in a frying pan（煎锅，咱们中国的圆底铁锅叫 wok）

deep-fried（油炸）the fish fillets（鱼片，这个是法语词，发音请认真听录音）

braised the pork（红烧肉）

grilled the shrimp and the fillets（grill 有点像国内的"烤串儿"）

tossed in a handful of spices / herbs（放进去一把调味儿的东东，比如 pepper，撒盐英文是 sprinkled the salt）

cooked it on high heat ＝ cooked it over a high flame（用大火，小火就把 high 改成 low 就可以）

When it started to boil（煮沸），⋯

I turned down（调低）the heat and let it simmer（炖）for like 10 minutes.

When the meat was brown, I turned off the burner.

还有一个法语词 sauté 是"煎⋯⋯"，有时候也能听到有人说说，比如 sautéed the chicken。

I put some noodle（面条，这里不要加复数）into the boiling water and boiled it until it was tender（面条软了）.

And then I ladled（用那种很长的大勺子）some sauce（在国外吃饭用得最多的就是

sauce, 几乎无菜不放 sauce, 很多刚去的朋友一开始都适应不了) over the noodle.

I poured some dressing (沙拉和 pizza 的调料) on the salad.

☆ 开始吃

My friend set the table. (放餐具)

served the dishes 端菜

We just helped ourselves to the food.

I made some coffee with the coffee maker.

After the main course, we had some ice cream as dessert (饭后甜点, 我又饿了, 写一个答案饿两次……)

We chatted over the meal.

He/She told me a whole bunch of funny things and they really cracked me up. (让我笑个不停)

☆ 还可以再说说吃完饭的事情

We took the serving dishes off the table.

And... cleared the table = wiped the table off.

Put the leftovers in the fridge. (把剩菜放进冰箱)

Really memorable. (很值得回忆啊)

Bonus (附送内容):

最后再给大家简单描述几句有中国特色的包饺子过程吧, 不过太复杂的 Pat 真的自己也说不出来:

marinated the meat (把肉腌一下)

chopped up the vegetables (切菜)

mixed them into a paste (和在一起) and that would be the stuffing (馅儿)

mixed the flour (面粉) with water

and kneaded the dough (揉面团)

we rolled out the wraps (擀皮儿)

wrapped the stuffing（包起来）

put the dumplings into boiling water

ladled them out into bowls…

Yummy！虽然前几天跟大家说过回答考官的问题时不推荐用 yummy，但是这里用 Yummy！却是最合适的。

> 　　如果需要描述 a cook，您不妨看一看这两个网站：www. gordonramsay. com/ corporate/theman/biography 和 www. jamieoliver. com，网站名字上的这两个人都是目前在英国红得发紫的厨师兼厨艺电视节目主持人，甚至连 Describe a TV presenter. 这个题也可以"一锅端"了。

Killer F

6. **双语感悟之　一堂科学课** Describe a science lesson that you had in school or university.

Pat 指南

　　貌似很多孩子连中文的物理、化学都还没学好，居然被要求用英语描述这类课程，实在是 ridiculous！不过如果您在国外上过中学的 science class，就会深感这边的科学课完全可以用"吃喝玩乐"四个字形容。英美中学阶段的科学课不是像国内把物理、化学划分得那么严格，在有的学校甚至几门课就一个老师讲，所以一般 science 老师都比较好说话（怕家长投诉）。而且为了吸引大家的兴趣（其实是食欲 appetite），science 老师们还经常会拿可乐（coke），柠檬水（lemonade）、葡萄干（raison）或者爆米花（popcorn）这类东西到教室做实验，有时微波炉（microwave）、烤箱（oven）这类厨具也会登场。最棒的是：因为这边的班级一般都比较小，也就十几个学生，所以做完实验大家往往就可以就把剩下的 food & drinks 分了。最近在北美的中学科学课里还特时髦地用一些不可逆的（irreversible）化学反应来展示 *Harry Potter* 7 里的魔法是怎么变出来的，所以连 magic wand（魔法棒）和 potion（神水）这类演出道具都用上了，完全是最真实的 *Harry Potter* 3D 版。所以 Pat 非常建议大家把这个题目说得轻松点，如果一定把这题说得跟国内的理科课堂那么抽象，考官反而会感到文化休克（culture shock）。

　　而且这题也还可以在回忆上课过程的同时顺带着讲讲老师的特色，不能太长，但短短几句话肯定是没问题的。比如 Pat 给您简单回忆一下我自己中学时在加拿大上过的一堂科学课吧：

Well, that was when I was in grade 10.（北美讲年级的时候很少说高一，高二之类

的词，一般都是象 grade 9, grade 10 或者 grade 11 这样讲的）. Back then, our science teacher was a really nice guy（请注意这个词跟中文的"家伙"不一样，其实只要是指某个男性在地道口语里这个词都巨常用）, you know, very amusing（说人搞笑也不一定非要说 funny）and understanding（善解人意的）. And just like many scientists, he was kind of balding（快秃顶了）and wore thick glasses. But he was not a nerd（说"书呆子"最常用的英文词）coz he always had some incredibly fun ways to make dead theories come alive（他能让枯燥的理论活起来）. I still recall（用这个词代替谁都用的 remember 怎么样）one of the most interesting science lessons he gave us. Our teacher came into the classroom with a huge beaker（烧杯）, a bag of raisins and a jumbo diet Pepsi（大瓶百事，还是不含糖的！）The whole setting made us thirsty and hungry! And he was like, "Guys！（今后对一堆人你就放心这么喊吧，即使有男也有女）Today I'm gonna show you some top secrets of density（密度）!" He opened the bottle and poured the Pepsi into the beaker and the soda（这个词可以泛指各种碳酸饮料，还有个词 pop 也差不多）just kept fizzing（嘶嘶嘶的响）in the beaker. Then the guy put a couple of raisins in the beaker. The raisins plumped up（变得胖大）coz they were soaked（泡湿了）. "See?" Our teacher asked, "The raisins are sinking fast coz their density is higher than the coke." Yeah, it was true. But then, right after the raisins hit the bottom of the beaker, they went back up! "That's because Pepsi is carbonated（含碳酸的）so it has lots of gas. Once the gas went into the raisins, the density of the raisins became lower, even lower than the soda." He explained, in a matter-of-fact voice（这个中文我想不出怎么翻译，总之是讲 science 老师特别合适，只可意会，不可言传）. "But once the raisins went to the surface of the Pepsi, the gas in them was squeezed out（被挤出去）," he pointed to the beaker, "so their density became high again and so you can see that they're starting to sink again!"

Geez, he was right! The raisins just kept going up and down in the Pepsi, for nearly twenty minutes, while we were enjoying the rest of the raisins in the bag... ☺

轮到你了 ///// It's Your Turn.

▶ **Word Bank on This Topic**

烧杯	beaker	实验	experiment
天平	balance	固体	solid
称重量	weigh	液体	liquid
悬挂	hang	加热	heat up

密度	density	冷却	cool off
质量	mass	元素周期表	the periodic table of the elements
体积	volume	化学公式	chemical equations
镊子	tweezers	化学反应	chemical reaction
勺子	spoon	显微镜	microscope
秤	scale	滴管	dropper
仪器	instrument	试管	test tube
仪表	meter	漏斗	funnel
搅拌	stir	温度计	thermometer

请参考Pat的思路，并适当借鉴这个词汇表里的单词，思考如果是您会怎么说

Pat 的海外生活英语实录

前文 Pat 已经说过，要描述音乐 "令人陶醉的"，那么非英语里的 **enchanting** 这个词莫属。但如果要用这个词来形容一节课上得很精彩，那就有点拍马屁（butter up the teacher）的嫌疑了。地道英文中说老师讲课 "引人入胜"，最准确的表达是 engaging，相应的它也可以用来形容 a speech，a TV show，a book，a childhood game 或者 a childhood story（这些话题我们已经在 Day 8 里全都 "无痛地" 练习过了）。

【剑桥例句】If a book doesn't engage my attention in the first few pages, I don't usually continue reading it.

Killer G

7. **帮别人准备的一个聚会** **Describe a party you prepared for others/another person.**

Pat 指南

Pat 一直认为准备雅思口语最好的心态就是把它看成国外留学生活的起点。各位进到任何一所英联邦大学里都会立刻知道 party 是白人校园文化何等重要的一个部分了。即使已经工作的年轻白人如果是单身那么每个月也总会有 N 次机去会参加各种 "派对"，只是这其中的分分合合到底给人带来的到底是消遣（recreation）还是更深的孤独感（loneliness）

就要靠自己去体会了。

对于国内的孩子们来说，生日聚会是最容易说到"点儿上"的话题，而且 birthday party 用"小词"也可以说得很曲折（full of twists and turns）。

Last month, a good friend of mine, Mia 's nineteenth birthday was coming up . I hoped it could be a really memorable birthday for her so I decided to organise a surprise birthday party for the birthday girl.

I called my friends Jillian, Chris, Evan and Matt who were also pretty close to Mia, and asked them if they'd like to join me in throwing a surprise birthday party for her. They were very delighted to hear my ideas and promised they wouldn't tell anyone about this "top secret ". I also called Mia's parents to make sure they would be okay with my plan.

On Mia's birthday, we went to her apartment, helped her parents decorate the living room and got a big birthday cake ready. Then we went into hiding. About ten minutes later, we heard footsteps and Mia stepped into the apartment. All of us jumped out and yelled , "SURPRISE!" Mia was totally surprised and she was like, "Oh my goodness ! What's going on here?" We said "Happy birthday!" to her in unison and then we brought out the cake and started singing the birthday song for her...

Mia told me it was the most special birthday she ever had. I felt my secretive planning really paid off...

（本节中的女配角 Jillian 将在 Pat 的另一本书《十天突破留学生活口语》中走到台前成为女一号，引领大家去深刻探寻一个长期被误读的真实西方世界）

轮到你了

It's Your Turn.

本文中所用的人名都是目前国外年轻人的常见名字，另外去年在英国最流行的男、女孩名字大家可以在后面的附录 B 里看到

过生日的男孩/女孩 the birthday boy /the birthday girl

（某一时间）临近了 approach / come up / is just around the corner

[剑桥例句] If you look out of the window on the left of the bus, you'll see that we're now approaching the Tower of London.

值得回忆的 memorable

为某人开一个"派对" hold / throw a party for sb.

与某人关系很亲密的 be close to / be tight with

高兴的 delighted（口语考试中代替 happy 的优秀选择）

[剑桥例句] We'd be delighted to come to dinner on Friday.

绝对机密 top secret　　　　　装饰 decorate

藏起来 hide / go into hiding　　脚步（声）footsteps

大声喊 yell

天哪! Oh my goodness!（比 Oh my God! 略微含蓄一点的常用感叹方式）

异口同声地说 say something in unison

[剑桥例句] Try to sing in unison if you guys can.

秘密的 secretive　　　　　　有回报 pay off

> 请参考Pat的思路，并适当借鉴这个词汇表里的单词，思考如果是您会怎么说

Pat 的海外生活英语实录

　　如果要说一个很成功的聚会是"精心策划"的，除了 It was carefully planned / carefully organised / carefully arranged. 这三个挺地道的表达之外，还有一个 Pat 从没听到过国内孩子用但在国外却听常用的表达：This was a well-thought-out party.

【剑桥例句】

(1) The training schedule wasn't very well-thought-out.

(2) Nothing can be more fun than going to a well-thought-out birthday party.

超短线
The Ultra-Short Track

近期还有一道卡片题偶尔也会上来冒个泡儿：

Describe a TV show host / presenter.

　　其实准备这道题，最好想的素材就是说加拿大的"大山"了，因为可以直接扯到学英语上面去，而且用词也不会很难。比如可以挑一个由他主持的语言教学节目（language education program），大致说说节目内容，然后说说他的外貌（tall, broad-shouldered, has pale skin 肤色浅，注意讲一个白人的皮肤白就不要用 has white skin 了，always wears a pair of glasses and a big smile，很有亲和力 very approachable / just like the guy next door...）。接下来就可以介绍"大山"的经历（born and raised in Canada，多伦多大学毕业 graduated from the University of Toronto），在北大学中文（studied Chinese at Beida / Peking University），又学习说相声（learned to perform the Chinese crosstalk comedy）等等。然后你还可以称赞他的中文说得多么多么完美（不一定要再用 perfect 那个俗词了，跟考官试试用 flawless 这个更拿分的词吧。Pat 在北京的时候不止一次地听朋友们说："大山"的中文比他们/她们自己的中文还好（His Chinese is better than mine!）。而且你还可以说他主持的节目给观众（the audience/ viewers）带来很多乐趣（pretty entertaining），同时也很有教育意义（educational as well），甚至还可以说你希望自己今后也能像他那样能成为完美的"双语人"（to be perfectly bilingual），blah, blah, blah...

有些 TV show hosts 很靓（gorgeous），有些却外表平凡（average-looking / plain-looking）；有的 TV show hosts 很煽情（emotional / provocative），有些却是以理服人型（a calm, well-reasoned approach）；有的 TV show hosts 很"炫"（flamboyant），有些则很恭谦（humble/modest）。

但不论主持人采用哪种风格，Pat 却总结出了中外所有成功电视节目主持人全都具有的四个英文特点：talented / gifted（有才华的），energetic（精力充沛的），articulate（表达清晰的）& engaging（确实能抓住别人注意力的）。

另外，下面这三个 TV show hosts 也都是 IELTS 考官们耳熟能详的，并且出国之后大家经常看到由他/她们主持的节目 www. aceshowbiz. com/celebrity/oprah winfrey/，www. ameri-canidol. com/bio/simon_cowell/，www. biography. com/articles/David-Letterman-9380239

Killer H

8. **小时候自己做过的一件淘气的事 Describe a naughty thing you did when you were a child.**

Pat 指南

首先要提示的是：准备这道题时最好不要套用太多的大词或者长难句。如果您先跟考官说"我来说说我小时候做的特淘的一事儿哈"，紧接着却给出一个极为生硬的书面语答案，那就是明摆着告诉考官刚开始你伪装出的一脸轻松根本是给他/她挖的一个坑。

平淡是真（But you'll be rewarded for being unpretentious.）。

讲这道题的时候很多同学倾向于把 naughty 这个单词连续擂上 N 次，其实 naughty 有个近义词叫 mischievous（发音是/'mɪsˌtʃɪvəs/，请注意重音是在第一个音节）。这个词在国外的使用频率虽然还没有 naughty 那么高，但确实也是生活中经常能听到的词。

　　此外还有两个相关词组，用来描述自己小时候很调皮时有可能用到：an unruly kid是指不服从管教的孩子，而 a disruptive student则特指上课时违纪的学生。

　　如果想说自己小时候超级淘气、很不听话，动词的表达是 act up。请注意"不听话"在地道英文里不要说 I didn't listen to my parents' words.（这听起来更像是在说"我这人就特爱一意孤行"），而应该说 I liked to act up when I was little.

　　对于低年级学生来说，最经典的不听话行为莫过于逃课（对于西方考官来说"上课说话"可不能算是调皮，反而极有可能被视为优点）。在地道英文中逃课称之为 cut class或者 skip school（请注意这个 school 前不能加 the），如果逃课就是很没出息地为了跟小男朋友/小女朋友出去疯玩儿，那么就说 I cut class /skipped school just to hang out with my little boyfriend/girlfriend；而如果逃课是为了去看电影那么当然就是 I cut class just to catch a movie/ I skipped school just to catch a flick.

　　最 naughty 的逃课方式毫无疑问是在老师刚一点完名之后立刻无耻地溜出教室，那就可以用英语说（假设逃的是英语课）I went to the English class, got my attendance checked and then sneaked out of the classroom.

　　在美国，21 岁之前是严禁买酒的，如果商家把酒卖给未成年人出了事故还要冒进监狱的危险。不过在北京时 Pat 倒是见过中学生把整箱啤酒往家搬的情形。和朋友们在酒吧喝高了当然也要算是 a naughty thing，除了 We got drunk in a bar. 这样的常规英文外，地道英语里有时还会讲 We got blasted drunk in a bar.

　　搞恶作剧捉弄别人，英文叫做 play pranks on sb.，也可以叫 play tricks on sb.，或者 play practical jokes on sb.（请注意这里的 practical jokes 并非"实用笑话"，而是恶作剧）。如果你的恶作剧让"受害者"（the victim）那一天都很不爽，则要讲 My prank reeeeeeeally ruined his/her day.

　　把一桶水放在门缝上面英文叫 put a bucket of water over a door；对方一推门水正好倒在他/她的身上英文说 He / She pushed the poor open. The bucket tipped over（翻了）and fell right on him/her. 浑身都湿透了叫 He / She got soaking wet. 水桶碰到头则要说 The bucket hit him/her on the head.

　　偶尔捉弄一下过于骄傲的某个同学（put a dent in his/her pride）倒也还是挺有社会意义的事情，但是必须要确保玩笑不能开得太出格了（I was lucky the prank didn't go too far.）……

　　如果你对别人做了恶作剧之后别人又找你"扯平"了，英文会讲 He / She managed to get even by doing sth.（get even 是个固定短语："扯平"的意思）。

　　如果你做的 naught thing 是告诉别人一条假新闻，则是 tricked people with a false news story。英文里还专门有个词是用来指这种传播假新闻的行为，叫做 hoax，比如在去年大家讨论得最多的 hoax 就是"千年极寒"（the Millenium Arctic），其实牛津科学史告诉我们人类从开始进行完整的气象记录开始到现在才只有 130 多年，真不知道这个"千年"是怎么出来的。注意如果你打算在描述 a naughty thing 时说自己告诉别人一条假新闻，那么 the false news you spread 一定不要涉及政治话题，因为 IELTS topics are supposed to be strictly politics-free. :)

当然，在这道题的开始部分还需要介绍一些时间、地点、相关人物等背景信息，但这些最好就自己设想了。千人一面才是 IELTS 口语备考中最大的误区，要敢于调动自己在中学或大学里学到的英语，即使它真的很有限。

Killer I

9. Describe something in your home that was broken or that didn't work.

近期被考到这道题的同学表示"鸭梨"很大……其实无非是被一个最简单的词给忽悠了：broken。

Pat 指南

相当多的同学误以为说这道题必须要描述一件"被打碎的东西"，其实 broken 在地道英文里极常用来指家电（home appliances）坏掉了。例如：

My iPad went broken but luckily, it was covered by Apple's warranty（保修）. 或者：My MacBook Air just arrived but sadly, it's broken...

了解了 broken 的含义，一切就变得豁然开朗了。下面 Pat 给您演示一下用高中程度的英语其实就可以把这道难题讲得非常清楚（简直是过于清楚）：

Let me talk about my laptop. It's a ThinkPad SL300. I bought it two years ago.

When I first bought it, everything was just fine... It was thin, light and super stylish. The screen looked gorgeous and typing on the keyboard felt totally comfortable. It also had a pretty decent hard drive that could hold lots of stuff and the battery could last up to four years.

But unfortunately it went out of order after I downloaded a file from an email attachment. I opened the file but ended up with a virus in my laptop. The virus was so powerful the operating system crashed right away and it destroyed the hard drive as well. The screen went black while the laptop was still running. So I turned off the laptop, only to find out it wouldn't even boot up anymore.

I began to worry that I wouldn't be able to get my valuable data back from the hard drive coz I didn't really have any backup plan. And by that time, my laptop was not covered by warranty anymore so I took the laptop to the local computer store immediately. The folks there fixed the problem and the hard drive data got saved as well.

And since then, I've always been extra careful any time when I pull stuff from the

Internet...

这段话中的 email attachment 当然是指电邮的附件；operating system 是操作系统；hard drive 在英文口语里就是电脑的硬盘，更麻烦的说法则是 hard disk drive; boot up 是一个与电脑有关的动词短语，（电脑）启动的意思；找回数据英文也可以说 recover data; backup plan 是指备份。

在使用某物品的时候操作错误，正式英文里叫 operated sth. improperly，口语里则可以说 I got it all mixed up. 如果自己在使用该物品之前压根儿就没看使用说明，则说 I really should have read （请注意 read 在这里是指过去，读成/red/）the user's manual/the user's guide first.

在很正式的书面语中，malfunction 可以用来指各种设备故障，这个单词也经常用作动词，比如可以写 It malfunctioned. 但在地道的英文口语里，电器出现小毛病则经常会用"调皮"这个拟人化的词来描述：It acted up. 短暂的失灵英文也可以说 It went on the blink；而电器工作不正常的情况极为严重时在地道英文里则说 It went haywire! 如果某个家电（home appliance）彻底报废，那么在国外日常生活里最常听到的一句就是 It was dead!

电视或手机的信号不好可以讲 The reception was awful. DVD 机"跳碟"叫 The DVD player skipped. 播放光盘时画面不流畅则可以说 The picture froze. （freeze 的过去时）

如果这道题您还是想说一个"被打碎"的东西，那么应该知道下面这些英文表达：

dropped sth. by accident 不小心掉了某物；

was broken into pieces 被摔成了碎片；

tried to glue the pieces back together 试着用胶把碎片粘起来；

It was precious to me. /It was invaluable to me. 某物对自己来说非常珍贵；

I just couldn't afford to lose it. 自己不能承受失去它。

可见，让一件物品 broken 的方式，在地道英文里其实远不止是 dropped it 或者 smashed it into pieces。

Killer J

10. 三道与环保有关的难题

Pat 指南

(i) **Describe a place where there was a lot of noise.**

噪声大的地儿，除了 airport（对于多数考生来说描述机场的挑战似乎有点大，即使用中文也难以说清）和 night club（让"小盆友们"描述这个也不是很合适），还可以有 shopping mall（是的，在国外 shopping mall 根本就不是有钱人去买东西的地方，而且多

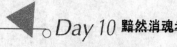

数 malls 里面的地下层 lower levels 都设有 food court 美食街，很多 malls 里还设有 video arcade / game arcade 让 gamer 们打游戏，所以跟社区 community 不同，大型 shopping mall 全都是巨吵无比的）或者也可以说 an open-air market（今天上半部分里的弱智话题 10）。

此外，说这道题时您虽然不必知道 80 ~ 90 分贝到底有多吵，但却不妨了解一下 The noise level can be as high as 80-90 decibels/ˈdesɪˌbelz/ 这句很地道的英文。

说噪音"很烦人的"，形容词是 annoying 或者 disturbing，但如果是长期持续的噪音则要用 depressing，或者说 It really bothers me. 此外还有个句型，叫 The noise really drives me up the wall. 比 The noise really drives me nuts. 要更加地形象 :)

（ii）Describe a job that can make the world a better place.

无数小将在考场里拿到这个话题之后当场晕倒——"能够让世界变得更美好的工作"话题实在过于宏大，让人完全丧失尺度感。其实现在英美年轻人最时髦儿的就是找 green job（亦称 green-collar jobs "绿领儿"工作），也就是能为地球环保做贡献的工作。请立刻登陆 http://www. careers-scotland. org. uk/GreenJobs/CareerPaths/CareerPaths_tpg. asp 点击下方的 Let's Start！您就能看到在 Scotland 与环保有关的各种工作介绍及该项工作所要求的教育背景。

（iii）Describe things that you can do to help improve the environment.

这个话题其实在 Writing 考试里早就考过无数次了，口语考试里描述时在前半段也可以先痛心疾首地讲一讲现在你所在的城市里污染已经严重到了何种程度。Pat 为您再简单地提示一下个人为环保做出的贡献常用的口语表达：

循环使用，当然是 recycle；自带购物袋则是 recycle shopping bags。

如果拒绝使用一次性筷子您可以说 take my own chopsticks to restaurants and decline disposable chopsticks（请注意这里的 decline 不是减少而是谢绝的意思）。

减少使用塑料制品可以说 cut down on the use of plastic bags and food containers；不乱扔垃圾叫 don't drop litter；把垃圾分类叫 sort out the household rubbish/household garbage。

多乘坐公交英文是 ride public transit/public transportation more frequently；总是骑自行车叫 always use a bike for short trips

节约用水叫 save tap water（自来水），捐献旧衣服则是 donate my old clothes。

英文里"有益于环保的"有太多说法，比如 environmentally-friendly, environmentally-beneficial, ego-friendly, 以及最简单却最常用的 clean 和 green。

此外，还有太多个人可以为环保做贡献的方法，比如有钱人少穿"皮草"，苦孩子打印资料时用双面打印……等等。与"低碳生活"（low-carbon living）密切相关的更多英文表达如果您还有深入兴趣的话可以再参阅《十天突破 IELTS 写作完整真题库与 6-9 分范文全解》Day 7。

附　录

Appendix

Pat's Guide
To the Speaking Test

Appendix A

雅思口语考试十大经典错误排行榜

这是 Pat 自己在长期教学中总结出来的中国考生犯得过多的口语错误 chart 之 top 10 countdown。

Top 10   无视 -ed 的存在 ⊠

悍然忘记动词过去时的杀伤力非常强，因为一旦忘记必然就是接连说错一串儿动词的时态。特别是对于 Part 2 卡片题的描述，行之有效的避免方法是在 1 分钟的思考时间里就把 V-ed 写在你手中白纸上的醒目位置，三个字母写得大一点也没关系，在这方面不需要给剑桥省纸，反正 1550 已经垫进去了。

Top 9   he/she 之不知 ⊠

有些孩子描述 an old man，一上来就是 she，但说了几个 she 突然又换成了 he... 我只能相信这位可敬的 old man 是一个 transsexual person。

Top 8   滥用······ how to say... ⊠

当一个考生想不出该用什么词汇的时候，他/她经常会这么说，可惜这真不是一个地道的英文插入语，却不知道为什么长期被国内孩子们挂在嘴边。下一次如果感觉被 "茬住了" 请改用 you know..., like..., basically... 这样在国外确实每天都有人用的 fillers。

Top 7   用 I just stay at home and relax myself. 麻痹考官 ⊠

其实完全可以直接使用更加地道的 I just stay at home and relax. 或者 get relaxed。

Top 6   拿 climb the mountain 吓唬考官 ⊠

这个倒算是正确的英文，可它的意思却是指用手去攀岩，属于极限运动的一种，难度相当大，普通人用脚爬香山的正确说法应该是 hike in the Xiang Shan Mountain。

Top 5   用 The colour is very suitable for me. 冒充领导

suitable 这个词在国外一般都是谈到很正式的事情才用，日常生活里面很少会听到人说 "The colour is very suitable for me." 这种沉重的说法，真不如就说 It just looks right on me.

Top 4 "How are you?" "I'm fine, thank you. And you?"

国内孩子们说这句的时候还要背着手，非常可爱。可惜比它好得多的说法是"Just fine. Thanks."而出国之后就说一个"Good."再给人点笑容儿就比什么都强了。

Top 3 humorous 并不幽默

严格来说用这个词不能算是错误，但是在口语里面听到它的次数却远不如 funny／amusing 这两个词的次数多，或者也可以说 He has a great sense of humor.

Top 2 In a word, ……自相矛盾

这个错得超多，包括看见过一些写作中的"范文"也喜欢用这个词开始一个长句子，其实这个词组在英文里面永远只能强调一个单词，比如 The music was, in a word, bad.

Top 1 -s 之殇

单复数永远是最常见的错误，名词要不要加 s ？动词要不要加 s ？对这两个问题在考试前应该形成条件反射。一点儿不夸张地说，如果能把这个错误完全改掉的话，你的口语成绩至少可以提高 0.5 分。遗憾的是很多孩子根本就不觉得这还算个事儿，但问题是在英文里加不加-s 往往会带来句意上的实质性差异

最后提醒大家一下，"Long time no see."其实是很地道的英文，而且有时候还可以在这个句子结尾用升调，引起对方的注意。

Appendix B

给自己一个容易听懂的名字

Pat 曾经在一个班里统计过，56 个孩子中，有 6 个 Alex，5 个 Cindy，4 个 Grace，4 个 Michael，3 个 Steven，3 个 Andy，2 个 Emma 和 2 个 Samantha。当然这些名字也都很不错，不过一个班里竟然出现这么多的 Alex，确实会让老师提问时相当不爽。

下面的 100 个名字是英国 2011 年最流行的男孩和女孩的名字（the most popular boy names & girl names in 2011），发音请大家听录音。大家如果还在为英文名字发愁，可以从里面选一个。雅思口试中如果想要说英文名字，那么一定应该是最大众化的那种。否则，如果你的非常另类的英文名字引起了考官的强烈兴趣，连问你几个你完全想不到的问题，那可就画蛇添足了（gild the lily）。

Top 50 Boy Names				
1. Joshua	2. Jack	3. Harry	4. Oliver	5. Charlie
6. Thomas	7. Daniel	8. Ethan	9. Noah	10. James
11. William	12. Max	13. Jacob	14. George	15. Alfie
16. Samuel	17. Joseph	18. Alexander	19. Dylan	20. Oscar
21. Lucas	22. Leo	23. Zachary	24. Nathan	25. Freddie
26. Luke	27. Liam	28. Benjamin	29. Matthew	30. Jake
31. Luca	32. Henry	33. Logan	34. Ryan	35. Alex
36. Archie	37. Adam	38. Lewis	39. Ben	40. Connor
41. Toby	42. Isaac	43. Jamie	44. Theo	45. Edward
46. Callum	47. Sam	48. Tyler	49. Sebastian	50. Harrison

Top 50 Girl Names				
1. Sophie	2. Isabelle	3. Emily	4. Olivia	5. Lily
6. Chloe	7. Isabella	8. Amelia	9. Jessica	10. Sophia
11. Ava	12. Charlotte	13. Mia	14. Lucy	15. Grace
16. Ruby	17. Ella	18. Evie	19. Freya	20. Isla
21. Poppy	22. Daisy	23. Layla	24. Megan	25. Amy
26. Abigail	27. Holly	28. Maisie	29. Hannah	30. Emma
31. Scarlett	32. Imogen	33. Caitlin, Kaitlyn	34. Phoebe	35. Eva
36. Molly	37. Ellie	38. Erin	39. Matilda	40. Annabelle
41. Amelie	42. Alice	43. Jasmine	44. Maya	45. Millie
46. Katie	47. Lola	48. Madison	49. Zoe	50. Niamh

Appendix C

老话儿的新生

国外年轻人爱说的话跟老年人经常有差异，比如说一个简单的"晚上上床睡觉"，年轻人就不一定要说 go to bed，而可能会说 turn in 或者是 hit the sack。

不过有些老话儿却是老年人和年轻人都常用的，这就是 proverbs（谚语）和 idioms（成语）。

下面的 40 句话是 Pat 总结出来的雅思口试必备的 40 个 proverbs / idioms，不管考官是老 SG 还是小 MM 皆宜。

……

There's no place like home.	这个说任何涉及家或者住所的话题都很合适
He/She's a walking encyclopedia.	是活字典。形容知识很丰富
He/She's a household name.	家喻户晓
He has the golden touch.	很会赚钱。形容成功人物常用
a whiz kid	神童
have two left feet	完全不会跳舞。Part 1 常用
get one's feet wet	意为"先尝试一下"，skill 技能话题常用
get the hang of it	初步掌握了……
know it backwards and forwards	精通……
Small is beautiful.	这是个俗语，可以用来形容任何可爱的小东西
It's a win-win situation.	是双赢的局面。Part 3 常用
have tunnel vision	目光短浅。Part 3 常用
It helps us stretch and grow.	某事物可以帮助我们发挥潜力，比 "helps us fulfill our potential" 这样的表达更口语化，用在 Part 1 和 Part 2 都不错

not let the opportunity slip away. 别错过机会。Part 3 常用

penny wise and pound foolish 小事儿聪明，大事儿糊涂。Part 3 常用

It's a dog-eat-dog world. 竞争很残酷。描述人的成功过程，Part 2 常用

give... the green light 批准……。Part 3 常用

Variety is the spice of life. 多样是人生的调味料。leisure 话题常用

He's sharp as a tack. 描述人反映很快，很精明

... is a notch above... 比……略胜一筹。很地道的英文

She's the apple of her parents' eye. 小孩是父母的掌上明珠。注意这里的 eye 不加复数

She's growing like a weed. 形容小孩长个儿快

Two heads are better than one. 这个 Part 2 说 advice 或者 a success 不错

... runs fast as lightning. 跑得像闪电一样。形容汽车或者人都可以

It fits like a glove. 形容衣服特合身

It's so quiet you could hear a pin drop.
别针掉在地上都能听见。这个形容安静的公园或者其他环境非常棒

It's smooth as silk. 形容人的皮肤、头发或者建筑和自然景观都可能用到

A dog is man's best friend. 这个说宠物不错，有的时候也会听到有人在 man 前面加个 a，都可以

in the first place 把这个短语放在一些否定句的句尾时很像中文的"压根儿"，比如 I didn't like that restaurant in the first place.

It's like putting the cart before the horse.
这个很像中文的"本末倒置"，不过在英文里它主要指做事情的顺序不对，应该先做的反而后去完成，很适合用在 Part 3 部分提出建议改变不良现状

402

When the going gets tough, the tough get going.

这里的第一个 tough 是"困难的"，第二个
tough 是"顽强的"，基本意思就是"坚持
就是胜利"。用在 Part 2 描述成功的任务
不错

... is a feast for my eyes/ ... is a great treat to me.

让我大饱眼福。这个说艺术品或者自然景色
都很好

It's the thought that counts. & It's always better to give than to receive.

这两个说 gift 非常好

He's a real Renaissance man. / She's a real Renaissance woman.

形容一个人多才多艺

of two minds about... / be born between A and B / in a dilemma / between a rock
and a hard place / be in a bind

左右为难。Part 2 描述 decision 时可以用

Blood is thicker than water.

血浓于水。回答和 family 有关的题时常用

A man is known by the company he keeps.

这里的 company 不是公司，而是陪伴你的
人。这句很像中文的"人以群分"，说
friends 相关话题时常用

A fault confessed is half redressed.

敢于承认，错误就已经改正了一半。这句在
Part 3 提出 solutions 时常用

Prevention is better than cure.

预防比有病之后再治疗要好。用法同上

It's a blessing in disguise.

这句话很像中文的"因祸得福"，在 Part 3
陈述事物影响时常用

If you want a friend, be a friend.

最后的这句最简单，但却最深刻，不仅在
friends 与 neighbor 话题中常用，到了国外
也是生活的至理名言。

Appendix D

紧张的 120 个小时

The Hop, Skip and Jump towards the IELTS Speaking Test

在你即将奔赴战场之前，请允许我把 the IELTS Speaking Test 的实战过程介绍一下：

☆ 星期六考试前的那一个星期四上午或者最晚星期四下午（如果你是报名参加星期四的加考，那就是在星期二下午）：

登陆 http://ielts.etest.net.cn/cn 查询自己的口语考试日期和时间。

☆ 星期六下午第一个考生是 2:00 开始，星期日和星期一上午第一个考生是 8:00 开始，星期日和星期一下午第一个考生是 1:00 开始。星期六上午的笔试结束之后，你就可以开始准备"蹲点儿"或者"网蹲"的时间了，还可以参考本书导读部分的问题 2 答案。"网蹲"其实也有它的好处，首先是安全，而且毕竟是全国各地的考生一起贴题目。同一个半天里面全国的考题是同步的，一个半天里的卡片题约 9~12 张，而且多数人考的是其中的 2~3 张。

星期四到星期一，整整 120 个小时。

☆ 口试之前 15'~20' 必须进场，全国多数的考场都是安排考生先到一个 waiting room 等候，会有中国监考官说一些考试纪律，看一下你的 ID。

☆ 到你的口语考试时间了，中国监考官会告诉你去你的考试房间，在多数考点考官会出门迎接你，但是也有些考点他/她把门打开考生自己走进去。

☆ 有时候会有简单的问候"How are you?"，也有很多考官现在把这个省略了，还可能问 mobile phone，Pat 的建议是干脆直接说"I don't have a mobile phone."，不要拿出来最省事了。咱们集中精力考试就好了，进到考场里你才会明白"套磁"那些东东在实战里面并不是很常用。

☆ 双方坐下。桌子上面会有录音装置，不要紧张，是为了保护你今后万一要申请 remark 的权利，是好东西。

☆ 常规部分，考官先说话：

Good afternoon/morning. My name is ... Can you tell me your full name please? ...

OK, can I see your ID card please?

☆ 正式开始问题部分，每部分都是考官先说话：

In this first part, I'd like to ask you some questions about yourself. So first of all let's talk about... (OK now I'm going to give you a topic and I'd like you to talk about it for one to two minutes...)

A Sample Topic Card

> Describe an important letter you received.
>
> You should say:
> when you received this letter
> what this letter was about
> how you felt when you read it
> and explain why it was important.

OK, we've been talking about a letter you received and now I'd like to discuss with you some general questions related to this...

☆ 考试结束时，有些考官会送你出来，但是也有很多就偷懒坐在那儿跟你告别了。如果看他/她没有要再多说什么的意思，你也不一定要再多说告别的话了，一切以自然最好。除了 "Have a nice day." 这样的说法，其实 "Have a good one." 在国外也极其常用，好处是你不用考虑是清晨还是快到黄昏了，挺万能的。还有一句 Pat 从没在国内听考生用过但在英美生活里有时周末会听到人讲的道别语，"Enjoy the rest of your weekend."（注意周四或周五加试的考生就一定不能这么说了）。但不管是你先说还是考官先说，答案永远都是 "You too."，而一句一定不要说的话是 "I hope I'll see you again soon..."

结束语 — "To the Next Step."

雅思口语的战役，就要开始。不知道您是不是已经听烦了，但 Pat 还是想最后一次提醒您："口语考试，交流的自然与真实永远才是最拿分的。"

另外，还很真诚地向您推荐 Pat 在近期将会完成的另一本新书《十天突破留学生活口语》。在那本书里，我将扮演一个 Spider-man 的角色，潜入到几所英语国家顶级大学的 cafeteria, gym, dorm 和 faculty buildings 中，向您汇报最真实的国外学生生活口语。Sounds like a lot of work, huh?

L'homme c'est rien — l'oeuvre c'est tout.
The man is nothing — the work is all.

P. S.

今晚正好看到一篇对 the Vice-Chancellor of Oxford University Andrew Hamilton 先生的一篇专访，Pat 决定就用"牛人中的牛人"——牛津校长的说话风格来作为您手中这本口语书的结束语，并且继续坚信您出国后会更深刻地理解 Pat 一直重复这句话的苦心："请从现在开始'下调'您的口语难度/ Please simplify your spoken English."

"When I moved from Yale to Oxford, I felt very familiar because there's a common emphasis on excellence in both Yale and Oxford."

"This is a form of education where the students have nowhere to hide, so they must be very well-prepared."

"That very often leads to success in whatever career an Oxford graduate chooses."

"It's providing an opportunity for the university to play an important role in the development of society."

"China now is a very significant source of students in the University of Oxford. The Chinese students at Oxford are very smart."

"We have never viewed an Oxford education as an industry. An undergraduate degree in Oxford costs around 17,000 pounds per undergraduate per year."

"Students shouldn't place too much emphasis on rankings. I spend little time worrying about the fluctuations in rankings. We are nearly 900 years old so the fluctuation of one or two places in some rankings for us isn't significant. We're focused on the long term. "

Shoot for the sky,

'cause even if you miss,

you'll still land among the stars

. . .